WORD ORIGINS
THE ROMANCE OF LANGUAGE

WORD ORIGINS

THE ROMANCE OF LANGUAGE

BY
CECIL HUNT

With Illustrations by
JOHN NICOLSON, A.R.E., R.B.A.

THE WISDOM LIBRARY

a division of

PHILOSOPHICAL LIBRARY
New York

First published 1949 by Philosophical Library Inc., 15
East 40 Street, New York 16, N. Y. as *A Dictionary of Word
Makers*; reissued 1962. All rights reserved. Printed in the
United States of America.

ISBN 0-8065-0685-7
Distributed to the trade by
CITADEL PRESS
A division of Lyle Stuart, Inc.
120 Enterprise Ave., Secaucus

FOREWORD

THIS book was a pleasure to write, and in itself this is a keen satisfaction to an author.

In twenty years of writing and work among authors I have heard from them, and found myself using, familiar literary references to persons unknown to me beyond that context. How many, for instance, speak of "Hobson's choice," a "lady bountiful" or a "Pyrrhic victory" without knowing the people who made the allusions current coin?

At my leisure I began a pursuit of these immortal personalities who are literally yours, but so often only in name. They offered a fascinating diversity and soon the spell of the chase was upon me and the interest quickened.

Other writers and book lovers will, I hope, share my pleasure and increase the richness of their writing and reading by this gallery of pen pictures of men and women who have added life, if not always lustre, to our language.

It would be simple to extend these sketches indefinitely; the scientists and mechanical inventors in particular have added a legion of names to our vocabulary. But in this book I have kept the accent upon literary allusions.

Other claimants for inclusion in this sketch book have occurred to me and still more may occur to readers. I shall hope for the pleasure of including them in a companion book. The works I have perused and the clues I have followed—often fruitlessly, but none the less enjoyably—far exceed in number the pages in this volume. Not easily now shall I relinquish this fascinating pursuit and I can only trust that readers will find comparable pleasure in these rewarding excursions along the unfrequented paths of literature and language.

CECIL HUNT

ACKNOWLEDGMENTS

I RECORD my thanks to the following persons and organizations for assistance in the compiling of specific entries in this volume:

Messrs. Ward Lock & Co., Ltd. (*Mrs. Beeton*);
The Monks of the Hospice of St. Bernard;
The Commissioner of Police, The Metropolis (*Black Maria*);
Messrs. Christie, Manson & Woods, Ltd. (*Christie's*);
The British Institute of Public Opinion (*Gallup*);
The Motion Picture Association (*Oscar*);
Rowton Houses, Ltd.;
Reginald W. M. Wright, Esq., Director of the Victoria Art Gallery and Municipal Libraries, Bath (*Sally Lunn* and *Dr. Oliver*);
The Shaftesbury Homes;
Toc H;
Madame Tussaud's, Ltd.;

and my friend, L. A. G. Strong, for much helpful criticism and suggestion.

Abessa, the personification of superstition. The term is taken from the name and character of Abessa in Spenser's *Faerie Queene* (1589–96).

She is the daughter of Corceca (blindness of heart).

In the pre-Reformation abbeys and convents she personified the superstition, seeking sanctuary from the truth behind closed walls.

Abigail. The prototype of the handmaid or lady's maid. In *1 Sam. xxv. 3*, Abigail was the wife of Nabal, the Carmelite, a woman "of good understanding, of a beautiful countenance," though he was "churlish and evil in his doings." By her strategy she prevented David's taking bloody revenge against her husband and his men. "Except thou hadst hasted and come to meet me, surely there had not been left unto Nabal by the morning light so much as one man child."

When Abigail returned to Nabal he was feasting and very drunken. "Wherefore she told him nothing, less or more, until the morning light."

In ten days Nabal was dead and David took Abigail to wife. She proclaimed herself his handmaid, "a servant to wash the feet of the servants of my lord."

Abigail, probably from the same derivation, is a character in Beaumont and Fletcher's *The Scornful Lady*. Vanbrugh uses the name for a character in *The Relapse*.

Abraham of Abraham's Bosom. The story of Abraham, or Abram (exalted father), the great Hebrew patriarch and ancestor of the Jews, is to be found in the book of *Genesis*. There are frequent references to Abraham in Mohammedan mythology.

The expression "Abraham's bosom" refers to the Jewish custom of reclining on couches at table. It brought the head of one person almost against the bosom of the one placed above him.

In the East the bosom was also the pocket, symbolizing the centre of secrecy and intimacy.

The allusion to resting in Abraham's bosom, *Luke xvi. 22*, refers to the repose of the faithful in death.

Absalom. Absalom is the epitomization of the erring, beloved son bringing upon his head the anguished cry of the father. David's lament, "O my son Absalom, my son, my son Absalom! Would God I had died for thee, O Absalom, my son, my son!" (*2 Sam. xviii. 33*) has echoed through the years.

Absalom was David's son by Maacah. "There was none to be so much praised for his beauty: from the sole of his foot even to the crown of his head there was no blemish in him." He was noted also for a profusion of hair, which was eventually to be his undoing. His army was routed when he fought against David's host. Absalom escaped on a swift mule, but his flowing hair caught and suspended him in an oak tree and the mule that was under him went on.

Joab, David's Commander, learning of his enemy's plight, thrust three darts into the heart of Absalom and Joab's armour-bearers slew the stricken man.

Absalom had first drawn his father's wrath upon himself by slaying Amnon, David's eldest son,

9

who ravished Absalom's sister, Tamar. He fled for three years, but by a woman's strategy David eventually admitted him to his presence. Absalom aspired to kingship and courted the support of the people.

He proclaimed himself king, David fled and Absalom ascended the throne.

Later he marched against his father's army, being routed on the edge of the forest of Ephraim.

When tidings of the victory were brought to David, he said to the Cushite messenger: "Is it well with the young man Absalom?

"And the Cushite answered, the enemies of my lord the king, and all that rise up against thee to do thee hurt, be as that young man is.

"And the King was much moved, and went up to the chamber over the gate, and wept . . ." (*2 Sam. xviii.*)

And as he went he uttered his anguished, immortal lament.

Academos of Academy and academic. Academos (or Akademos) was the reputed founder of the original garden near Athens where Plato taught. Plato's Academy was

The Royal Academy to-day

divided into three schools—the Old, the Middle and the New.

The French Academy, whose forty members are known as the Immortals, was founded by Richelieu in 1635. Its function was to labour diligently to give exact rules to the French language and to render it capable of treating the arts and the sciences.

The English Royal Academy of Arts, in Burlington House, Piccadilly, was founded by George III in 1768. Its first President was Sir Joshua Reynolds, whose statue stands in the forecourt.

The British Academy, for the promotion of the study of learning and the moral and political sciences, was founded in 1902. Sir Israel Gollancz was its first secretary. There is also an Irish Academy of Letters.

Achates, the faithful companion or bosom friend. The allusion is to Achates, the constant attendant of Aeneas, legendary founder of the Roman nation, in his wanderings after the fall of Troy. He was remarkable for unswerving fidelity. Achates figures frequently in Virgil's *Aeneid.*

Achilles of Achilles' Heel. Achilles, greatest and noblest figure of the Trojan War and hero of *The Iliad*, was the child of Peleus and the Goddess Thetis, who had been bestowed upon him by the gods as a reward for his chastity.

Tradition asserts that Thetis plunged her son into the Styx, thereby rendering him invulnerable in every part except the heel by which she held him.

The Achilles' heel is now accepted as a description of a person's or a nation's one vulnerable weakness. The tendon at the back of the heel is named after the hero who, instructed by the Centaur, Chiron, acquired such wonderful strength, skill and agility that he surpassed all his contemporaries.

Post Homeric legend asserts that Achilles was wounded in his vulnerable heel by an arrow from Paris.

Tradition claims that Alexander the Great, at Achilles' tomb, proclaimed, "O fortunate youth, who has found a publisher of thy valour in Homer." "Peter Pindar" (Dr.

John Wolcot, 1738–1819) added a piquant postscript in his *A Moral Reflection* (To George III)

> *A great deal, my liege, depends*
> *On having clever bards for friends,*
> *What had Achilles been without his Homer?*
> *A Tailor, woollen-draper, or a comber!*

Robert and James Adam of the Adam Style. Robert Adam (1728–92), the Scottish architect, was born at Kirkcaldy, the son of an architect. He entered Edinburgh University.

He visited Italy with the distinguished French architect, C. L. Clérisseau, and closely studied and sketched classical architecture. He resigned his post as architect to the King and Queen on election as M.P. for Kinross in 1768 but he continued to follow his profession.

With his brother, James, who died in 1794, he built the Adelphi, which is named after them, as brothers, from the Greek. It lies between the Strand and the Embankment, near Charing Cross. Many famous literary men and artists have lived there and for years the noted Savage Club occupied one of the most characteristic houses in the Adelphi.

The Adam brothers recorded their achievements in *Works in Architecture, 1773–78*. They include the screen to the Admiralty Office, Lansdowne House, Glasgow Infirmary, Caen (Ken) Wood House and part of Edinburgh University. James Adam is believed to have designed Portland Place.

Robert Adam, the predominant partner, had a profound influence upon architecture and upon furniture, designing much himself. He regarded the furnishings of a house as an essential part of its design and collaborated with, and largely influenced, Chippendale.

He was a man of considerable scholarship, first-hand knowledge of classical architecture and a prodigious energy. The work of the brothers is distinguished by a grace and refinement that had a profound effect upon the development of English architecture and allied arts and crafts.

Parson Adams. Parson Adams is the prototype of the simple-minded, industrious and learned country curate.

The character is from Henry Fielding's *Joseph Andrews* or, to give it its full title, *The History of the Adventures of Joseph Andrews and his friend Mr. Abraham Adams*, published in 1742.

It was the first of Fielding's novels and was begun as a skit upon Richardson's *Pamela*, with the characters many of its counterparts. Its real hero is the simple, generous but slightly ridiculous Parson Adams, curate in Sir Thomas Booby's family.

Abraham Adams is described as "an excellent scholar," with many languages. "He had applied many years to the most severe study, and had treasured up a fund of learning rarely to be met with in a university. He was, besides, a man of good sense, good parts, and good nature; but was at the same time as entirely ignorant of the ways of this world as an infant just entered into it could possibly be . . . As he never had any intention to deceive, so he never suspected such a design in others."

The character was drawn from William Young, with whom Fielding collaborated in translations.

Adam of the Adam's Apple. The Adam's apple is the familiar name for the projection of the thyroid cartilage of the larynx. Tradition has it that the name derives from the superstition that a piece of apple, given to Adam by Eve from the forbidden tree, stuck in his throat.

In fact there is no mention of apples in the Biblical story, which refers only to the fruit of the tree in the midst of the garden of which God hath said, "Ye shall not eat of it, neither shall ye touch it, lest ye die" (*Gen. iii. 3*).

"Adam's ale" is a euphemistic expression for water.

Paul refers to Adam as the figure of Him who was to come and Christ is referred to as the second Adam (*Rom. v. 14-19*).

Adonis, the beautiful youth.

Adonis, in Greek mythology, was a youth of surpassing beauty, beloved by Aphrodite. He was killed by a wild boar while hunting and the Goddess, arriving too late to rescue him, changed his blood into flowers. Some accounts specify the anemone.

Proserpine restored him to life with the not unduly irksome condition that he should spend annually six months with her and six months with Aphrodite, a symbol of summer and winter.

His death and revival were marked by ceremonies in many countries, and frequently his image was surrounded by beds of flowers whose transient beauty symbolized the cycle of life and death in the vegetable world.

Leigh Hunt was sent to prison for libelling George IV when Regent in the phrase "a corpulent Adonis of fifty."

In the 18th century, the term "adonis" was given to a particularly elegant type of wig.

Adullam of Adullamites. The ad-

herents of Lowe and Horsman, who seceded from the Liberal Party in 1866, were called Adullamites by John Bright. Their secession was a protest against a Liberal Franchise Bill then introduced.

The term is frequently used for seceders from prominent parties and beliefs, who gather about them discontents.

The reference is to *I Sam. xxii. 1-2*, in which David in his flight from Saul "escaped to the cave of Adullam: and when his brethren and all his father's house heard it, they went down thither to him. And every one that was in distress, and every

one that was discontented, gathered themselves unto him; and he became captain over them: and there were with him about four hundred men."

Æsop of the Fables. Æsop, the

traditional Phrygian author of the famous Greek fables about animals, is said by Herodotus to have lived in the 6th century B.C. and to have been a deformed slave of Iadmon, the Thracian. He is reputed to have gained his freedom and to have been employed by Crœsus for important missions.

He was, in some accounts, a witty, wise but profane talker and through these gifts appears to have incurred the wrath of the priests, so much so that he was thrown over a precipice at Delphi.

Socrates, in prison, is said to have rewritten such of Æsop's fables as he remembered.

W. S. Landor, in *Imaginary Conversations*, presents the fabler and his fellow-slave, Rhodope, a Greek courtesan.

Aladdin of Aladdin's Lamp. The

phrase "Aladdin's lamp" signifies a talisman which enables its owner to gratify any wish.

The allusion is to Aladdin in *The*

Aladdin and his Lamp

Arabian Nights, who utilized the lamp's magic to build a castle for his marriage to the daughter of the Sultan of China. He lost the lamp and his palace was transported to

Africa. If the lamp became rusty through neglect it lost its potency.

The phrase an "Aladdin's window" is frequently used to describe a task of great magnitude which defies completion. In the story Aladdin's castle had twenty-four windows framed in jewels. The last was left incomplete for the Sultan to finish, but he exhausted his treasures and then abandoned the work as hopeless.

Prince Albert of the Albert Hall, etc. Albert, Prince Consort of England (1819-61), is commemorated by name in several ways which are not always nowadays attributed to him.

The Albert Hall and Memorial are so ascribed by the majority, but the Albert watch-chain, with which he set a fashion, has passed into period history, and not all associate the Albert Medal with the Prince.

He was born the second son of the hereditary duke of Saxe-Coburg-Gotha, in the same year as his cousin, Queen Victoria, whom he married on February 10, 1840, at the Chapel Royal, St. James's.

Albert had been described by Victoria as "extremely handsome" and possessed of all the qualities she desired for her happiness.

He was keenly interested in the application of science and art to industry, and it was from a suggestion of his at the Society of Arts that the Great Exhibition of 1851 originated. He carried it through in the face of sustained opposition. The Commons claimed that it would result in an influx of foreign rogues and anarchists, trade spies and subversive propagandists. The Lords challenged the right to hold the Exhibition in Hyde Park.

The Exhibition was a brilliant success in every way and from the profits the South Kensington Museum was established and endowed. It was later renamed the Victoria and Albert.

Albert, who had to fight personal animosity and political prejudice almost to the end of his life, was granted the title of Prince Consort by Letters Patent in 1857.

He died after a brief illness, and while planning an international exhibition, in 1861.

Among the many memorials to "Albert the Good" were the Albert Hall (1867), and the Albert Memorial (1876). The former vast amphitheatre does not commend itself to all, nor does the over-decorativeness of the Memorial find general approbation. In earlier years there was a typical quip of a guide explaining these two phenomena as: "On my right the memorial to Albert Hall; on my left, the Kensington Gasworks."

The Albert Medal, for gallantry in saving life, was instituted by the Queen in 1866, and the Order of Victoria and Albert four years before.

William Almack of Almack's Club and Assembly Rooms. Almack's famous assembly rooms in King Street, St. James's, were celebrated in the 18th and 19th centuries and are mentioned frequently in contemporary literature.

Their founder is said to have been William Almack, a tavern keeper who built the first premises. Some accounts say that he was a Highlander McCaul or M'all, which name he used as the basis of his business cognomen when he came to London. He is thought to have come south as valet to the Duke of Hamilton.

From the opening of the rooms, in 1765, they achieved such celebrity and the support of a committee of women of high rank that admission to Almack's bestowed the highest possible social prestige.

The premises were later known as Willis's Rooms, from the name of Almack's heir, his niece, Mrs. Willis.

Almack's Club, noted for its high play, became Brooks's Club in 1778. Many famous 18th-century names in politics and art were associated with it.

Almack died in 1781, leaving a considerable fortune.

The Amazons. The term amazon, applied to female warriors, masculine women and women of outstanding physical development and courage, derives from a mythical race of warrior women. They were associated with the territory adjoining the river Thermodon in Cappadocia.

There were no males in the Amazonian tribes, whose members only tolerated temporary union with the males of adjacent tribes for the purpose of procreation. The male infants resulting therefrom were banished or destroyed.

The Amazons are credited with taking part successfully in many wars.

An instance of the importance attached to their achievements is the inclusion among the tasks of Hercules (*q.v.*) of the wresting of the girdle from the Amazon queen, Hippolyte.

The name in many Greek accounts is said to derive from *a*, not; *mazos*, breast; the Amazons being said to remove their right breasts by cutting or burning in order to handle the bow more· efficiently. In art they are generally depicted as armed and with the right breast bared.

Ananias, the lying deceiver. The reference is to Ananias, a member of the church at Jerusalem, who with his wife, Sapphira, sold land and retained a part of the price before presenting the balance to the apostles. When challenged by Peter, who said, "Thou hast not lied unto men, but unto God," Ananias fell down and died. His wife, entering some three hours later, maintained the deception and when told of the death and burial of her husband, expired also.

The Biblical reference is *Acts v. 1–10*.

There are other men of the name of Ananias mentioned in the Bible, notably the high priest when Paul was brought before Felix (*Acts xxiii.*).

Aphrodite of Aphrodisiac. Aphrodite (foam) was the Greek Venus, so called because she sprang from the foam of the sea. She was the daughter of Zeus and Dione, the goddess of moisture.

Aphrodite first touched land at Cyprus, which island was held sacred to her. She was the goddess of beauty and sexual love.

The celebrated girdle of Aphodite, the Cestus, was love-begetting and its owner was constantly concerned in passionate association with the gods and even with certain chosen mortals. There are many legends of her love for Adonis, who was killed while hunting the wild boar. Zeus agreed to restore his life on condition that he spent part of his time in the shadows and the remainder in the domain of the gods.

Aphrodite had a wider significance than is assumed· by the meaning of the word deriving from her name. There was an Aphrodite Urania, concerned with the fertility of the soil, and an Aphrodite Pontia who controlled maritime prosperity.

The seasons and the graces waited upon her. She is one of the three goddesses in the famous legend of the golden apple inscribed "to the fairest." Paris gave her the decision against the claims of Hera and Athène.

The Cestus, which bestowed irresistible powers upon its wearer (and was not infrequently mislaid by its owner), is mentioned often in literature, notably by Spenser in *The Faerie Queene*.

Apollo, a man of great beauty and physical perfection. The Greek god, son of Zeus and Leto, was the deity associated primarily with the ideal arts, with medicine and music and, in some accounts, with prophecy and the care of flocks and pasture. He is often identified with Helios, the sun god.

He was held in high honour as a great athlete and the winner of the first Olympic Race. He built cities, and Troy is said to have owed much to his gifts. Statues of him reveal a man of physical perfection and classic grace.

In Roman mythology Apollo is accorded similar attributes with prominence given to his patronage of healing and the gifts of oracular pronouncement and prophecy. He was the god of mice. The most frequent attributes in representations of Apollo are the bow and the lyre.

> *The fire-robed god, Golden Apollo.*
> *Winter's Tale, iv. 4.*

Argus, the Watchful Guardian. The attributes of watchfulness derive from Argus, the hundred-eyed guardian in Greek mythology. The allusion may have been to the starry heavens.

Juno employed Argus to watch Io, of whom she was jealous, but Mercury induced the watchful guardian to sleep, and then slew him. This may have been the representation of the eclipse of the stars by the coming of dawn.

Juno revived Argus in the form of a peacock, his "eyes" appearing in the tail. In many countries the peacock's feather is still regarded as a symbol of the Evil Eye and an indication of the presence of a traitor. The bird is regarded as unlucky and even to-day there are British publishers, guided by market reactions, who will not include the peacock in their published designs.

Armageddon, the supreme disaster or conflict between nations. The reference is to the Apocalypse from *The Revelation of St. John the Divine, xvi. 16.* The narrator hears the voice out of the temple commanding the angels to pour out the vials of wrath of God upon the earth. The first poured out his vial "and there fell a noisome and grievous sore upon the men which had the mark of the beast" (*xvi. 2*). The second caused the sea to turn to blood, as of a dead man, and every living soul died in the sea. The third caused the rivers

and fountains of water to become blood. The fourth caused the sun to scorch men with fire. The fifth angel "poured out his vial upon the seat of the beast; and his kingdom was full of darkness; and they gnawed their tongues for pain" (*xvi. 10*). The vial of the sixth angel dried up the waters of the great Euphrates.

At the climax of the great fight between the powers of good and evil, the foul spirits were gathered together "into a place called in the Hebrew tongue Armageddon" (*xvi. 16*).

The seventh angel poured out his vial into the air; and there came a great voice out of the temple of heaven, from the throne, saying, "It is done." There were thunderings and lightnings and an earthquake of unequalled magnitude, and the cities of the nations fell and great Babylon came in remembrance before God. ₁

The name, Armageddon, derives from Megiddo (*Judges v. 19*), where the chief battles of the Israelites were fought.

Jacob Arminius of Arminianism. Jacob Arminius, or Jakob Harmensen, founder of Arminianism, was born in South Holland in 1560. He studied in Geneva and later, as a minister in Amsterdam, he was to be the centre of much religious controversy. His doctrine was that God gives forgiveness and eternal life to all repentant believers, in contrast with the contemporary doctrine of predestination, by which God had ordained by eternal decree which persons should be saved.

Arminius died in 1609.

The Ashes. "The Ashes" is the most famous phrase in the history of cricket. Its true story was told by the Dowager Lady Darnley in 1930 at a luncheon given to the visiting Australian cricket team.

In 1882, she said, the *Sporting Times*, after England had been thoroughly beaten by Australia at the Oval, published an obituary in affectionate memory of English cricket "whose demise was deeply lamented and the body would be cremated and taken to Australia."

Her husband, then the Hon. Ivo Bligh, took the next team to Australia and *Punch* printed a poem which contained the line "When Ivo comes back with the urn."

Bligh wiped out the defeat and Lady Clarke, wife of Sir W. J. Clarke, who had been a firm friend of the English XI, burnt a bail, put the ashes in a little urn and, wrapping it in a velvet bag, gave it to the English captain.

The urn with its ashes is now one of the treasures of Lord's.

Elias Ashmole of the Ashmolean Museum, Oxford. Ashmole was born in Lichfield in 1617 and abandoned law to enter Brazenose College to study philosophy and allied subjects, including astronomy and astrology. A marriage which brought Ashmole wealth enabled him to pursue his studies at ease. He received several important appointments, including that of Windsor Herald, but declined the office of Garter King of Arms, offered to him after the successful publication of his *History of the Order of the Garter*.

Ashmole was throughout his life an enthusiastic collector of books, medals and coins. He also acquired a collection of John Tradescant of considerable importance.

Ashmole planned to present the collection to Oxford University, and a suitable building for their reception, the Old Ashmolean, was completed in 1682. Meantime a fire in the donor's chambers caused substantial losses, but the gift was still a remarkable one. Ashmole, who died in 1692, was the recipient of many foreign honours.

In 1897 the Ashmolean collection, which had been augmented by substantial bequests in the donor's will, was removed to new buildings known as the Ashmolean Museum of Art and Archæology.

Asklepiades, of asclepiad. Asclepiad, verse consisting of a spondee, two or three choriambi and an iambus. The name comes from the inventor, the Greek poet, Asklepiades (3rd century B.C.).

The first Ode of Horace is Asclepiadic.

A spondee is a metrical foot ($--$); a choriambus is a metrical foot ($- \cup \cup -$) and an iambus is the metrical foot ($\cup -$).

St. Athanasius of the Athanasian Creed. The great bishop of Alexandria lived about A.D. 296–373. At an early age he made his mark in the Councils of Nicea and was a consistent opponent of the doctrines of Arius. He was made patriarch of Alexandria and primate of Egypt. He refused to reinstate the banished Arius when he was restored to favour owing to the support of the Emperor Constantine.

Athanasius was exiled, restored to favour and again banished. In Rome he was supported by the Italian bishops and threats of war eventually led to his re-establishment, only to meet with much intrigue and persecution. He went into exile again, supported by the leaders of the Egyptian Church, who refused to facilitate his capture.

Athanasius was a great leader of the church, whose influence never waned during his persecutions. He was a noted orator and though the forty-odd years of his primacy were interrupted by four periods of banishment, his was a remarkable reign.

The creed perpetuating his name was not established until several centuries after his death, which was the occasion of widespread religious persecution. The origin of the creed has been an issue of much controversy.

Athene of Athenæum. Athene, the Greek virgin goddess of wisdom, identified with the Roman Minerva, was the origin of the name Athenæum for the famous school or academy founded by Hadrian in the 1st century B.C. It was situated on the Capitoline Hill in Rome.

Athene is said to have sprung fully armed from the head of Zeus. Everything essential to the spiritual, intellectual and physical welfare of mankind was reputed to derive from this goddess.

The owl, accounted a wise bird, was among the many things sacred to her.

The Athenæum, one of London's most distinguished clubs, was established in 1824.

Tommy Atkins, the private soldier. The name Tommy Atkins arose from the former custom of issuing to recruits record papers for completion, with a specimen form for instruction which was completed in the hypothetical name of "Tommy Atkins."

In legal circles the sample name John or Richard Doe is always employed for a similar purpose.

Kipling and other writers have frequently used Tommy Atkins and Tommy to represent the typical soldier in the ranks.

Atlas of Atlas. In Greek mythology Atlas was one of the Titans who, because of his attempt to overthrow Zeus, was compelled by him to support the pillars of the heavens upon his broad shoulders.

Milton refers in *Paradise Lost, Book II*, to "Atlantean shoulders, fit to bear the weight of mightiest monarchies."

Some accounts show Atlas as artfully relieving himself of his load by persuading Heracles to support the heavens while Atlas fetched the apples of Hesperides. He revelled in his newly-found freedom, but Heracles persuaded Atlas to resume his load while he arranged a more comfortable cushion for his back.

Heracles left the guileless Atlas in his former straits and made off with the apples.

Another account makes Atlas a King of Mauretania who, for his want of hospitality to Perseus, was changed into a mountain.

The traditional Atlas

The use of the word Atlas for a book or collection of maps has an added justification. Mercator, the great cartographer, used the figure of Atlas, bearing the world upon his back, on the title-page of his 16th-century collection of maps.

Augustus Cæsar of August. In the old Roman calendar August was named *Sextilis*, as the sixth month of the year, and it consisted of twenty-nine days. Julius Cæsar, in his calendar reform, extended it to thirty days. When Augustus gave the month his name he took a day from February and added it to the month of August. September was his birth month, but many fortunate events occurred for him in August and it had the added significance of being next to July, the month of his famous predecessor. In August Augustus was first made consul and he celebrated many triumphs, reduced Egypt, and settled the civil wars.

Augustus was the grand-nephew of Julius Cæsar. His mother was the daughter of Cæsar's sister. In 45 B.C. he was made a patrician and master of Cæsar's horse. After the murder of Cæsar, Augustus was appointed heir to the great ruler. The succession met with much opposition, but the reign of Augustus was marked by distinguished progress and reconstruction and an almost unrivalled flowering of literature.

September derives its name from the fact that it was originally the seventh month. Augustus took from it the thirty-first day which had been allotted by his predecessor, Cæsar, in his calendar reform.

October similarly derives its name from the fact that it was originally the eighth month. It was named by the Saxons *Wyn monath*, the wine month. The best and strongest ale was often called "October."

November likewise has root in its original place as the ninth month. It was called by the Saxons *Wint monath*, or the wind month, from the prevailing gales; or *blot monath*, the bloody month, from the customary slaughter of cattle for winter use. Some accounts also link this name with the bloody sacrifices at one time prevalent during this season. In the French Republican calendar it was called Brumaire, the fog month.

December derives its name from the original position as tenth month in the calendar. The French Republicans gave it the name Frimaire, the month of hoar frosts.

Aurora of Aurora Borealis. The aurora, or luminous atmospheric phenomenon at the magnetic poles, is named from the Roman goddess of the dawn.

At the north pole the phenomenon is known as the Aurora Borealis (see *Boreas*) and at the south, Aurora Australis.

Aurora was a sister of the sun god and the moon goddess. She rose in her beauty—rosy-fingered, as Homer says—and harnessed her bright horses that she might precede the sun god and announce the dawning day.

Erasmus claimed that Aurora was friendly to the Muses. The name is frequently employed by poets and the dew has been poetically described as "Aurora's tears."

Sinclair Lewis of Babbitry. "Babbitry—the moral and social tone prevalent among average business men; acceptance of the group standards (always in a derogatory sense)"—*O.E.D.*

Babbitt is the creation of Sinclair Lewis, one of the great contemporary American novelists, born in 1885 and awarded the Nobel Prize for Literature in 1931.

The novel of that name, published in 1922, presents the self-satisfied, not precisely scrupulous but very lovable, modern business man. As Sir Hugh Walpole said in the Introduction to an English edition ". . . not only is Babbitt a warning, he is also a friend. And, through him, the country of which he is a citizen."

The citizen of Zenith is described as having made "nothing in particular, neither butter nor shoes nor poetry, but he was nimble in the calling of selling houses for more than people could afford to pay."

He is in fact the astute, successful man, setting too much store upon local esteem and outward prosperity.

At the close of the book, Babbitt's son defies his father's wish that he should go ahead to the University. Instead he announces his secret marriage and the fact that he intends to "get into mechanics." Babbitt "crossed the floor, slowly, ponderously, seeming a little old. 'I've always wanted you to have a college degree.' He meditatively stamped across the floor again. 'But I've never . . . Now, for heaven's sake, don't repeat this to your mother, or she'd remove what little hair I've got left, but practically, I've never done a single thing I've wanted to in my whole life! I don't know's I've accomplished anything except just get along. I figure out I've made about a quarter of an inch out of a possible hundred rods. Well, maybe you'll carry things further. I don't know. . . . Don't be scared of the family. No, nor of Zenith. Nor of yourself, the way I've been. Go ahead, old man! The world is yours!' "

Babbitt is one of the major creations of contemporary literature.

Bacchus of Bacchanalian. Bacchus, the Roman equivalent of the Greek Dionysus, was the god of wine and vineyards. He symbolizes the fruitfulness and blessings of autumn. He planted the vine, and soon succumbed to its potency. Encouraged by education at the hands of Silenus, son of Pan, Bacchus began to spread the gospel of wine to which he was an addict.

Bacchus

The triennial festivals, held in Rome (and later in Greece) in honour of the god, were eventually characterized by much drunkenness and lechery, although originally they followed a more sober and symbolic pattern. They were more in the nature of harvest thanksgivings, allied with celebration of Bacchus' marriage to Ariadne.

To-day the adjective bacchanalian is reserved for a drunken orgy on a grand scale.

Francis Bacon of Baconian. Francis Bacon, Lord Verulam (1561–1626), is known as the father of the inductive method of scientific enquiry.

He was called to the Bar and represented Taunton, Liverpool and Ipswich in Parliament. He was a favourite of the Queen and held high offices in the State, including that of Lord Chancellor. He was convicted as a judge, deposed and subsequently pardoned.

Bacon's chief works were *Novum Organum, The Advancement of Learning* and *De Augumentis Scientiarum.*

The wisdom and wit of his famous *Essays* led to the formation of the Baconian Theory that he wrote the plays attributed to Shakespeare.

After the sacred volumes of God and the Scriptures, study, in the second place, that great volume of the works and creatures of God, strenuously, and before all books, which ought to be only regarded as commentaries.
To Trinity College, Cambridge.

The Duke of Beaufort of Badminton. The game of Badminton, played with rackets and shuttlecocks, takes its name from the country seat of the Duke of Beaufort, Badminton Hall, Gloucestershire. It was there extensively played and popularized towards the end of the 19th century. It had previously been played in India. The Badminton Association in England was formed in 1895.

The now arbitrary rules and dimensions evolved from contrived domestic fittings rigged up at Badminton for private playing of a personal game.

The name Badminton has also been given to a type of claret cup, doubtless originally associated with the playing of the game in its first English setting.

Karl Baedeker of the Guides. The word Baedeker is almost synonymous with exhaustive guides to the world's great cities and places of historic importance. Even Hitler, when proposing to destroy our cities of great historical, architectural and ecclesiastical interest, announced that he would make "Baedeker raids."

The origin of the word was a German bookseller, born at Essen in 1801, the son of a local printer and bookseller. Karl set up similar businesses in Coblenz, and soon began the series of guide books which eventually covered most of the world and were printed in many languages. They were so ably compiled and so authoritative that they became almost essential to travellers. The firm, which later generations continued, was transferred to Leipzig in 1872.

The guide books owed almost everything to the acumen of Karl Baedeker and his ability in his wide travels to assess exactly the information, whether it be historic or a question of cuisine, which the traveller required. He died in 1859, having added unexpectedly in a comparatively short life a new word to the language.

Balaam, the disappointing prophet or ally. The reference is to the Midianite soothsayer, Balaam, whose disappointing prophetic efforts are described in *Num. xxiv.*

It was believed that whomever was blessed by Balaam was truly blessed and likewise his curses were potent.

Balak sent for Balaam to curse Israel, but though willing he was unable to fulfil the command. "Balak's anger was kindled against Balaam, and he smote his hands together and said . . . I called thee to curse mine enemies, and, behold, thou hast altogether blessed them these three times. Therefore now flee thou to thy place . . ." (*xxiv. 10*).

The term Balaam is also frequently used for time-serving officials.

The incident of Balaam and his prescient, talking ass, referred to frequently in literature and literary allusion, is found in *Num. xxii.*

Balaam was also formerly a term for journalistic "fills"—matter kept standing in type for filling or use in emergency. The name was also given to the receptacle for such type. Lockhart, in his biography of Scott, claims that the allusion is to the asinine character of such fill matter —fit subjects, perhaps, only for the "gooseberry season."

Banbury of the Cake. The familiar spiced cake derives its name from the Oxfordshire town of Banbury.

The name Banbury was also synonymous with cheese-paring and is frequently found in literature. In this connection it was often applied to Puritans and bigots. The reference may have been drawn from the special cheese associated with Banbury, a cream cheese which was very thin—about an inch in thickness—compared with most characteristic British cheeses.

Bantam of Bantams. The name Bantam, applied to a diminutive species of fowl with a particularly pugnacious cock, derives from Bantam in Java, whence they were possibly brought, though some authorities suggest Japan as the country of actual origin.

The term is also applied to a particularly spirited small fighter, it is a category of recognized boxing weights (8 st. 6 lb.) and was given admiringly to battalions raised in the First World War of men below normal physical standards.

William Banting of Banting. William Banting (1797–1878), a London cabinet-maker, owes his inclusion in the dictionary to the slim distinction of weight-reducing.

In 1863 he published, with humanitarian desires, a remarkable *Letter on Corpulence.*

This little man of sixty-six should have weighed, according to current medical tables, about 142 lb. In fact he weighed 202 lb.

Banting claims in his *Letter,* with likeable earnestness, that his corpulence and obesity were not through self-indulgence or a lack of exercise.

Even so, "I could not stoop to tie my shoe, nor attend to the little offices humanity requires without considerable pain and difficulty." He was compelled even to walk downstairs backwards to reduce the pain in his distended joints, though he had worn knee bandages for twenty years.

On medical advice he adopted a diet. It included several ounces of meat for breakfast, tea without milk or sugar and toast or biscuit.

Dinner included five or six ounces of any fish except salmon, any meat except pork, any vegetable except potato, poultry or game, cooked fruit, several glasses of wine. Champagne, beer and port were barred.

Tea consisted of fruit, rusks or toast and the drink without milk or sugar.

Supper was three or four ounces of meat or fish with vegetables and a glass or two of claret.

By modern standards the fare sounds Lucullan, but in little more than a year (and remember Banting was in his late sixties) he lost 46 lb. and reduced his waist line by 12$\frac{1}{4}$ inches.

He reported himself as a new man and lived to a ripe age, hearing his name become an adjective for slimming.

Barkis of "Barkis is willing." The expression, to convey willingness or consent, is taken from Dickens' *David Copperfield.*

It was the message sent by Barkis, the carrier, to Peggotty by Copperfield conveying his desire to marry (*Chapter V*).

The Barmecides of Barmecide and Barmecide's feast. A barmecide is a giver of benefits that are illusory, imaginary or disappointing.

The name was the patronymic of a family of Princes ruling in Bagdad just before Haroun-al-Raschid. The family achieved great power under the Abbasid caliphs.

The allusion is to the story in the *Arabian Nights* of the Barber's sixth brother, Shakálik. In a state of penury Shakálik seeks sustenance from the Barmecide family and is served with an imaginary banquet, his host miming all the ritual of hospitality and the serving of the feast. Shakálik "observed in his own mind, Verily this is a man who loveth to jest with others," and eventually decided, "By Allah, I will do to him a deed that shall make him repent before God of these actions."

So, pretending to be intoxicated by the imaginary wine, he struck his host "such a sharp blow upon his neck that the chamber rang at the blow."

The host, after his first fury, recognized the justice of the assault and confessed that he had tried the trick many times, but Shakálik was the only one who had endured it. He had not found "any who had sagacity to conform to all my actions, save thee."

Dr. Thomas John Barnardo of Barnardo's Homes. The English philanthropist whose name is indelibly associated with the care of destitute children, was born in Dublin in 1845. His father was of Spanish origin, born in Germany, his mother an English Quaker. The doctor described himself as "a bit of all sorts." He studied medicine at London Hospital, at Paris and in Edinburgh.

His work in the East End of London during the cholera outbreak of 1865 diverted him from his original interest in foreign missionary endeavour among the Chinese to a fruitful life work of pioneer philanthropy and healing. That magnificent career was carved by a puny child who, at the age of two, had been pronounced dead. The coffin was in the house and the undertaker preparing to embalm the child when the heart fluttered. Many millions the world over must be thankful for that deliverance.

The first of Dr. Barnardo's homes, all of which subscribe to the Charter, "No destitute child ever refused admission," was opened in Stepney Causeway in 1867. Barnardo, who met fierce opposition, was a pioneer in educational and industrial training methods and medical care and he lived to see his influence spread all over the world. He initiated successful emigration schemes, and maintained and proved that "heredity counts for little, environment almost everything." He was insistent on religious teaching, according to the denomination of the child's parents.

He had a keen sense of fun, was much beloved and had no time for long-faced religion.

He died in 1905 and was buried in the church of his own girl's village home at Barkingside.

Phineas Taylor Barnum, the super-showman. The name of Barnum, the American super-showman, has become synonymous with ingenious, bravura self-advertisers. But Barnum was more than an astute advertiser and "barker."

He was born in 1810, the son of an inn- and store-keeper. After an unsuccessful start in lotteries, business and journalism, he began as a showman with the exhibition of a coloured woman, said to be the nurse of George Washington and aged over 150. He was a past master of unorthodox and highly ingenious advertising and his tours were spectacular. He had the super showman's flair for novelty, and his star turns included the celebrated dwarf, General Tom Thumb, and a tour of America presenting Jenny Lind, the Swedish Nightingale, at prodigious expense.

His circus, menagerie and general exhibition toured the world as the "Greatest Show on Earth." Its magnificence gave some justice to the slogan. Certainly he was the prince of showmen. Whether he was attracting the public by a chain of three or four men continually entering his premises (and returning from the rear to repeat the performance) or ploughing with his elephants during the slack season (only when traffic was passing), he was the king of money extractors from the masses.

He died in 1891, deserving the tribute of a dubious but legitimately earned adjective.

St. Bartholomew of "St. Barts."

The world-famous London hospital at Smithfield was founded in the 12th century by Rahere, a monk. Many famous figures in medicine have been associated with it.

St. Bartholomew, apostle and martyr, is commemorated on August 24. He is frequently depicted as holding a knife and sometimes headless or bearing his own skin, a reference to his having been flayed alive. He is thought to have died in Armenia about A.D. 44.

He is supposed to be identical with Nathanael, mentioned in St. John's Gospel, but is generally referred to as Bartholomew and associated with Philip. He was present at the Resurrection (*John xxi. 2*) and at the Ascension (*Acts i. 4, 12–13*).

"St. Bartholomew's Day" is a term used to describe an outrage of unprecedented cruelty, from the Massacre of the Innocents in France on the saint's day, 1572, at the instance of Catharine de Medici, acting as regent for her son.

A famous fair was held for centuries at Smithfield on St. Bartholomew's Day. A feature of it was a pig roasted whole and sold hot. This custom gave rise to the expression "a St. Bartholomew's pig." Falstaff uses the expression to describe himself in *2 Henry IV*. Jonson's *Bartholomew's Fair* was published in 1614.

A "Bartholomew doll" was once favoured to describe an over-dressed woman, from the cheap, gawdy dolls that were a feature of the Fair.

Bavius and Mævius, inferior poets or poetasters.

Bavius and Mævius were two inferior poets who were criticized and satirized by Virgil.

The Baviad was a fierce satire by William Gifford (1757–1826), published in 1794. It was followed two years later by *The Mæviad*. The subject of the satire was the dubious and sentimental poetry of the Della Cruscans who, towards the end of the 18th century, published in England much extravagant and self-laudatory verse. The leader of the set, which claimed association with Florence, was Robert Merry, who used the pseudonym Della Crusca.

George Baxter of Baxter Prints.

The famous lithographer and wood-engraver was born in 1804 and was largely self-educated. He began his working life as a printer in Lewes, Sussex.

He was a craftsman by instinct and practice and his desire was to place beautiful work within the reach of all.

Baxter's particular process, based upon a steel engraving and involving numerous blocks, often as many as thirty, produced a work of singular beauty and delicacy of colour. He printed his works extensively, eager to secure the widest circulation but without lowering his very high standards of art and execution. As a result, Baxter prints are too numerous still to be very rare but certain plates are now sold for large sums and all have an appreciable value.

His work is recognized as a signal contribution to the progress of art and printing.

The artist died bankrupt in 1867, but the formation of a Baxter Society was a tribute to his work, the appreciation of which still persists and is enhanced with the years. The first London Exhibition of Baxter Prints was held in 1909.

Pierre du Terrail Bayard of

Sans peur et sans reproche. Bayard is a dictionary synonym for a chivalrous person because of the exploits of Chevalier Pierre du Terrail Bayard, born at the Château de Bayard in

Dauphine in 1475. His family was one of great military distinction, soon to be adorned by the exploits of the youth who was placed in the service of the Duke of Savoy.

At the age of nineteen, Pierre accompanied Charles VIII against Naples and won glory at the Battle of Fornovo. He served in the Italian wars of Louis XII and was taken prisoner at the Battle of the Spurs. He was knighted by Francis I and was mortally wounded when defending Bonnivet in Northern Italy against Charles V. As such the record could be shared by many. What distinguished *"le bon chevalier"* was the brilliance of his fearless fighting and the gentle, pious nature of the man himself. He was the perfect cavalier. His exploits are a golden thread through the tapestry of his times. Like Nelson, he had never seen fear.

His end was typical. The French troops were retreating under relentless pressure from the Imperial Army under De Bourbon. Bayard was implored to take command. "It is too late," he said, and in him it was no affectation, "but my soul is God's, and my life is my country's."

He went to the head of a body of men-at-arms and defied the enemy until shot from his horse.

Mortally wounded, he still refused to retire, saying he had never shown his back to the enemy.

His comrades propped him against a tree, facing the advancing hordes. He had no cross, so he kissed his sword. There was no priest, so Bayard confessed to one of his company.

De Bourbon, expressing regret for the fall of his enemy, was told, "Weep for yourself, sir. For me, I have nothing to complain. I die in the course of my duty to my country. You triumph in betraying yours." That was in 1534.

The signal tribute, *"Le bon chevalier; sans peur et sans reproche,"* has since been applied to our own gallant Sir Philip Sidney.

The Marquis de Béchamel of Sauce Béchamel. The noted white sauce, thickened with cream, was named after its inventor, the Marquis de Béchamel, steward to Louis XIV of France, 1636–1715.

Beelzebub, the devil. There are Biblical references to Beelzebub, prince of the devils, in *Mark iii. 22,* and *Luke xi. 15.* Milton also uses the name for one of the fallen angels, next to Satan in power, in *Paradise Lost.*

Isabella Beeton of Mrs. Beeton's Cookery Books. Isabella Beeton was born at 24 Milk Street, off Cheapside, in 1836. Farther down the street, at No. 39, was a boy of five, named Samuel Orchart Beeton.

Isabella was one of a remarkable family of twenty-one children. Her stepfather was Henry Dorling, who owned the Grand Stand on Epsom

Mrs. Beeton

Downs and printed the race cards—"Dorling's Correct Card." In the late forties, as a widower with four children, he married Elizabeth Mayson, a widow with a family of four, of whom Isabella was one. The Dorlings subsequently had thirteen children of their own.

Isabella married in 1856, at Epsom Parish Church, and the reception was held in the Grand Stand. Her husband, Samuel Orchart Beeton, was now a well-known young editor and publisher, with offices in the Strand. He published numerous reference books. His production of *Uncle Tom's Cabin* was a remarkable success and though he was not required by law to recompense the author, he made a special journey to the United States to present Harriet Beecher Stowe with a cheque for £750.

Mrs. Beeton's first home was at Pinner. She had studied gastronomy at Heidelberg and pastry making under the supervision of the Epsom confectioner. Despite her studies, Isabella was a spirited young woman, fashionable and extremely pretty. She bought all her clothes in Paris. She wrote fashion as well as cookery articles for her husband's periodicals.

Her famous cookery book, which took her four years to collect and test, was published in twenty-four monthly parts at 3*d*. (1858–61). Economy was its main object and no other cookery book contained an equally large proportion of recipes for those with very limited means. Her *Household Management* swiftly became a bestseller. She was caricatured in print and on the stage for an extravagance of outlook, which was completely contrary to the facts.

Mrs. Beeton, who was a linguist and an accomplished pianist and pupil of Sir Julius Benedict, confessed that if she had known beforehand the labour that her book involved, she would not have been courageous enough to begin it. But she had "always thought that there was no more fruitful source of family discontent than badly cooked dinners and untidy ways."

Conan Doyle, in *A Duet, with an Occasional Chorus*, makes one of his characters say: "Mrs. Beeton must have been the finest housekeeper in the world . . . her book . . . has more wisdom to the square inch than any work of man."

Mrs. Beeton died at the age of twenty-six, two days after the birth of her fourth son, who became Sir Mayson Beeton. Her portrait is in the National Portrait Gallery.

Bellona, the personification of war. Bellona was a Roman goddess of war, particularly of the fury of war. She is related to Mars, in some accounts as sister, in others as wife. There was a temple to her in Campus Martius, the scene of the athletic exercises of Roman Youth.

The Greek counterpart of the goddess was Enyo.

The name Bellona is frequently used as an epithet for a woman of commanding presence.

St. Benedict of Benedictine and a Benedict. St. Benedict, founder of Western monasticism, was born near Spoleto late in the 5th century. He lived as a hermit for some years and attracted many to his retreat. He left an abbey to found his own monasteries and composed a *Regula Monachorum* which required implicit obedience and imposed celibacy, strict austerity and religious observance and intense industry.

The Benedictine Order was founded about 530 at Monte Casino, near Naples, and is known as the Black Monks. The Black Friars are the Dominicans. The Benedictines are renowned for their learning, though its founder was not a man of scholarship. In the early centuries they rendered outstanding service to literature and science, particularly in the preservation and transcription of classic literature.

St. Benedict is frequently represented as accompanied by a raven, which sometimes bears a loaf in its beak. Other presentations depict the saint as surrounded by thorns or threatening devils.

The saint's day is March 21. The term "benedict" does not imply a vow of celibacy, but is used to describe an eligible man who has not married.

A "benedick," to describe a sworn bachelor who is at last caught in the toils of matrimony, derives from

Shakespeare's character of that name and reputation in *Much Ado About Nothing*.

Benjamin the youngest or best beloved child. The reference is to Benjamin (son of my right hand), the younger son of Jacob and Rachel (*Gen. xxxv. 18*). His mother, who named him Ben-oni (son of my pain), died at his birth. Jacob changed the child's name to Benjamin. There are many references to the favour he enjoyed.

The preference bestowed is symbolized in the phrase "Benjamin's mess." When Joseph feasted his brethren "Benjamin's mess was five times so much as any of theirs" (*Gen. xliii. 34*).

The tribe of Benjamin was one of the twelve tribes at the Exodus, the smallest but one.

Jeremy Bentham of Benthamism and Benthamite. Jeremy Bentham (1748–1832) was a noted writer on ethics and jurisprudence. He was trained to the law but never practised. He made a life-long study of legal theory and government. Briefly his guiding ethical principle was the greatest happiness for the greatest number.

Carlyle was a noted opponent of Bentham's teachings. He protested against the implied low estimate of a man's soul as a mere balance for weighing against material goods and physical pleasures.

The only merit he saw in Benthamism was its evidence of the material crises which would surely be succeeded by a regeneration of mankind and mankind's philosophy.

The sacred truth that the greatest happiness of the greatest number is the foundation of morals and legislation.

Works, vol. 10.

Berenice of Berenice's Hair. Berenice, daughter of Magas, King of Cyrene, was the sister-wife of Ptolemy III, Euergetes.

Ptolemy invaded Syria to avenge the death of his sister and in his absence Berenice offered her hair to Venus against his safe return. It was placed in the temple at Zephyrium.

The hair disappeared and Colon, the sage of Samos, poetically explained the theft by announcing that the hair had been carried to heaven and placed among the stars. The constellation *Coma Berenices* is to be found near the tail of *Leo*.

Savinien Cyrano de Bergerac of the prodigious nose. Cyrano de Bergerac, probably the only man whose nose has made history, finds his name given to anyone whose nose assumes diverting proportions.

de Bergerac (1619–55) was a Gascon, son of the Seigneur de Mauvières et de Bergerac, and an eccentric of remarkable comic powers. His nose was of such preposterous proportions that he is said to have fought countless duels in vindication of it.

Cyrano de Bergerac

He served as an officer in the Guards for several years and his adventures became the subject of legend, though they were, including his fight with a hundred men, actual fact.

Cyrano turned to writing and produced notable comedies, tragedies and satirical scientific romances. His comedy, *Le Pédant Joué*, considerably influenced Molière.

His most notable romances, *L'Histoires Comiques des états de la lune* and

L'Histoires Comiques des états du Soleil (the latter published posthumously), are in the Rabelaisian tradition, and are regarded by some as the inspiration of Swift's *Gulliver's Travels*.

The famous play, *Cyrano de Bergerac* (1897), was written by Edmond Rostand (1868–1918) and founded on the hero's adventures.

The title role was created by Coquelin *ainé* and has since been interpreted by many great actors.

St. Bernard of the St. Bernard Dogs.

St. Bernard, founder of the famous Hospice, whose name is perpetuated thereby and in the famous dogs, was born in the 10th century in Menthon, Savoy.

He came of noble family and completed his studies in Paris. He declined a noble marriage planned by his father and surrendered his wealth to become a Canon Regular of St. Augustine's Cathedral, Aosta. He

A St. Bernard dog

was later appointed Archdeacon and Preacher.

At that period pilgrims to Rome from several European countries were often robbed and ill treated when crossing the Mons Jovis pass. Bernard converted these mountain dwellers and built the hospice for travellers. His parents visited him there and supported the project with their wealth.

The Castle of Menthon still exists and St. Bernard's room is a chapel visited by the Fathers of the Hospice on St. Bernard's Day, August 20.

The Hospice, built on a pass between Switzerland and Italy, is 8,000 feet above sea level. The top of the pass is snow-bound for ten months of the year and in winter is often impassable. Avalanches are frequent, vegetation is scarce, even in summer.

In 1883 the St. Bernard Fathers were the first to use skis in Switzerland. They were obtained from Norway. The hospitality of the Hospice is freely available to all, and the monks and the dogs assist every traveller in difficulty. Sometimes several hundred travellers may be accommodated on a single night and many royalty and famous people have visited the monks.

The monks are Canons Regular of the Order of St. Augustine and only the strongest can survive the severe conditions and then only for a limited period. Many have died through exposure and accident. They do all the work and the nursing. They pursue classical and scientific study.

Many of the famous dogs, of which there are generally about fifteen at the Hospice, are capable of carrying a man. They are magnificent guides and rescue workers and their training is long and arduous. Their lives are short, owing to the severe conditions.

The St. Bernard breed is a cross between a bulldog and a Pyrenean shepherd's dog. Those with long hair are discarded as it is a handicap in the snow. The line of dogs has been bred for four centuries.

Alphonse Bertillon of the Bertillon System.

Alphonse Bertillon (1853–1914) was inventor of the Bertillon system, or Bertillonage, for the identification of criminals by means of anthropometry. He described his system in *Photographic Judiciare*. He was a distinguished anthropologist and son of a doctor who was one of the founders of the School of Anthropology in Paris.

Alphonse was an expert witness in the famous Dreyfus case.

Sir Benjamin Hall of Big Ben.

Sir Benjamin was Chief Commissioner of Works, 1855–8, and it was during his term of office that the great bell was cast for the clock tower of the Houses of Parliament.

The bell was to have been called "St. Stephen," but a random use in the Press of the sobriquet "Big Ben" immediately caught the public's fancy and it has persisted.

George Birkbeck of Birkbeck

College. The eminent English physician and philanthropist, George Birkbeck (1776–1841), was born at Settle, in Yorkshire. He studied medicine at Leeds and Edinburgh, and after graduation he was appointed to the chair of Natural Philosophy at the Andersonian Institution, Glasgow.

In the following year he delivered a free course of scientific lectures to working men and founded a mechanics' institute.

Birkbeck removed to London and there, in 1823, he was largely responsible for founding the Mechanics' Institute. He became director and the name was later altered to the Birkbeck Institution or College, in honour of its director who substantially endowed it.

The buildings and the scope of the College have been frequently extended and in 1920 Birkbeck College became a college of London University.

Augustine Birrell of Birrellisms.

Birrellisms: passing comments, pungent yet kindly, characteristic of Augustine Birrell.

Birrell (1850–1933), the noted English author and man of letters, was born near Liverpool, the son of a Nonconformist Minister. He became a Q.C. and was Professor of Law at University College. He entered Parliament first for West Fife as a Liberal in 1889.

His writings on literary subjects and even his legal treatises revealed an original and sparkling style enlivened by much wit. The use of these gifts in the House of Commons led to the coining of the words "birrelling" and "birrellisms."

Birrell was Minister for Education and for some years Chief Secretary for Ireland. He wrote studies of Andrew Marvell and William Hazlitt and several volumes of *Obiter Dicta*. He was regarded as among the leading literary critics of his day and all his work is distinguished by a brilliant originality and pungent wit.

James Tait Black of the James

Tait Black Literary Prizes. James Tait Black was a partner in the publishing house of A. & C. Black, Ltd., and the annual Memorial Prizes were inaugurated by his widow. She substantially endowed the fund, which provides prizes annually for the best biography or similar work and the best novel.

The Hawthornden Prize (William Drummond of Hawthornden was known as "The Petrarch of Scotland") was founded by Miss Agnes Warrender in 1919. It is for the best imaginative work in prose or verse by a British author under forty-one years of age.

The Stock Prize (formerly the *Femina Vie Heureuse*) is for the best imaginative work produced by young British authors or those not considered previously to have received adequate recognition.

The John Llewellyn Rhys Memorial Prize was founded by the widow of J. L. Rhys, who was killed while serving with the R.A.F. in 1940. It is intended to encourage young writers.

The Rose Mary Crawshay Prize, founded in 1888 by Rose Mary Crawshay, is awarded annually to a woman of any nationality for an historical or critical work on a subject connected with English literature. Preference is given to studies of Byron, Keats, or

Shelley, which authors formed the subject of the original prize terms.

The Cromer Greek Prize was founded by the late Lord Cromer to encourage the study of Greek. Full details of the other Literary Prizes and Awards will be found in *The Artists' and Writers' Year Book.* The Nobel Prize and the *Prix de Goncourt* are the subject of separate entries in this book (pp. 114 and 76).

Maria Lee of Black Maria. The tradition in Scotland Yard is that the name for the van used for conveying prisoners from the courts to jail derives from one, Maria Lee.

This negress, of fearsome proportions and fiery spirit, kept a sailors' lodging-house in Boston, Philadelphia. Her reputation was such that even hardened offenders went in dread of her and when the police required help in the tracing and capture of them, Maria's assistance was often sought. Her physical assistance, eagerly given, was equally welcomed.

Charles Blondin, the "tight-rope walker" in any circumstances. The feats of Charles Blondin, the French acrobat and tight-rope walker, were so prodigious and so universally proclaimed, that his name has become descriptive of anyone achieving a feat of perilous negotiation.

Blondin was born at St. Omer, in France, in 1824, and as a small child his skill was so outstanding that he was called "The Little Wonder."

His most spectacular exploit was to cross the Niagara Falls on a tight-rope over a thousand feet long and slung 160 feet above the water.

Not content with this amazing feat, he repeated the performance, frequently adding to his fame by executing it blindfold, carrying a man across on his back, wheeling a barrow and crossing the rope on stilts.

He died at Ealing, London, in 1897, after a career of almost unparalleled showmanship and skill.

Mrs. Amelia Bloomer. To edit a journal entitled *The Lily*, even in Seneca Falls, New York, must require courage, despite the flower's advantageous comparison with Solomon in all his glory. The more so, perhaps, when it is a temperance journal.

The Bloomers

Editor Amelia Bloomer was therefore not unequipped for her mission, and when the U.S. Women's Rights Movement developed about 1849, she launched her offensive. Her press view was a ball held in July, 1851, at the cotton-manufacturing town of Lowell, Mass. She left the upper part of the revolutionary costume to the taste of the wearer, but below "we would have a skirt reaching down to nearly half-way between the knee and the ankle, and not made quite so full as is the present fashion. Underneath this skirt, trousers moderately full, in fair, mild weather, coming down to the ankle (not instep) and there gathered in with an elastic band. . . . For winter, or wet weather, the trousers also full, but coming down into a boot, which should rise some three or four inches at least above the ankle."

In *The Lily* Mrs. Bloomer defended her fashions against charges of immodesty or inelegancy. "If delicacy requires that the skirt should be long, why do our ladies, a dozen times a day, commit the indelicacy of raising their dresses, which have already been sweeping the side-walks, to prevent their dragging in the mud of the streets? Surely a few spots of mud added to the refuse of the side-walks, on the hem of their garment, are not to be compared to the charge of indelicacy to which the display they make might subject them!"

The fashion found some favour in the United States and was generally absolved from the charge of indelicacy.

When Mrs. Bloomer lectured in this country, backed, it would seem from an illustration in *The Lady's Newspaper of 1851*, by a bloomered beauty chorus in alternating dark and light colours, there was more censure than conversion. The hygienic advantages were apparently not disputed, but the English lady was suspicious of any movement from a dangerously democratic country. What was liberty of limb compared with dignity and respect. The bloomers have shrunk to shorts and dignity, as my lady would know it, has diminished.

Not for Mrs. Amelia Bloomer of *The Lily* was Herrick's "Sweet disorder in the dress." She put her temperate faith in the elastic ankle band—and it was sufficient to preserve the name.

Bluebeard, the murderer of many wives. Bluebeard, the prototype of the wife murderer, is generally attributed to the story of Charles Perrault (1628-1703), to whose *Contes du Temps* are traced the origin of many of the best known fairy stories.

Perrault was a Frenchman of letters who followed a legal career. He also wrote *Parallel des Anciens et des Modernes* in which he sought to prove by comparison that the ancients were inferior in everything to the moderns.

Bluebeard, a wealthy seigneur, leaves his wife, Fatima, in charge of his castle with instructions not to unlock any of the rooms. She uses the keys, only to discover the remains of former wives locked in one of the rooms.

Her sin is discovered and she is saved from death only by the arrival of her brothers who dispatch Bluebeard.

Some writers detect in the story a satire upon notorious wife killers, including Henry VIII. Various names are given to the original of Bluebeard, including Chevalier Raoul and the Marquis de Laval who was accused in Brittany during the 15th century of murdering six of his seven wives.

The use of the term Bluebeard with these associations is frequent in literature and there is a similar story in *The Arabian Nights*.

Landru, a 20th-century French wife killer, was called "The Modern Bluebeard."

Boanerges, the loud-voiced orator or preacher. Boanerges, meaning the sons of thunder, was the surname given by Christ to James and his brother John. When the Samaritans declined to receive Christ the two disciples said, "Lord, wilt thou that we bid fire to come down from heaven, and consume them?" They were rebuked for the suggestion (*Mark iii. 17* and *Luke ix. 54*).

Captain Bobadil, the vain braggart. The word derives from the characteristics of Captain Bobadil, one of Ben Jonson's finest creations. He appeared in *Every Man in his Humour*, which was produced in 1598, with Shakespeare in the cast.

Bobadil is an old soldier, a cowardly braggart who clothes his boasting in a grave decorum. He is a "Paul's man," a reference to the secular uses of St. Paul's Cathedral in the 16th and 17th centuries. The centre aisle was known as "Paul's Walk" and was a noted promenade and recognized centre for gossip, business transactions and secret assignations. Servants could be hired there, which custom is referred to by Falstaff.

Jonson himself used this strange Cathedral traffic as the background for part of *Every Man Out of his Humour*, produced in 1599.

Sir Thomas Bodley of the Bodleian. Thomas Bodley was born in the West Country in 1544. He received his early education in Geneva, whither his Protestant father had fled from the religious persecutions under Queen Mary. He returned in 1559 a good scholar and at this early age entered Magdalen College, Oxford. He was made a Fellow of Merton in 1563. He lectured on Greek and Natural Philosophy. For several years he travelled the Continent studying modern languages. He was made a Gentleman Usher to Queen Elizabeth or, according to more robust accounts, "Esquire of the Body."

In 1585 Bodley married a rich widow of Bristol and entered diplomacy, frequently travelling abroad. He was recommended by Burleigh as Secretary for State in conjunction with his own son, but the jealousy of Essex prevented the appointment and Bodley retired in chagrin to devote himself to restoring and refounding the public library. He gave his own magnificent library and supplemented it with substantial financial assistance.

He was knighted by James and laid the foundation stone of the Bodleian in 1610 but died two years later before it was completed.

Will Boniface, the Inn-Keeper. The name is taken from the character in Farquhar's comedy, *The Beaux Stratagem*, produced in 1707.

The scene is set at Lichfield and Boniface is landlord of the inn. He is the first character to speak and is shown rousing his staff to attend to the Warrington coach, whose passengers have been waiting an hour and threaten to go elsewhere.

He boasts a good cellar, reveals a smooth, comic tongue and claims that he has "lived in Lichfield, man and boy, above eight-and-fifty years, and, I believe, have not consumed eight-and-fifty ounces of meat."

Aimwell: "At a meal, you mean, if one may guess your sense by your bulk."

Boniface: "Not in my life, sir: I have fed purely upon ale; I have eat my ale, drank my ale, and I always sleep upon ale."

Boreas, N. or NNE. wind. Boreas was one of the four winds, children of Eos (Aurora), goddess of the dawn by Titan Astræus.

Boreas was characterized by rude violence and was dreaded as a ravisher of maidens. One of them, Orithyia, became by him the mother of Calais and Zetes, who figure in the story of the Argonauts.

The Athenians erected an altar to Boreas.

Cease, rude Boreas, blustering railer!
The Storm, G. A. Stevens
(1710–84).

James Boswell, the prototype of biographers. James Boswell, (1740–95), whose classic biography of Dr. Samuel Johnson has made him an immortal, the name instantly used to describe the perfect biographer.

He was born in Edinburgh, the son of a Scottish judge, and early showed a talent for writing and desire for the company and admiration of literary men.

He met Dr. Johnson, after much persistence and surviving many rebuffs, and immediately became a devoted admirer and constant companion. The period they spent together, however, was relatively brief, which makes the biographer's brilliant, exhaustive portrait the more remarkable.

Boswell toured the Hebrides with Dr. Johnson and published the *Journal* of the tour. The *Life* was not published until five years after its subject's death in 1784.

Boswell, who eventually succeeded to his father's estates, Auchinleck House (locally called "Place Affleck") in Ayrshire, with a considerable income, was a man of intemperate habits and dubious morals, vain often to the point of absurdity. Some would dismiss him as no more than a sycophant. They do well to remember the brilliance of his biography and the discerning doctor's constant reiteration of his affection for Boswell and his merits as a boon companion.

George Farquhar of Lady Bountiful. The term for the benevolent lady of the village or any community is taken from the character Lady Bountiful in *The Beaux' Stratagem*, by George Farquhar (1678-1707).

Farquhar, born in Londonderry, relinquished the stage after accidentally wounding a fellow actor while fencing. He made his mark as a comic dramatist. *The Beaux' Stratagem* was written on his death-bed.

Thomas Bowdler of Bowdlerizing. Dr. Thomas Bowdler, born near Bath in 1754, published in 1818 a "Family Shakespeare" in ten volumes. He claimed that nothing was added to the text, but in it "those words and expressions are omitted which cannot with propriety be read aloud in a family."

The publication immediately added several derivative words—bowdlerize, bowdlerism, etc., to the language.

The doctor produced a similarly expurgated edition of Gibbon's *History of the Decline and Fall of the Roman Empire* in 1776.

It is to be noted, in contrast with the general public ridicule aroused by the project, that Swinburne, in *Studies in Prose and Poetry*, praised the doctor's intention and its execution.

J. M. Morton of Box and Cox. The expression "to play Box and Cox" originated in the farce, *Box and Cox* (1847), by John Maddison Morton (1811-91).

The point of the saying lies in the duplicity of Mrs. Bouncer, the lodging-house keeper, who has let her room to Box and Cox, concealing the existence of each from the other.

Box is a journeyman printer out all night; Cox, a journeyman hatter, out all day.

The plot is revealed when Cox gets an unexpected holiday. The play is further complicated by the fact that Box and Cox have separately proposed to Mrs. Bouncer.

Captain Boycott of To Boycott. Captain Charles Cunningham Boycott (1832-97), victim of the treatment that assumed his name, was agent for the estates of the Earl of Erne in Co. Mayo, Ireland.

In 1880, when he refused to accept rents at figures set by the tenants of the estates, he was subject to a system of ostracism which proceeded to a criminal degree. The nationalist plan of campaign against him included threats upon his life. Servants were forced to leave the estates, physical damage was done to property, the captain's correspondence was intercepted and attempts were made to curtail his food supplies. A large force of troops was eventually drafted to the estates to protect the gatherers of the crop.

The spreading of the criminal process was dealt with by the Crimes Act of 1887.

The word boycott was swiftly adopted by the world's press and at once passed on to common usage.

George Bradshaw of the Railway Guides. The Manchester map engraver and printer who made his name synonymous with railway guides was George Bradshaw (1801-53), a Quaker.

In October, 1839, he first issued an occasional *Railway Time Table*, the title of which was changed in the following year to *Railway Companion*. A supplementary sheet was published in the first week in each month and endeavoured to include the changes up to within a few days of publication.

As the result of strenuous efforts the railway companies were persuaded to alter their times only at the beginning of each month. Thereafter the first monthly *Railway Guide* appeared in December, 1841. It covered only some forty-two lines in England alone. The *Bradshaw* gradually extended to its present comprehensive volume and its plan was copied in many countries. *Bradshaw's Continental Railway Guide* was first issued in 1847.

Louis Braille of Braille. The inventor of the reading system for the blind was born on the outskirts of Paris in 1809. He was blinded by an accident at the age of three. In 1826 he became professor of the *Institution Nationale des Jeunes Aveugles,* of which he had been a distinguished pupil. He worked, in his efforts to invent a system that the blind could read and write, upon the earlier Barbier letter, which consisted of six

Braille Symbols

points, but occupying an area, in Braille's opinion, too long to be covered by the finger-tip.

He eventually evolved the system which has been so universally and successfully adopted. It consists of six embossed points in an oblong of which the horizontal line can contain two and the vertical three points. There are sixty-two possible combinations, so that not only the alphabet but punctuation and contractions can be provided for. The system also covers musical notation.

Braille died in 1852.

The Vicar of Bray of the song. The term is used to describe anyone with weathercock tendencies, prepared to adjust himself or herself to every changing breeze.

The source of the term is Simon Aleyn, or Alleyne, Vicar of Bray, in Berkshire, and Canon of Windsor in the reign of Henry VIII. Under this King he was a Papist. In the reign of Edward VI he was a Protestant. Under Mary he was again a Papist, reverting to Protestantism in the reign of Elizabeth.

When his versatility provoked scandal he claimed that he was true to his principle that "Whatsoever King shall reign, still I'll be Vicar of Bray, sir."

In the song, which is attributed to a soldier in the Dragoons in the reign of Charles I, the time-serving vicar is depicted as maintaining his principle through the reigns of Charles II, James II, William III, Anne and George I.

Dr. E. Cobham Brewer of the *Dictionary of Phrase and Fable.* The author of one of the most fascinating of all literary reference books was born in London, 1810. His father, a distinguished scholar and historian, was given the Crown living of Toppesfield to provide leisure for his research.

Ebenezer Cobham was ordained in 1836 and was LL.D. four years later. He lived in Paris, London and Sussex. The *Dictionary of Phrase and Fable* was published in 1870. The doctor wrote and compiled several other literary works. He died at Edwinstowe Vicarage, Newark, in 1897.

Lord Brougham of the carriage. The carriage, generally one-horse or electric and of a closed type, was named after Henry Peter Brougham, Baron Brougham and Vaux (1778–1868).

He was first known as a scientist and was elected F.R.S.

He was called to the Scottish Bar and afterwards to the English Bar. He made a reputation in Whig politics and was employed on a diplomatic mission to Portugal in 1806. He was one of the first and frequent contributors to the famous *Edinburgh*

Review. He was a zealous worker in the cause of slave abolition.

Brougham made a swift and considerable reputation in Parliament, which he entered in 1810. He sustained political eminence over a long period and enjoyed Royal confidence and support. He was noted as a speaker and introduced many Bills. The closing years of his career were less distinguished and were marred by vanity and the clash of personalities.

Robert Browne of the Brownists.

Robert Browne (1550–1633), founder of the Brownists and one of the founders of the Congregational Church, was born in Rutland and after education at Cambridge became a schoolmaster.

He took Orders in the Church of England but rebelled against ecclesiastical discipline, particularly the ordination by bishops and the parochial system.

Browne suffered several terms of imprisonment for his views and eventually crossed to Holland where he formed a church. His work, *A Booke which showeth the Life and Manners of all True Christians*, propounded the system upon which Congregationalism was developed.

He was a turbulent Puritan controversialist and, though he returned to England and accepted teaching and ecclesiastical office, Browne suffered further terms of imprisonment, once during a long period as vicar of a Northampton church, for a civil offence.

The sect which he had established continued despite its founder's misdemeanours, and some of its members migrated to America.

In England the sect became known as Independents or Congregationalists.

Shakespeare puts into the mouth of Sir Andrew Aguecheek, in *Twelfth Night*, the line:

I'd as lief be a Brownist as a politician.

Beau Brummell and Beau Nash.

George Bryan Brummell was born in London in 1778 and educated at Eton and Oriel College, Oxford.

He inherited a considerable fortune and became a conspicuous society figure. As a leader of fashion and elegance he displayed originality which never descended to blatant eccentricity.

He was an intimate of the Prince of Wales, afterwards George IV, but they quarrelled in 1813 and gambling debts drove Brummell to France. Later he was appointed Consul at Caen, but died in the local asylum in 1840.

Beau Nash (Richard) was born at Swansea in 1674 and educated at Jesus College, Oxford.

"Beau" Nash

He flirted with the army and the law, but his zest for pleasure and gaming led him to Bath where, as Master of the Ceremonies, he quickly established the city's fame as a spa and a fashionable, cultural centre.

The sobriquet "Beau" was bestowed for his foppery, but Nash ruled the social and cultural life of the city with arbitrary power.

He combined a certain profligacy with a considerable generosity and undoubtedly earned his title as "The King of Bath."

He died in 1761, aged 87, and the great public occasion of his burial in Bath Abbey was a merited tribute to his development of the city's prosperity.

The Corporation voted a marble

statue to be erected in the Pump Room, which Nash had made famous, between the busts of Newton and Pope.

Lord Chesterfield's caustic epigram thereon:

> The statue placed these busts between
> Gives satire all its strength;
> Wisdom and Wit are little seen,
> But Folly at full length,

could scarcely be justified by a considered judgment.

Admiral Sir William James of "Bubbles."

Admiral Sir William James was model, as a child, for the famous Pears' painting, "Bubbles," depicting a curly-headed child in a velvet suit blowing bubbles from a bowl of soap-suds.

The picture, painted by the famous artist, Sir John Everett Millais, President of the Royal Academy, became such a byword that the title "Bubbles" is still in general use for a curly-headed child.

Admiral James, who has had a distinguished naval career, was Commander in Chief, Portsmouth, during the 1939–45 war. He describes his experiences in *Portsmouth Letters*.

He has notable literary antecedents as his grandmother, Effie Gray, was married first to Ruskin and afterwards to Millais. She was a noted beauty.

The admiral has written a book dealing with the two marriages, based upon letters found under the floorboards of Ruskin's house and others in a secret drawer of his grandmother's.

He called the book *The Order of Release* (1948), after another famous Millais picture for which Effie Gray sat as model.

Alexander Buchan of Buchan's Cold Spells.

Alexander Buchan, the Scottish meteorologist (1829–1907), wrote several works, including *The Handy Book of Meteorology* and *An Introductory Text Book of Meteorology*. He was also responsible for the reports on the "Challenge" Expedition, 1889–95.

From a long experience and study of records he gave the following weather periods as likely to occur. Nowadays it is chiefly the cold spells to which reference is made when his forecasts prove correct.

BUCHAN'S WEATHER PERIODS

Cold		Warm	
1. February	7–10	1. May	22–26
2. April	11–14	2. July	12–15
3. May	9–14	3. August	12–15
4. June 29–July 4		4. December	3–9
5. August	6–11		
6. November 6–12			

Buddha of Buddhism.

Buddha, the Enlightened, otherwise known as Gautama or Sakya-muni, was a Hindu who lived in the 5th century B.C. He was the son of a king and he resisted all temptations to abandon the contemplative life to which he retired in solitude at the age of thirty, leaving his wife and child. At the end of a long period of contemplation and study he came forth as the Buddha, preaching and gaining many disciples for a creed which was concerned primarily with salvation and not with speculation upon God and His purpose for the world. He urged that "desire is the cause of sorrow."

Buddhism imposes a high moral code, concerned with the mortification of passions and the dispersal of the weight of accumulated sins. He preached universal love and accepted the doctrine of reincarnation. The eventual obliteration of sin secures the achievement of the spiritual peace of Nirvana. He regarded salvation as a release from the wearisome cycle of death and rebirth.

Buddhism supports a strong monastic system and the canonical books, which were not written by the prophet but accumulated several centuries after his death, are known as the Tripitaka, or triple basket; the Sutras, concerned with discipline, the Vinaya, works on doctrine, and the Abidharma, devoted to metaphysics.

Col. William F. Cody of Buffalo Bill. The name "Buffalo Bill," now generally applied to any rough-riding showman, was given originally to William Frederick Cody (1846–1917). He was born in Iowa and first used his remarkable horsemanship in the service of the "Pony Express" mail system, transporting letters by pony relay from St. Joseph, Missouri, to Sacramento, California, a distance of nearly 2,000 miles.

When the service was superseded by telegraphic facilities, Cody joined the U.S. Army as scout and later saw service in the cavalry.

His name arose from a contract fulfilled between several periods of military service, whereby Cody maintained a supply of buffalo meat to men working in remote areas during the building of the Kansas Pacific Railway.

He became world famous as organizer of a sensational Wild West Show which toured Europe and visited England.

Cody combined brilliant horsemanship and show knowledge with considerable acumen. He was elected a member of the Nebraska House of Representatives in 1872.

John Bull, the typical Englishman personified. The name John Bull, generally depicted as a bluff, sturdy farmer type, is taken from a character in a satire by Dr. John Arbuthnot (1667–1735), an eminent physician and man of letters. He was an intimate of Pope and Swift. His *History of John Bull*, originally called *Law is a Bottomless Pit*, and published in 1712, depicted the character as bluff, honest and well fed. The Church of England is represented as his mother.

The term "Uncle Sam," as his U.S. counterpart, derives from the initials U.S.A.

Lieut.-Colonel Cyril McNeile of "Bulldog Drummond."; Lt.-Col. Cyril McNeile (1888–1937), the creator of "Bulldog Drummond," was a regular Army officer, whose writings as a regular Engineer officer in the First World War attracted the attention of Lord Northcliffe and were popularized by him. The author used the pseudonym "Sapper" by which he was widely known.

The famous character, which appeared in many highly successful novels, plays and films, gave his name to any typically British adventurer of considerable physical strength and courage; the embodiment of masculine fearlessness and cheerful ingenuity.

Gerard Fairlie, from whom the author is said to have drawn many of the attributes of "Bulldog Drummond," was a friend of the author's and sustained the life of the character after "Sapper's" death.

Bumble, the fussy official. Bumble was the over-bearing, officious beadle in Dickens' *Oliver Twist*. Bumble-dom is used to designate fussy officialdom, especially on the part of parish officials or of any collection of jacks-in-office.

John Burke of the Peerage. The standard reference book, known briefly as *Burke's Peerage*, is named after its originator, the English genealogist, John Burke (1787–1848). The family came from Tipperary.

In 1826 Burke issued *A Genealogical and Heraldic Dictionary of the Peerage and Baronetage of the United Kingdom*.

He was assisted by his son, Bernard, a genealogist and barrister, who was subsequently knighted and held the office of Ulster King at Arms and became keeper of the state papers in Ireland.

William Burke of "To Burke." "Burke: avoid, smother (publicity inquiry), hush up, suppress (rumour, book)"—*O.E.D.*

The origin of the verb was William Burke, a notorious Irish criminal, born 1792.

His associate was William Hare, and these two Irish labourers kept a lodging house in Edinburgh.

It was the period of the body-snatchers, or Resurrectionists, and when one of the lodgers, an army pensioner, died, Burke and Hare sold the body to Dr. Robert Knox, a prominent Edinburgh anatomist, for dissection.

The price they received—£7 10s.—suggested a profitable traffic in corpses, and their system was to encourage likely lodgers, make them drunk and suffocate them without leaving evidence of violence.

The wives of the two murderers assisted and at least fifteen bodies were thus disposed of, at prices ranging from £8 to £14.

The suspicion of neighbours attracted the police and the two criminals were arrested. Hare turned King's Evidence and Burke was hanged in Edinburgh.

It is thought that Stevenson's *The Body Snatcher* may have derived from Burke's infamous exploits.

C.A.B.A.L. of Cabal. The word cabal, or cabbala, to denote a private organization or secret party intrigue, is of ancient origin, but the word acquired a new significance and an added use in this country in the reign of Charles II.

By a curious coincidence the initials of the members of the King's infamous ministry formed the word Cabal — Clifford, Ashley (Shaftesbury), Buckingham, Arlington and Lauderdale. Its enemies were swift to notice the coincidence and to apply the most sinister interpretation of the word to the conspirators.

Cab(b)ala is also applied to Jewish oral tradition, to mystic interpretation, esoteric doctrine and occult lore.

Cadmus of Cadmean victory. Cadmus, in Greek mythology, was son of a king of Tyre. He was sent to find his sister, Europa, who had been carried off by Zeus. A dragon overcame his companions, but Cadmus was saved from it by the intervention of Athene. He destroyed it and when he sowed its teeth, warriors sprang up, but turned upon each other until all perished but five. These five, Sparti (*Spartoi*, sown men), helped to build the city of Thebes.

A Cadmean victory is a victory with disastrous results (see Pyrrhus of Pyrrhic victory).

Cæsar of the Cæsarian birth. Caius Julius assumed the cognomen Cæsar (taken by all male members of the dynasty) as part of the imperial dignity. His birth by extraction from the womb, after cutting the abdomen, caused his name to be given to this operation.

He was born in 100 B.C. and as Governor of Gaul he subdued the province to the rule of Rome. His democratic success aroused the jealousy of Pompey, who sided with the aristocrats, and Cæsar was recalled.

Cæsar crossed the Rubicon with triumphant troops and visualizing the complete conquest of Italy, pursued and defeated Pompey in Greece.

After distinguished service there and in Egypt he returned to Rome and initiated vast schemes for the benefit of the city, whose inhabitants idolized their ruler.

He was assassinated, after a soothsayer's warning, on the Ides of March (March 15, 44 B.C.).
Why, man, he doth bestride the narrow world
Like a Colossus . . .

　　　　　　　　Julius Cæsar, i. 2.

Cæsarianism is the absolute rule of man over man, recognizing no divine law and no human will other than that of the dictator.

Pompeia of "Cæsar's wife must be above suspicion." The phrase is used frequently, but many could not name the wife nor the circumstances that gave origin to the phrase.

Julius Cæsar (100–44 B.C.) divorced his wife, Pompeia, on the grounds of allegations against her and Clodius.

According to Plutarch's references in his *Lives* of Cæsar and Cicero, Cæsar offered no evidence against Clodius and declared that he knew nothing of the allegations. He divorced his wife, he said, because he would have his wife and her chastity not only clear of crime but of the very suspicion of it.

Cain of "To raise Cain." The expression "to raise Cain" and the nomination of a fratricide and murderer as a "Cain," derive from the Biblical character (*Gen. iv.*).

He was the son of Adam and Eve, and "a tiller of the land." His younger brother, Abel, was "a keeper of sheep."

The brothers brought offerings to the Lord, "but unto Cain and to his offering he had not respect. And Cain was very wroth and his countenance fell." He slew his brother in the field, and when the Lord said unto Cain, "Where is Abel thy brother?" the first murderer responded with the famous words, "I know not: Am I my brother's keeper?"

And the Lord put a curse upon Cain, saying, "When thou tillest the ground, it shall not henceforth yield unto thee her strength; a fugitive and a vagabond shalt thou be in the earth."

And the Lord set a mark upon Cain, lest any finding him should kill him.

The Mohammedan tradition gives both Cain and Abel a twin sister and Cain would not consent to Adam's plan that each should marry his brother's twin. Adam proposed to submit the problem to God by means of a sacrifice and the Lord's rejection of Cain's offering signified His disapproval of Cain's objection and his plan to marry his own twin.

Cain-coloured hair is red or reddish-yellow. This colouring, of hair and beard, was attributed by tradition to Cain and to Judas Iscariot, possibly because men of this colouring are sometimes of a choleric nature.

Caliban, a degraded, bestial man. Caliban is the famous deformed half-human son of a devil and a witch in Shakespeare's *The Tempest*. It is an astonishing creation, this slave of Prospero, the rightful Duke of Milan, and speaks its own language.

All the infections that the sun sucks up
From bogs, fens, flats, on Prosper fall, and
    make him
By inch-meal a disease! His spirits hear me.
And yet I needs must curse. But they'll not
    pinch,
Fright me with urchin shows, pitch me i' the
    mire,

Nor lead me, like a firebrand, in the dark
Out of my way, unless he bid them: but
For every trifle are they set upon me . . .
. . . Sometimes am I
All wound with adders, who, with cloven
    tongues,
Do hiss me into madness . . .

John Calvin of Calvinism. John Calvin, or Cauvin, the great religious reformer, was born in Picardy in 1509. As a Protestant he became involved in religious disputes in Paris which necessitated his fleeing for safety. After sojourns in various cities, during which, at Basel, Switzerland, he wrote his great book, *Institutes of the Christian Religion*, he settled in Geneva. The magnitude of the book was the more remarkable because the author was still in his twenties.

Geneva, from which Calvin was expelled for a period, became indissolubly linked with Calvin and the doctrines he propounded. He was regarded as the head of the Reformed Churches in many countries. He imposed a rigid code and visited offenders with an extreme severity.

The principal characteristics of Calvinistic doctrine are centred upon predestination, irresistible grace, original sin, particular redemption and the final perseverance of the saints.

Canaan, the land of promise. Canaan, the Old Testament name for Palestine, was named after Canaan, the fourth son of Ham (*Gen. x. 6, ix. 22–7*). Its boundaries are described in *Gen. x. 19*.

It was the Promised Land which God promised to give to Abraham for his obedience (*Exod. xii. 25*), "a good land and a large, unto a land flowing with milk and honey" (*Exod. iii. 8*).

Earl of Cardigan of Cardigan. The popular knitted over-waistcoat, or garment superseding the waistcoat, was named after the 7th Earl of Cardigan (1797–1868). He led the charge of the Light Brigade at Balaclava and afterwards became Inspector-General of Cavalry.

Andrew Carnegie of the Trust and Libraries. Andrew Carnegie (1835–1919), the great iron and steel master and philanthropist, was born at Dunfermline, Fifeshire, the son of a damask-linen weaver. When it was once suggested to Carnegie that he was descended from Scottish Kings, he said, "I am sorry to hear that because my wife married me under the impression that I was the son of a weaver."

The family emigrated to America when Andrew was a youth. He entered a cotton factory and became a bobbin boy. He was later a telegraph boy.

When he joined the Pennsylvania Railroad, his progress was rapid. He introduced sleeping cars and was a successful investor. After Government service as superintendent of military railroads he began his amazing development of the Pittsburgh iron and steel industries.

When Carnegie retired in 1901 he was in control of vast co-ordinated enterprises. They were sold to J. Pierpont Morgan, who confessed afterwards that if he had been asked $100,000,000 more he would have paid it. Carnegie was delighted to be free.

He returned to his native Scotland and lived at Skibo Castle in Sutherland, using his vast wealth to become a munificent philanthropist and probably the greatest financial benefactor of education.

He gave £10,000,000 for the establishment and equipment of libraries in England and the Colonies. He made handsome gifts to English and American universities and gave £2,000,000 for Scottish educational facilities and student grants. He founded the Dunfermline Trust for the development of his native town and endowed the Carnegie Hero Fund.

He was of gentle, affectionate disposition, a great reader and lover of the country; in fact, the complete antithesis of the so-called authentic magnate. No commercial success gave him as much satisfaction as the private assistance he was able to give to innumerable friends. He felt that it was a disgrace to die rich, but few men died richer in friendship and esteem.

Carnegie was buried, as he had chosen, in Sleepy Hollow Cemetery, near Tarrytown, New York. Nearby lies Washington Irving whose graceful pen had made the district known through the English-speaking world.

René Descartes of Cartesian. René Descartes, the French philosopher (1596–1650), was born in Touraine and after a Jesuit education entered the army of the Prince of Orange. He later lived in Holland, pursuing his philosophical studies, until he went to Stockholm at the invitation of Christiana of Sweden. He was an eminent mathematician.

Descartes' philosophy is based on the phrase, *Cogito, ergo sum*—I think, therefore I exist. Man is not wholly material, as thought proceeds from the soul and that soul must come from some spiritual Being, who is God. He attempted to apply the mathematical method of strict deduction from self-evident premises to metaphysics and science.

His two chief works are *Discourse on Method* and *Meditations*.

Enrico Caruso. The frequently-heard phrase, "He's a regular Caruso," pays tribute to one of the greatest tenors in the history of music—Enrico Caruso. He was born in Naples, in 1873, of a large family in humble circumstances. With a comparatively slight musical training he reached world-fame as an opera singer. Recordings of his voice, the first of which was made in Milan in 1902, brought him a fortune and increased his world audience.

He enjoyed spectacular and sustained success in England and in America. A man of boyish, light-hearted temperament and erratic yet lovable, his voice was one of rare power, range and sympathy.

While singing in 1920 he ruptured a blood vessel in his throat and died in Naples on August 2 in the following year.

The Maidens of Caryæ of Caryatid.

A caryatid, the female figure frequently used as a pillar or column, derives its name from the maidens of Caryæ, a town in Laconia.

At the festival of Artemis these maidens performed ritual dances in which they often assumed the poses represented in the statues.

Originally the caryatids were used instead of columns to support the entablature of the temples. Now the use is more widespread.

Some accounts say that these women supported the Persians at Thermopylæ and that the victorious Greeks made them slaves. Praxiteles, as a constant reminder of their disgrace, used representations of their figures instead of columns.

The male figures similarly used were called Atlantes.

Casanova de Seingalt.

The name is synonymous with the amorous adventurer and polished intriguer.

Giacomo Casanova de Seingalt was an accomplished adventurer born of a distinguished family in Venice in 1725. He alienated his family by entering the theatrical profession and had already given a hint of what was to follow by being expelled from his seminary for immoral conduct.

He visited many of the capitals of Europe, leading a vicious and sensuous life. His wit and undeniable accomplishments enabled him to insinuate himself into the most distinguished circles and he met men of the eminence of Frederick the Great and Voltaire.

He left racy memoirs, written in faulty but vigorous French, in which he describes with typically blatant zest his incessant amours and intrigues. Many passages are licentious, but a very vivid picture is presented of 18th-century European Society.

Casanova, who died in 1798, is not to be confused with the brothers Francesco and Giovanni Casanova de Seingalt who were distinguished painters in Paris and Dresden respectively during the same century.

Cassandra, the disregarded baleful prophet.

The name familiarly applied to the foreboding prophet who is unbelieved but eventually justified, derives from the beautiful Trojan princess.

Cassandra was the daughter of Priam and Hecuba and was endowed by Apollo with the gift of prophecy. She refused his suit and in consequence he caused all her prophecies to be discredited and disregarded.

Her warnings concerning the imminent fate of Troy were dismissed as mad ravings, but they were proved by events.

In the destruction of Troy the Locrian Ajax entered the Temple of Pallas, dragged Cassandra from the sanctuary of its altar and overturned the statue of the goddess. For this offence he was drowned. Cassandra was among the spoils of Agamemnon, King of Mycenæ, and leader of the Greeks at the siege. Like her new protector, Cassandra suffered death by murder.

Cassandra: Cry, Trojans, cry! lend me
ten thousand eyes,
And I will fill them with prophetic tears . . .
Troy must not be, nor goodly
Ilion stand;
Our firebrand brother, Paris,
burns us all . . .

Troilus: Because Cassandra's mad:
her brain-sick raptures
Cannot distaste the goodness
of a quarrel . . .

Troilus and Cressida, ii. 2.

Cassiopea of the constellation. Cassiopea was the wife of Cepheus, king of Ethiopia. She was the mother of Andromeda.

Cassiopea offended the Nereids, or sea maidens, by boasting that she herself, or her daughter, was more beautiful than they.

The boaster was changed into the northern constellation.

St. Catherine of St. Catherine's **Wheel.** The popular firework depicts the form of the reputed martyrdom of the virgin of royal descent whose day is November 25. She is said to have died on Mount Sinai on a spiked wheel after torture.

The association is also seen in the name Catherine applied to a circular spoked window or window compartment (a "rose" window), and in the phrase "to turn Catherine wheels," i.e. to turn lateral somersaults.

There are several other St. Catherines; notably de Ricci (16th century), of Bologna' (15th century); of Genoa (15th century); of Siena (14th century); of Sweden (14th century).

The name is often spelt Catharine. "To braid St. Catharine's tresses" means to remain a virgin. Longfellow employs the allusion in his *Evangeline.*

William Cecil of "Cecil's fast." The term "Cecil's fast" for a meal of fish derives from William Cecil, Lord Burghley (1520–98), for many years Chief Secretary of State to Queen Elizabeth.

Cecil introduced a Bill to provide for the eating of fish on certain days to restore the trade.

Cerberus of "a sop to Cerberus." The expression "to give a sop to Cerberus" means to tender a bribe to placate a troublesome customer or opponent.

Cerberus was Pluto's three-headed dog which guarded the gates of the infernal regions. The ancient Greeks and Romans placed a sop in the hands of their dead so that Cerberus would allow them to pass without interference. The ancient Egyptians guarded their graves with dogs. The Greeks placed a small coin, or obolus, in the mouths of their dead to ensure that Charon, the ferryman on the Styx, did not turn them back.

It was one of the prodigious tasks of Hercules to bring up the hellhound, Cerberus, from the infernal regions. It was regarded as one of his most daring feats. He was required to master the dog without the use of weapons.

The name, Cerberus, is sometimes applied to a hard, tyrannical taskmaster; a reference to the dog's fierceness and intractability.

Chadband, the unctuous hypocrite. The character with these traits, who became a synonym for them, is found in Dickens' *Bleak House* (1852–3). He is a pious humbug.

Sir Francis Chantrey of the Chantrey Bequest. Francis Chantrey, born in Derbyshire in 1781, was the son of a carpenter who worked a small farm.

At an early age the son revealed marked talent for carving and modelling and studied in the provinces and in Dublin before coming to London. Here the boy, who had been left an orphan at twelve, but had been helped by a wealthy local woman, studied at the Royal Academy.

Chantrey was soon in request as a portrait painter and sculptor and portrayed many of the leading figures of his age, including Watt, Wordsworth, Pitt and Wellington. He did a series of busts of great British admirals for Greenwich Hospital. He was successful in 1808 in competition for the statue of George III for Whitehall. His group, "Sleeping Children," in Lichfield is notable.

Chantrey was elected an R.A. in 1818 and knighted in 1835, but he refused a baronetcy.

The sculptor left a fortune of

£150,000 and bequeathed to the Royal Academy a sum yielding about £3,000 a year, of which the President was to receive £300 and the Secretary £50. The balance was to be devoted to the purchase of works of art executed in Great Britain. Since the first purchase, in 1877, many works have been acquired and the collection is housed in the Tate Gallery.

Chantrey died in London in 1841.

An exhibition of the complete collection in London in 1949 aroused much controversy.

Chauvin of Chauvinism. Chauvinism, an excessive, almost idolatrous worship of military might and national prowess, derived from Nicholas Chauvin of Rochefort. This much-wounded veteran of the First Republic became an idolator of Napoleon and his blind enthusiasm reached such lengths that it was soon the subject of public jest and ridicule. Cogniard, in a famous vaudeville, *La Cocarde Tricolure*, produced in 1831, recognized and exploited the public's reaction when he included the line: *"Je suis français, je suis Chauvin."*

Lord Chesterfield of the Chesterfield. The name Chesterfield for a popular type of couch or settee (and for a fashion of overcoat) derives from

A Chesterfield

Philip Dormer, the 4th Earl (1694–1773).

He was a statesman and diplomat, an ambassador at The Hague and Viceroy of Ireland, but he is chiefly remembered for "Letters" to his natural son, Philip Stanhope. They were designed to equip the recipient with full worldly knowledge and courtly accomplishment. They were not intended for publication.

Dr. Johnson describes them as teaching "the morals of a whore and the manners of a dancing master." He was not, however, an entirely unprejudiced judge. He had sought the patronage of Chesterfield for his great Dictionary. The Earl's complete neglect of patronage and interest until the vast work was published and well received drew from Dr. Johnson a letter which is one of the most noted passages of invective in the English language.

The Chimera. A chimera, representing a bogy or fanciful conception, takes its name from the Greek mythological animal which devastated the land.

According to Hesiod it had three heads, those of a lion, a goat and a dragon. In some accounts it had the head of a lion, the body of a goat and the tail of a dragon. It was the child of Typhon and Echidna.

The Chimera was killed by Bellerophon who, mounted on the winged Pegasus, slew it with arrows.

James Christie of Christie's. The founder of the world-famous Christie's, the art sale rooms of St. James's, was James Christie (1730–1803), who, on his mother's side, was related to the Scottish heroine, Flora Macdonald.

He resigned a commission in the Royal Navy before he was twenty to devote himself to business. His first art sale is recorded in 1766, though he had started on his own account three years previously. In 1768 he had moved to premises in Pall Mall with a specially built auction room designed by the Free Society of Artists, namely, George III's Royal Academicians, who used Christie's rooms as their exhibition galleries.

Garrick, Reynolds and Gainsborough were among the many distinguished friends of this man of "gentle refinement of manners" and a connoisseur's knowledge.

James Christie, Junior (1773–1831), was also not only an auctioneer but an antiquary of distinction.

The sale rooms have continued to be one of the great art and social centres of the world. A sale in the auction rooms is the subject of a water-colour by Rowlandson.

Christie's in both wars was offered free of charge for remarkable charity sales.

On the night of April 16–17, 1941, Christie's was destroyed by an enemy raid, only the door remaining as an earnest of the indestructability of a great institution.

Lord Derby placed Derby House at the disposal of the firm. With this munificent assistance and aid from many other well-wishers, including Earl Spencer, the name and work of Christie's survived vigorously until the leasing of Spencer House, St. James's Place, from Earl Spencer, pending the rebuilding of Christie's King Street premises.

Though it is over a half century since the family connection with the business ceased, with the death of James H. B. Christie, it is still a national institution, invested with the spirit of its founder. It was claimed for the original James Christie, and it is still applicable, that he made Christie's auction rooms the most important in Europe for the distribution of works of art and the rendezvous for people of rank and fashion.

Cicero of Cicerone. The term Cicerone, to designate a guide who points out the chief points of interest, derives from the great Roman orator Marcus Tullius Cicero. He was born in 100 B.C. and soon distinguished himself as an orator at the Roman Bar. He was an elegant writer and prose stylist whose work has always been taken as a model for students.

Cicero attained Consulship in 63 B.C. He delivered a Philippic against Antony, by whose soldiers he was eventually killed in 43 B.C.

The Cimmerii of Cimmerian. Cimmerian: thick, gloomy, nocturnal darkness.

The adjective is taken from the Cimmerii, or Cimmerians, who, according to Homer, lived upon the extremities of the world, in the stream Oceanus. It was shrouded in darkness which the sun never penetrated. It was there that Odysseus visited the spirits of the dead.

According to Herodotus, the Cimmerians were an historical people who invaded Assyria and Asia Minor.

In post-Homeric times they were regarded as an historic people inhabiting the shores of the Black Sea—hence the word Crimea.

Milton, in *L'Allegro*, refers to "the dark Cimmerian desert."

Cincinnatus, the great man in retirement who is recalled in crisis. The term arose from Lucius Quinctius Cincinnatus, one of the early Roman heroes, who was noted for his simplicity and dignity. The record is that about 458 B.C., when the Roman army was facing disaster, the former consul was recalled from his plough to assume dictatorship. He overcame the enemy, tidied up the political field and returned to his plough and simple life. Many years later he was again recalled in extreme old age to become dictator and to avert civil war. He was again successful.

George Washington was known as the Cincinnatus of America in part because he was first president-general of the Society of Cincinnati, so called after the Roman hero and founded in 1783 by the officers of the Revolutionary Army. Membership was hereditary and its purpose was to sustain a settled policy and to look after the dependents of those who had died in the war.

Cinderella, the person of un-recognized merit or beauty. The allusion is to the famous Cinderella fairy tale of very ancient origin.

In it, Cinderella is the drudge and scapegoat, left at home while her ugly sisters attend the fine ball.

The disconsolate, neglected Cinderella is visited by a fairy godmother, who transforms her raiment and gives her magic transport to the said ball. The one condition is that Cinderella must leave the ball by midnight and resume her humble guise.

Caught up in the excitement of the ball and enjoying the attention of the Prince, she leaves her departure until the last minute and in her haste loses one of her glass slippers. The Prince, determined to find its charming owner, causes a search to be made for the person whose foot the slipper fits.

At last the unsuspected Cinderella is identified, with commendably romantic results.

The *glass* slipper is thought to be an error of translation and association. The original is believed to have been *pantoufle en vair*, a fur or sable slipper, which would have been in keeping with royal custom. The similar-sounding *verre* (glass) is believed to have been a substitution in the course of time.

A "Cinderella Dance" is one ending at midnight.

Circe the enchantress. In Greek mythology Circe was the daughter of Helios, the sun god.

Odysseus (Ulysses) finds the enchantress on coming to her home, the island of Æææ. She turns his companions into swine but Odysseus is protected by a herb, moly, given to him by Hermes. He persuades Circe to restore his companions.

The enchantress releases the company after a year and instructs Odysseus to consult Tiresias in Hades, where he sees the ghosts of many dead heroes and talks with them.

Circe bore him a son, Telegonus, who, in later years, when coming to Ithaca to make himself known to his father, slew Odysseus in ignorance of his identity.

The name is used for any woman who brings out the worst in a man.

Milton, in *Comus*, refers to Circe as

The daughter of the Sun, whose charmèd cup
Whoever tasted lost his upright shape,
And downward fell into a grovelling swine.

Pope's translation of *The Odyssey* describes the mythical herb as

Black was the root, but milky white the flower.

The name moly is given to a number of plants, especially of the garlic family.

Lionel, Duke of Clarence, of Clarenceaux King of Arms. The name of the second King of Arms, whose office includes the supervision of funerals of baronets, Knights and Squires south of the river Trent, derives from the Dukedom of Lionel of Antwerp (1338–68), third son of Edward III. He was created Duke

Norroy King of Arms

of Clarence when he married the heiress of Clare, in Suffolk.

The College of Heralds, or College of Arms, was founded in the 15th century and now controls armorial matters, the recording of pedigrees and the granting of armorial bearings and other heraldic privileges. It is in Queen Victoria Street, London, E.C.4.

The first King of Arms is the

Garter, the third, Norroy, who holds Jurisdiction north of the Trent.

The heralds are Windsor, Chester, Richmond, Somerset, York, Lancaster: the pursuivants, Rouge Croix, Bluemantle, Rouge Dragon and Portcullis.

The chief herald in Scotland is the Lyon King of Arms, so named from the lion on the Royal shield.

E. C. Bentley of Clerihew. The name Clerihew for a novel poetic form derives from the unusual second Christian name, Clerihew, of its inventor, E. C. Bentley, born 1875.

Its compact, comic form has been brilliantly exploited by its creator, and Clerihews have competed in popularity with limericks. (The name Limerick, applied to the familiar five-line form used for nonsense verse, especially by Edward Lear (1812–88), is thought to have derived from the chorus line, "Will you come up to Limerick?" sung after extempore verses recited at parties.)

The most frequently quoted Clerihew, which shows the form, is

> Sir Christopher Wren
> Said 'I am going to dine with some men:
> If any one calls,
> Say I am designing St. Paul's.'

Bentley, father of Nicolas Bentley, the noted humorous artist, wrote one of the classic detective stories, *Trent's Last Case*, published in 1912.

G. K. Chesterton dedicated *The Man Who Was Thursday* in verse to Edmund Clerihew Bentley, who was one of his closest friends.

Bentley began writing Clerihews at school and a notable collection was subsequently published under the title, *Biography for Beginners*, which G. K. C. illustrated.

Bentley was for many years on the editorial staff of *The Daily Telegraph*.

Richard Cobden of Cobdenism. Richard Cobden, the political economist and apostle of Free Trade, was born in Midhurst, Sussex, in 1804.

After experience in the cotton industry he toured the Continent and the United States in the study of political economy. He did great work in the abolition of the Corn Laws. He became M.P. for Stockport in 1841.

Cobden secured wide acceptance of his policy of free trade, international co-operation, retrenchment and peace. He received the public acclamation of Britain and Continental countries and concluded a commercial treaty with France. He refused all civic honours and died in 1865.

Edward Cocker of " According to Cocker." Edward Cocker (1631–72) was a schoolmaster by profession and an arithmetician whose book upon arithmetic, published after his death, had remarkable sales. It was regarded as the prototype of all such works and the phrase "according to Cocker" was widely used as meaning "according to the rules," much in the same category as "is it cricket?"

It was further popularized by use in a successful farce, *The Apprentice*, produced in 1756.

The American equivalent of the expression is "according to Gunter," implying unquestionable correctness. Its derivation was in fact British, the original was Edmund Gunter (1581–1626), born in Hertfordshire and intended for the Church. He became Professor of Astronomy at Gresham College, London, in 1619 and his *Canon Triangulorum* was the first table of logarithmic sines and tangents. His inventions included Gunter's Chain and Gunter's Scale for use in surveying, etc.

Confucius of Confucianism. Confucius (550–477 B.C.) was born of a noble but impoverished family in Lu, in the present Shanghtun Province. Confucius is the Latin form of K'ung Fu-tze, the philosopher or master K'ung.

He married early and had a family. He travelled widely in China, preaching a high standard of social ethics and personal virtues. Returning to his own kingdom he filled high legal and ministerial office and effected remarkable reforms and an enlightened administration. He was a scholar and eager teacher who secured a large and influential following. He left no substantial writings which embodied his gospel, but his epigrammatic sayings have become part of the literature of China and are widely quoted and revered to-day.

Confucius laid no claim to deity or even divine revelations. His was a philosophy, based on theism, which claimed that the universe was generated by a heavenly principle, that man had fallen by his own sin from a state of grace and through his own efforts could recover it. His political precepts envisage the sovereign state with strict obedience from the family of subjects.

His descendants retained their nobility and were untouched by all the political changes of the succeeding centuries. They became a sacred caste. The burial place of Confucius, wherein he is praised in tributes from the leaders of many dynasties, is still a place of homage.

It is required that there shall be temples to Confucius in every district and the Emperor did regular homage in Pekin, thus paying tribute to the wisdom of the Sage and his undoubted vital and beneficial influence upon the development of China.

Thomas Cook of Cook's Tours.

Thomas Cook (1809–92) turned "the grand tour," which was the privilege of the wealthy, into the pleasure of the masses. He added a phrase to the language of travel.

He was an enthusiastic writer, and lecturer on temperance, and in 1841 ran a cheap trip from Leicester to Loughborough and back—the first public railway excursion privately organized and personally conducted. The distance was 24 miles and 370 passengers were conveyed at a fare of one shilling return.

Four years later Cook determined to conduct the business on a regular commercial basis, and applied to the Midland Railway to place trains at his disposal, he to find the passengers. He advertised his first pleasure excursion to leave Leicester on August 4, 1845, for Liverpool, with visits to North Wales, the Isle of Man and Dublin. He compiled, printed and issued a small guide to the places of interest *en route*, and the sights to be visited.

In less than ten years after the running of the first excursion, the system Cook originated had become an important feature in the travel arrangements of the railway companies. He had, in fact, created a new industry.

The great London exhibition of 1851 was visited by 165,000 persons from the provinces under Cook's arrangements. The Dublin exhibition of 1853, the Paris exhibition of 1855 and the Manchester exhibition of 1857, gave the excursion system an immense impetus.

The success of the 1855 Paris exhibition turned Cook's thoughts to the Continent generally, and in the following year began those "Circular Tours" which in turn were the genesis of the European Tourist System that to-day embraces the world. He initiated International Travel Tickets and Hotel Coupons, which are in universal use to-day.

In 1870 Cook was called on to assist in conveying relief to the starving citizens of Paris when the trains were controlled by the German military authorities. In the same year he was appointed by the Khedive to act as the Agent of the Egyptian Government for passenger traffic on the Nile. When the British Government organized its expedition to Khartoum for the relief of Gordon in 1884, Cook's transported about 18,000 troops and 40,000 tons of stores and war material as far as the Second Cataract.

Cook organized (at the request

of the Viceroy) the Pilgrimage of Mohammedan Indians to Mecca; the arrangements for the Kaiser's famous tour to Palestine in 1898, and the transportation of British nationals stranded on the Continent at the outbreak of war in August, 1914. For this service Cook's received a vote of thanks from Parliament.

Emile Coué of Couéism: "Every day, and in every way . . ." The inventor of one of the most familiar psycho-therapeutical methods of healing was born at Troyes, France, in 1857. At first he was a chemist who studied hypnotism and later he developed his own methods.

In 1910 he established a free clinic at Nancy and put his theories into successful practice. He stressed the powers of auto-suggestion to clear the mind of causes of illness and disease. The kernel of his teaching was his formula which became a byword: "Every day, and in every way, I am becoming better and better."

Coué was a public figure in France and achieved much publicity in England and the United States, where he made lecture tours. The sensation soon subsided and although his formula caught the public's imagination, rather more credence was given to the current story of the bowlegged man who repeated the formula too frequently and became knock-kneed.

Coué died at Nancy in 1926.

Sir Roger de Coverley. The Sir Roger known to us in literature through *The Spectator*, in which he appears continually and with charming detail, is described by Steele (*The Spectator, No. 2*) as the great grandson of the "inventor of that famous country dance which is called after him."

The portrait, drawn by Steele and adorned by Addison, is one of the liveliest in literature.

"He is a gentleman that is very singular in his behaviour, but his singularities proceed from his good sense, and are contradictions to the manners of the world, only as he thinks the world is in the wrong. However, his humour creates him no enemies, for he does nothing with sourness or obstinacy; and his being unconfined to modes and forms, makes him but the readier and more capable to please and oblige all who know him. When he is in town, he lives in Soho-square. It is said, he keeps himself a bachelor by reason he was crossed in love by a perverse beautiful widow of the next county to him. Before this disappointment, Sir Roger was what you would call a fine gentleman, had often supped with my Lord Rochester and Sir George Etherege, fought a duel upon his first coming to town, and kicked bully Dawson in a public coffee-house for calling him youngster. But being ill-used by the above-mentioned widow, he was very serious for a year and a half; and though, his temper being naturally jovial, he at last got over it, he grew careless of himself, and never dressed afterwards. He continues to wear a coat and doublet of the same cut that were in fashion at the time of his repulse, which, in his merry humours, he tells us, has been in and out twelve times since he first wore it. It is said Sir Roger grew humble in his desires after he had forgot his cruel beauty, insomuch that it is reported he had frequently offended in point of chastity with beggars and gypsies: but this is looked upon, by his friends, rather as matter of raillery than truth. He is now in his fifty-sixth year, cheerful, gay, and hearty; keeps a good house both in town and country; a great lover of mankind; but there is such a mirthful cast in his behaviour, that he is rather beloved than esteemed. His tenants grow rich, his servants look satisfied, all the young women profess to love him, and the young men are glad of his company. When he comes into a house, he calls the servants by their names, and talks all the way up the stairs to a visit . . ."

"As the knight is the best master in the world," (*The Spectator, No. 106*), "he seldom changes his servants; and as he is beloved by all about him, his servants never care for leaving him . . . you would take his valet de chambre for his brother, his butler is gray-headed, his groom is one of the gravest men that I have ever seen, and his coachman has the looks of a privy counsellor. You see the goodness of the master even in the old house-dog, and in the gray pad that is kept in the stables with great care and tenderness out of regard to his past services, though he has been useless for several years."

Announcing Sir Roger's death in *The Spectator, No. 517*, Addison quotes the letter from Sir Roger's butler, Edward Biscuit: ". . . his death, which has afflicted the whole country, as well as his poor servants who loved him, I may say, better than we did our lives. I am afraid he caught his death the last county-sessions, where he would go to see justice done to a poor widow woman, and her father-less children, that had been wronged by a neighbouring gentleman . . . Upon his coming home, the first complaint he made was, that he had lost his roast-beef stomach, not being able to touch a sirloin, which was served up according to custom . . . we were once in great hope of his recovery, upon a kind message that was sent him from the widow lady whom he had made love to the forty last years of his death . . . He was buried, according to his own direc-tions, among the family of the de Coverleys . . . It was the melan-choliest day for the poor people that ever happened in Worcestershire . . ."

Hazlitt wrote, "Who can be insen-sible to his unpretending virtues and amiable weaknesses; his modesty, generosity, hospitality, and eccentric whims; the respect for his neighbours and the affection of his domestics?"

The Admirable Crichton. James Crichton (1560–83/5) was born probably in Dumfriesshire. His father was a Lord Advocate and his mother one of the noble Lindsay family. Crichton entered St. Andrew's University at ten and graduated, being third on the list, at fifteen.

His father became a reformer, but James refused and went to France. From the University of Paris he issued challenge to the world to hold discussions on any subject in any twelve languages named. He main-tained a successful discussion for nine hours. He gave similar manifesta-tions of his amazing knowledge and memory in Rome. He was lionized in Venice. He retired to Padua in ill health and there improvised a poem in Latin for six hours, extolling the virtues of the city.

He was a man of remarkable grace and athletic prowess and a consider-able musician.

The Duke of Padua made Crichton a tutor to his son, but jealousy caused the eventual assassination of the re-markable personality. He was set upon in the streets by a masked gang among whom Crichton recognized his pupil.

His title, "The Admirable," is said to have been bestowed by Sir Thomas Urquhart.

Sir James Barrie's Admirable Crichton, of the play, is "this perfect butler . . . the man who could never tell a lie . . . and an enigma to the last." In the directions Barrie says, "It would not be good taste to des-cribe him, who is only a servant . . . to be an indoor servant at all is to Crichton a badge of honour; to be a butler at thirty is the realisation of his proudest ambition."

William Crockford of Crockford's Club. William Crockford (1775–1844) was born in London, the son of a fishmonger, which trade he appears to have followed until he made a considerable fortune at cards. He built a gaming house, making it a club to secure exclusiveness, and it became the rage of London. The wealthiest and most famous frequented Crockford's Club, where stakes were prodigiously high and hazard was the most favoured game.

The proprietor made a fortune out of the property but dissipated it in speculation after his retirement from ownership.

Crœsus of "as rich as Crœsus."

Crœsus was King of Lydia in the 6th century B.C. He possessed such fabulous wealth that his name became the criterion of riches.

When Solon, the great Athenian lawgiver and one of the sages of Greece visited him, Crœsus asked him if he knew of anyone happier than his questioner.

The sage replied, "Call no man happy until he is dead."

His meaning was not that happiness is only acquired in an after life, but that the catastrophes are so unpredictable that the happiness of a life can only safely be assessed when it is complete.

Crœsus had cause to remember the answer when he was defeated by Cyrus and condemned to death by burning. As he approached the pile Crœsus called upon the name of Solon and his captor, learning the reason, pardoned Crœsus and availed himself of his counsels. On his deathbed Cyrus commended Crœsus to the care of his son.

Alexander Cruden of the Concordance.

The name Cruden is almost synonymous with Concordance, so universal is the use of his great Bible reference.

He was born in 1701, educated at Marischal College, Aberdeen, and intended for the ministry. He was an eccentric, though a likeable man, and was several times placed in confinement by his friends. Once he escaped from an asylum in which he had been chained to his bed. He brought an action against the author-

ities, but unwisely decided to plead his cause himself.

Cruden was continually projecting plans which he thought were for the public's weal and when he was rebuffed he issued accounts of his motives and disappointments.

In his early twenties he came to London as tutor and bookseller. Sir Robert Walpole appointed him bookseller to the Queen of George II.

The famous *Complete Concordance of the Holy Scriptures* was published in 1737 and dedicated to Queen Caroline. His standing must have been appreciable as he was allowed to present a copy in person to Her

Alexander Cruden

Majesty. Her death a fortnight later, before she had bestowed the expected tangible proof of her indebtedness (£100 from her own purse), was a disappointment to Cruden. The first edition brought the author only £20.

His eccentricity increased. He assumed the title of "Alexander the Corrector" and suggested to the King that by Order in Council, or by an Act, Cruden should be formally constituted Corrector of Morals. He developed religious mania, with a Sabbatarian bias, and spent much money on tracts which he distributed while admonishing passers-by to observe the Sabbath more religiously.

Cruden sought Knighthood and a Parliamentary seat, only to further his plans for the regeneration of mankind. He conducted an incredible and unsuccessful courtship of Elizabeth, the daughter of Sir Thomas Abney, a wealthy City merchant. The fantastic courtship is described in one of Cruden's most remarkable pamphlets.

He died in Islington in 1770. In fact he was found dead, in an attitude of prayer, by a prostitute to whom he had given sanctuary and who became his devoted servant.

Charles Cruft, of Cruft's. Charles Cruft, whose name is synonymous with the blue ribbons of the dog world, was born in London in 1852, son of a jeweller. Cruft became salesman to a firm making dog-cakes. He was impressed] by the sales possibilities of dog shows in local districts. He organized his first London show in 1886. It was a marked success. He enjoyed further prestige by the patronage of Queen Victoria, whose entries, he instructed, were to be judged as dogs.

His annual shows increased in world renown and success in them is the highest honour.

Cruft died in 1938.

Cyclops, the one-eyed person. The employment of the word "cyclops" for a one-eyed person and especially a one-eyed giant, derives from mythology.

The Cyclops were of different types, but all distinguished by their one eye, in the centre of the forehead. The name is given to a tribe of savage giants, to a group of Titans who worked the forges for Vulcan and to a class of master builders in Thrace.

It is suggested by some that the legend of the single eye arose from a lantern worn on the head by the quarry workers, much as the miners' head lamp is worn to-day.

Many ruins in Greece and Italy built of huge blocks of unhewn stone and without cement were called Cyclopean walls or masonry from the assumption that they could have been built only by such giants and skilled craftsmen as the Cyclops.

Louis Jacques Mande Daguerre of Daguerrotype. Daguerre (1789–1851), a French painter and physicist, was formerly a Government revenue official and theatrical scenery painter. He staged famous Diorama exhibitions in Paris and London. The latter was destroyed by fire in Regent's Park in 1839.

With Niepce, who had previously been working separately on similar lines, Daguerre developed a photographic process of heliographic pictures, achieving permanent prints by the action of sunlight. The process, which Daguerre developed, improved and wrote upon, involved the use of a metal plate treated with iodide of silver and exposed in a camera. It was later developed by means of mercury vapour.

The process was a milestone in the history of photography and produced results of remarkable beauty and integrity.

Daguerre was appointed an officer of the Legion of Honour and he and the heir of his early collaborator, Niepce, received financial recognition from the State. Joseph Niepce died in 1833.

Damocles of the Sword of Damocles. Damocles was a court sycophant at the time of Dionysius the Elder, tyrant of Syracuse. Cicero records that the flatterer, after extravagantly extolling the enviable happiness of Kings, was invited by Dionysius to sample the alleged felicities. He accepted and was invited to a magnificent banquet, only to discover that above his head was a gleaming sword suspended by a single hair.

In consequence the banquet was an agonized torment instead of a delight, and the expression "The Sword of Damocles" became generally used to typify a threatening and imminent danger.

Damon and Pythias, the inseparable friends. The celebrated inseparables were two Pythagoreans of Syracuse in the age of Dionysius I.

When Pythias was condemned to death he sought leave to settle his affairs and Damon pledged his own life in the event of Pythias defaulting. He was preparing to redeem his pledge at the place of execution when Pythias arrived and insisted upon placing his own head upon the block.

The devotion of the friends so moved the tyrant that he pardoned the offenders and encouraged their counsel. Spenser mentions their indissoluble friendship in *The Faerie Queene*.

Dandie Dinmont of the Terriers. Dandie Dinmont, a character in Sir Walter Scott's *Guy Mannering* (1815), was a sturdy hospitable farmer of Liddesdale in the Lowlands. The character, despite the author's claim that it was an entirely fictitious creation, is generally thought to have been drawn from James Davidson, of Hindlee, on the edge of the Teviots, to whom the name was subsequently attached.

Dandie Dinmont is presented as possessing a notable breed of terriers. Davidson was also noted for his terriers, named Mustard or Pepper, according to their colour.

The story is set in the 18th century and is concerned with the kidnapping of a laird's son, who is carried to Holland by smugglers.

Dandy Dinmont comes to the help of the gipsy, Meg Merrilees, in frustrating plots concerned with the disposition of family estates.

Daniel of the Lions' Den. Daniel, of the sayings "A Daniel in the lions' den" and "A Daniel brought to judgment," is the prophet whose history is told in the Old Testament. He was carried off to Babylon, where he received the Chaldean name of Belteshazzar. He rose to be chief of the governors and governor of Babylon.

He it was who interpreted the writing on the wall at Belshazzar's feast (*Dan. v.*).

After Cyrus took Babylon, Daniel, whose name means "God is my judge," was still in a position of great authority under Darius, and highly esteemed. His integrity brought him into jeopardy when his rivals secured the signing of a royal statute which decreed that no one for thirty days should make a petition to any god or man, save the King. The penalty was that the offender should be cast into the den of lions.

Daniel, knowing the interdict, knelt in prayer to God before his open window, "three times a day" (*vi. 10*). The King, against his will, was compelled to commit Daniel to the lions, but was confident that "Thy God whom thou servest continually, he will deliver thee" (*vi. 16*).

The stone was rolled across the entrance of the lions' den and the King sealed it "with his own signet and with the signet of his lords."

The King spent the night sleepless and fasting, and early next morning went to the lions' den and called to Daniel "with a lamentable voice." Daniel replied, "O king live for ever. My God hath sent his angel, and hath shut the lions' mouths, and they have not hurt me; for as much as before him innocency was found in me" (*vi. 21–2*).

And the accusers of Daniel and their families were cast to the lions and Darius proclaimed the God of Daniel as "the living God, and steadfast for ever, and his kingdom that which shall not be destroyed" (*vi. 26*).

David and Jonathan, the devoted inseparables. David (beloved), the youngest son of Jesse, was a man of beautiful countenance and at first a shepherd, battling with wild beasts. He was chosen to succeed Saul as King (*1 Sam. xvi.*). He slew Goliath and the victor's popularity aroused the jealousy of Saul, from whom he fled.

Jonathan, Saul's eldest son and David's faithful friend, tried to make peace between them (*1 Sam. xx.*). "What have I done?" asks David. "What is mine iniquity? and what is my sin before thy father, that he seeketh my life?"

Jonathan replies: "God forbid; thou shalt not die."

When Jonathan was slain by the Philistines (*1 Sam. xxxi. 2*), David, in grief for his death, wrote "the Song of the Bow" which contains so many magnificent and oft-quoted lines (*2 Sam. i. 19–27*).

How are the mighty fallen! Tell it not in Gath, publish it not in the streets of Ashkelon; lest the daughters of the Philistines rejoice . . . Saul and Jonathan were lovely and pleasant in their lives, and in their death they were not divided . . . I am distressed for thee, my brother Jonathan: very pleasant hast thou been to me: thy love to me was wonderful, passing the love of women . . .

The Delilah. Delilah, the seductress, who lived in Sorek, was a daughter of the Philistines. Samson met her in Timnah (*Judges xiv.*). When his father demurred against his son's taking a wife of the uncircumcised Philistines, Samson said: "Get her for me: for she pleaseth me well."

Delilah was bribed by the lords of the Philistines to learn from Samson the source of his strength, but three times she failed. At the fourth attempt he confessed that "if I be shaven my strength will go from me" (*Judges xvi. 17*).

Delilah persuaded Samson to sleep upon her knees and called a man to shave his head. Samson's strength departed from him and he was blinded and brought down to Gaza. He pulled down the temple of Dagon upon his tormentors, crying, "Let me die with the Philistines," and was among the three thousand slain.

Demosthenes of Demosthenic. Demosthenic is one of the great adjectives of oratory. It is applied to Demosthenes and his oratory and in addition to eloquent, patriotic and often denunciatory speech.

The great Athenian orator of the 4th century B.C. attained his pre-eminence by perseverance in the face of usual handicaps. It is said that he overcame a stammer by practising with pebbles in his mouth and that he trained himself in declamation by speaking on the seashore against the roar of the ocean. He mastered language by copying many times Thucydides' *History of the Peloponnesian War.*

The classic orator is particularly associated with denunciatory speech because of his fifteen years' denunciation of Philip of Macedon, against whom he pronounced his classic *Philippics.*

Demosthenes poisoned himself rather than fall into the hands of Antipater, the Macedonian general.

Derrick of the Derrick. Derrick, whose name and association with the gallows gave the name to the crane, was a 17th-century Tyburn executioner. He served under the Provost Marshal in the Earl of Essex's expedition against Cadiz.

While there, Derrick was sentenced to death for rape, but was pardoned by Essex, possibly on account of his usefulness, and he was subsequently responsible for many executions.

By an ironic turn of fate he was eventually responsible for the execution of Essex. A contemporary ballad, entitled *Essex's Good Night,* mentions twenty-three executions and concludes:

> *But now thou seest myself is come*
> *By chance into thy hands I light;*
> *Strike out thy blow, that I may know*
> *Thou Essex loved at his good-night.*

Diana, the riding and hunting woman: a woman intent upon remaining single. Diana, the Roman goddess of the moon and of hunting, is identified with the Greek Artemis. She was regarded as the protectress of women and was invoked by them in childbirth. She prized her virginity and Actæon is said to have been changed into a stag perhaps because he boasted of greater hunting prowess than the goddess possessed, but more probably because he surprised the virgin goddess while she was bathing. She delighted to bathe with her nymphs after the day's hunt. She was the patron of virgins until their marriage.

Diana

Diana was the daughter of Zeus and Leto, and twin sister of Apollo, whose physical beauty she shared. She was a beneficent goddess of nature, but capable of inflicting destruction. A temple and groves were sacred to her.

"Diana of the Ephesians," mentioned in *Acts xix. 24–28,* was the Ephesian Artemis, a separate Asiatic deity.

The phrase, "Great is Diana of the Ephesians" (*Acts xix. 28*), is often used to imply that self-interest can breed self-deceit. The cry is uttered in its Bible context, because Demetrius, the silversmith, who kept the local trade busy with orders for the goddess's temple, sensed that Paul's teaching would affect business. The apostle proclaimed that there were no gods made with hands and Demetrius stirred up his fellow craftsmen to praise Diana whose worship brought their orders.

Late revellers are sometimes called Diana's worshippers because they place themselves under her protection as goddess of the moon. Or it may be of the chase.

Diana, to the alchemists, was the symbol for silver, due also to her association with the moon.

In art Diana is generally depicted as a woman of slender grace and beauty. A bow and quiver and sometimes an animal are among her identifying symbols.

Charles Dickens of Dickensian. Charles John Huffham Dickens, one of the greatest figures in English literature, was born at Landport, Portsea, in 1812. The adjective Dickensian applies more to the remarkable vitality of his host of immortal characters than to their creator. It implies a colourful and robust distinctiveness of which such figures as Pickwick are typical examples.

The novelist started work in a blacking warehouse at Old Hungerford Stairs. From the first he had an acute observation, an intense interest in people, in social problems and in literature. He entered journalism as a parliamentary reporter. His first *Sketches by Boz* appeared in the *Monthly Magazine* in 1833.

The Posthumous Papers of the Pickwick Club created a sensation. A new creative genius had arisen.

Many of Dickens' novels exposed social evils and achieved reforms. His *Christmas Carol*, 1843, did much to revive the genial spirit of Christmas. He created a gallery of immortal characters, brilliantly named and unrivalled in the literature of any country. Such figures as Oliver Twist, Dombey, David Copperfield, Little Nell, Mrs. Gamp and the Artful Dodger are part of our national heritage, recognized far beyond the bounds of book-lovers.

Dickens' illustrators included the noted Cruikshank and "Phiz."

For a short period he was editor of the *Daily News*, but the post was uncongenial.

The Dickens Fellowship, founded in 1902 to encourage the study and discussion of Dickens' works, has a large membership all over the Empire and in the United States.

When Dickens died in 1870 mourning was national and memorial cards were sold in the streets to "England's most popular author . . . he was a sympathizer with the poor, the suffering, and the oppressed."

Jeremy Diddler of diddling. Diddler and diddling as the slang description of a petty swindler and his methods are taken from Jeremy Diddler, the chief character in James Kenney's first play, a farce entitled *Raising the Wind* (1803). Diddler's methods of petty duping were imaginative and productive.

James Kenney, who was born in Ireland in 1780, was the son of one of the founders of the famous London club, Boodles. He was for some years a London bank clerk.

Raising the Wind had a remarkable success at Covent Garden. Kenney was a prolific author responsible for comedies, dramas and operas, many of which long survived his death in 1849. He numbered Charles and Mary Lamb and Samuel Rogers among his friends.

Edgar Allan Poe wrote an essay on "Diddling considered as one of the exact sciences."

Dives, the rich, insensitive man. Dives has, since Biblical times, given his name to the worst manifestations of material wealth. He is identified (although he is not named in current versions) with the rich man of the parable recorded in *Luke xvi. 19-31.* Dives "was clothed in purple and fine linen, faring sumptuously every day."

Lazarus, the beggar, lay at his gate, full of sores and desiring, in vain, to be fed with the crumbs that fell from Dives' table. The dogs came and licked his sores.

When both died, Dives, in the torment of Hades, saw Lazarus afar off in the bosom of Abraham.

Dives cried, "Father Abraham, have mercy on me, and send Lazarus, that he may dip the tip of his finger in water, and cool my tongue; for I am in anguish in this flame" (*verses 23–4*).

Dives is reminded that in his lifetime he received good things. "Now here he is comforted and thou art in anguish. And beside all this, between us and you there is a great gulf fixed."

Dives begs Abraham to send to his brethren to warn them, but is told, "They have Moses and the prophets, let them hear them."

Dives pleads that if one went to them from the dead they would repent while there was time. Abraham replies that if they will not hear Moses and the prophets, "neither will they be persuaded, if one rise from the dead."

Doiley of Doily. The fabric was named after a 17th-century inventor and the original use was thought to have been primarily in the form of small napkins placed below finger glasses or bowls.

The name is spelt Doiley, or Doyley, and in some accounts he is placed as a linen draper in the Strand. Sir Hans Sloane describes him as a great searcher after curiosities and as having given his name to stuffs worn in summer. There is a *Spectator* reference to his fame and to his making a fortune out of such materials "as might at once be cheap and genteel."

Don Juan, the polished libertine. Don Juan Tenorio, the prototype of rakes, libertines and heartless seducers, was the son of a leading Seville family in the 14th century. He killed the commandant of Ulloa in a duel after seducing his daughter.

Tradition says that, to cramp his style, the Franciscan monks enticed him to a monastery and killed him, announcing that he had been taken off to hell by the statue of the commandant which stood in the grounds.

Another version says that Don Juan, after the crime, prepared a feast and invited the tomb-stone statue of the commandant to partake of it. The statue compelled the seducer to follow it and delivered Don Juan to the confines of hell.

The aristocratic libertine is the subject of many operas and plays. in Mozart's *Don Giovanni*, first produced at Prague in 1787, the dubious hero's valet, Leporello, says that his master had "in Italy 700 mistresses, in Germany 800, in Turkey and France 91, in Spain 1,003."

His exploits have been included in the writing of many famous authors, including Molière, Corneille, Dumas, and in the present century by Shaw in *Man and Superman*, 1903.

Byron follows Don Juan's adventures in many countries in his epic satire of the same name, which, although incomplete, runs to sixteen cantos. Byron's hero, however, is not the essential profligate of the original.

Dorcas, sewing woman or meeting to make clothes for the needy. Dorcas societies still persist and derive their name from the woman of Joppa referred to in *Acts ix. 36–41*. She was also called Tabitha.

She was "full of good works and almsdeeds which she did." She fell sick and died and Peter was brought to her body, around which the widows were weeping. They showed him the coats and garments Dorcas had made.

Peter "put them all forth, and kneeled down and prayed: and turning to the body, he said, Tabitha, arise. And she opened her eyes; and when she saw Peter, she sat up. And he gave her his hand, and raised her up; and calling the saints and widows, he presented her alive."

The Count D'Orsay of Quai D'Orsay.

The *Quai D'Orsay* is seized upon so frequently by romantic writers to give the "authentic" touch to a Parisian setting that the origin of the name deserves some recognition. Happily he fills the bill brilliantly. He was the last of the Paris dandies (1801–52), the son of the distinguished General D'Orsay, from whom he inherited remarkable distinction of appearance. Alfred Guillaume Gabriel joined the army and entered the bodyguard of Louis XVIII. In 1823 he met the Count and Countess of Blessington and began the peculiar relationship which can be pursued at least with interest in Lord Byron's correspondence after he had met the trio in Italy. D'Orsay's marriage to a girl of fifteen, the daughter of Lord Blessington by a previous marriage, scarcely made less complicated the intricacies of the *ménage*. A separation took place and after Lord Blessington's death, D'Orsay returned to England with the widow.

D'Orsay had the accomplishments of a wit and dandy. He had considerable skill in painting and sculpture. He and the Blessingtons moved in the highest literary and artistic circles. D'Orsay was also, however, a considerable athlete, a skilled horseman and a good boxer and fencer. He wrote well and talked and entertained brilliantly.

Carlyle, to whom D'Orsay paid homage in Chelsea, talks of his amazing good looks and stature after he had come "whirling hither in a chariot that struck all Chelsea into mute amazement with splendour."

He was appointed Director of Fine Arts in Paris, a gesture from Louis Napoleon, whom D'Orsay had befriended in London before the *coup d'état*, but did not live to enjoy the position.

Sir Henry Doulton of the pottery.

Sir Henry Doulton (1820–97) revived, and unexpectedly from Lambeth, London, the fortunes of the pottery industry when they declined after the death of Wedgwood.

Doulton, in contrast with his predecessor, enjoyed the benefits of a good education, though his father was in a small way of business, chiefly concerned with the manufacture of blacking bottles and other similar utilitarian articles of earthenware.

Sir Henry discovered the art of making glazed earthenware, which invention revolutionized sanitation. Hitherto drains had been mostly channels of bricks which absorbed and distributed the deleterious matter they conveyed.

The Doulton pottery works, on Thames-side, became the largest in the world and Sir Henry turned his attention from industrial earthenware to the demands of the domestic market. He did much to revive and develop the standard of art in the design and manufacture of pottery and made Doulton ware famous throughout the world.

Downing of Downing Street.

The name derives from Sir George Downing (1623(?)–84), a noted

The entrance to No. 10

soldier, diplomat and politician of the reign of Charles II. Sir George was Scout-master-general to Cromwell's

army in Scotland in 1650 and led The movement to offer the crown to Cromwell. He was Secretary to the Treasury in 1667.

Downing was British Resident at The Hague for several periods and sat for Morpeth in 1670.

It was another Sir George Downing, his grandson, the proceeds of whose estates, after prolonged litigation, made possible the founding of Downing College, Cambridge.

M. B. Drapier of Drapier's Letters. M. B. Drapier was the pseudonym of Jonathan Swift (1667–1745), Dean of St. Patrick's Cathedral, Ireland, in one of the most unusual incidents in English literature.

The Duchess of Kendal had been granted a patent by George I for supplying copper coin to Ireland. The Duchess, the King's mistress, sold it for a substantial sum to a William Wood who proposed to circulate his own coinage. The Duchess was to have a handsome share in the profits.

In 1723 the Irish Houses of Parliament protested against the transaction and Swift, who was a distinguished pamphleteer and often a paid publicist, took up their cause. Writing as a Dublin draper (hence the associated name) he explained in four letters that the circulation of "Wood's halfpence" would bring national ruin.

The effect of the Drapier's Letters, published in 1724, was so swift and so great that the scheme was abandoned and Wood was compensated by the Government.

Drawcansir, the burlesque tyrant. Drawcansir is the blustering swashbuckler in *The Rehearsal* (1671), by George Villiers, Duke of Buckingham (1627–88). The character was a caricature of Almanzor in Dryden's *Conquest of Granada.*

I drink, I huff, I strut, look big and stare,
And all this I can do, because I dare.

Buckingham, son of the Duke who was favourite of James I and Charles I, became a minister of Charles II. He was a dissolute character.

The Dromio of the identical brothers. The term is taken from Shakespeare's *Comedy of Errors*, wherein Dromio of Ephesus and Dromio of Syracuse are twins. They are servants of the two Antipholuses and the duplications cause much of the comedy of the play.

Galsworthy uses the term for characters in *The Forsyte Saga.*

Sir William Drury of Drury Lane. The London street and the famous theatre, properly called The Theatre Royal, are named after Sir William Drury, whose Drury House stood to the south of the present Drury Lane, in what is now Aldwych, during the reign of Henry VIII. The first of the four theatres upon the site was opened in 1663.

Dr. Dryasdust, the dull, laborious antiquarian or historian. The phrase, to describe a dull and uninteresting scholar, originated in the fictitious character, Dr. Jonas Dryasdust of York, to whom Sir Walter Scott addresses the prefaces of several of his books.

He is a prosy, ponderous person, given to frequent quotation.

"I chew the cud of sweet and bitter fancy, in a state betwixt sleeping and waking, which I consider as so highly favourable to philosophy, that I have no doubt some of its most distinguished systems have been composed under its influence. My servant is, therefore, instructed to tread as if upon down; my door hinges are carefully oiled, and all appliances used to prevent me from being prematurely and harshly called back to the broad waking-day of a laborious world . . ." from the Introduction to *Peveril of the Peak*, in which Dryasdust has an amusing conversation with the author, whom he vividly describes.

Dulcinea, the worshipped and idealized mistress. Dulcinea is the idealized mistress of Rabelais' *Don Quixote*. Her real name was Aldonza Lorenzo, but Don Quixote, after an intricate description of the descents to which she lays no claim, calls her Dulcinea del Toboso as "she derives her origin from a family of Toboso, near Mancha."

Don Quixote's squire, Sancho Panza, describes her as a sturdy wench of considerable muscular power.

The name, however, is generally used in literature to personify a female inspiration in a spiritual and æsthetic sense. Laurence Sterne, for example, says, "I must ever have some Dulcinea in my head—it harmonizes the soul."

John Duns Scotus of Dunce. John Duns Scotus was a 13th-century learned schoolman (d. 1308), who was so called from his birthplace, Dunse, in Scotland.

His numerous followers maintained the doctrine of the Immaculate Conception in opposition to St. Thomas Aquinas. The school were called Dunsers or Scottists and the name dunce came to be applied therefrom by the 16th-century humanists to apparently stupid enemies of learning and progress.

Tyndal records that the school, when its views were menaced, raged in every pulpit, and Butler in *Hudibras* and Pope in his *Essay on Criticism* refer to the sect in association with the modern interpretation of the term.

Duns Scotus was buried in Cologne.

Lord Dundreary of the Whiskers. Lord Dundreary was a character in *Our American Cousin*, by Tom Taylor, published in 1858.

The character of the witless, indolent peer was made doubly famous by the stage presentation in New York, in which the noted E. A. Sothern made a rich study of the part. His Lordship's long dismal whiskers became current coin.

Tom Taylor (1817–80) was a Fellow of Trinity College, Cambridge, a successful playwright and editor of *Punch*, 1874–80.

Alexander Mack of Dunkers. The Dunkers or Tunkers (the Dippers) were a body of German-American Baptists who administered Baptism only to adults and by triple immersion. They were founded in Germany by Alexander Mack in 1708. They settled in Pennsylvania early in the 18th century and spread to Ohio and other States. Many appear to have been doctors and to have devoted themselves to healing, particularly among the Indians. They upheld celibacy as a virtue but did not make it binding upon members.

The name was revived during the 1939–45 war in Britain when the people were extorted in official broadcasts to become Dunkers, dipping their bread in the gravy and clearing their plates to secure the maximum nourishment at a time of short rations.

St. Dunstan of St. Dunstan's. St. Dunstan, a noted Archbishop of Canterbury in the 10th century, and an outstanding statesman of his age, was born near Glastonbury, of noble line. He was called from a life of meditation to become Abbot of Glastonbury, whose abbey he restored and rebuilt.

Dunstan was a great political force during the reigns of Edgar and Edmund.

He died, in retirement at Canterbury, in 988 and was buried in the Cathedral.

The most familiar story associated with St. Dunstan, who appears to have practised austerities on occasion to an almost fatal degree, is that of his temptation by the devil in the form of a woman. Dunstan, who is regarded as the patron saint of blacksmiths and goldsmiths, was working at his forge. He waited until his tongs were red hot and then seized in them the nose of the temptress.

There is an allied legend that the devil, accosting St. Dunstan in his forge, asked him to shoe his single hoof. St. Dunstan, recognizing his visitor, pinned the devil to the wall and carried out the operation so painfully that the devil begged for mercy.

St. Dunstan agreed to release him on condition that he promised never to enter a place where a horseshoe was displayed.

The saint is often depicted in art as working at his craft, dressed in episcopal vestments.

The name of the saint in association with the work among blinded Service men and women arises from the headquarters of the movement, St. Dunstan's Lodge, Regent's Park, London. It was founded in 1915 by Sir Arthur Pearson, the pioneer periodical publisher, who was then blind.

Egeria, the eminine counsel and inspiration. Egeria was a Roman goddess of childbirth and of fountains. The vestal virgins drew water for their rituals from her sacred spring at Porta Capena. There, according to legend, she would meet King Numa by night and give him wise counsel. The king, whose life was written by Plutarch, is said to have reigned over a golden age and to him are attributed many Roman customs, laws and the construction of the Royal Palace, etc.

Some accounts name Egeria as his wife.

Queen Eleanor of the Eleanor Crosses. Eleanor (1244–90), Queen of Edward I of England (named Longshanks) and sister of Alfonso X of Castile, accompanied her husband to the Crusades in 1269. She is said to have saved the King's life by

An Eleanor Cross

sucking the poison from a wound inflicted by a poisoned arrow.

Her body was brought from Harby, Nottinghamshire, to Westminster for burial and at each stopping place of the cortège an Eleanor cross was set up. Several survive. The places so marked were Lincoln, Newark, Grantham, Leicester, Stamford, Geddington (Northants), Northampton,

Stony Stratford, Woburn, Dunstable, St. Albans, Waltham, West Cheap (Cheapside) and Westminster. The last Westminster resting place was in fact marked by the Charing Cross, in the ancient village of Charing which stood between the cities of London and Westminster. Its site was on the south side of Trafalgar Square.

The original cross was destroyed by the Puritans and the existing copy was moved to its present site in the forecourt of Charing Cross station in 1865.

The Earl of Elgin of the Elgin Marbles. The seventh Earl of Elgin (1766–1841) entered the Army at the age of sixteen and became a general. During his subsequent diplomatic career he was Envoy to the Porte, 1799–1803. While in residence at Constantinople, at his own cost he had models made of the principal sculptures of the Parthenon and obtained permission from the Turkish Government to view and explore the ancient temples of the Acropolis of Athens, then a Turkish Fort, and to acquire statuary of interest.

On the strength of this authority Elgin removed the collection, now called the Elgin Marbles, which cost him some £70,000.

After the envoy's recall they were shipped to England and the vessel carrying them was wrecked near Cerigo. The collection was salvaged.

The Marbles, chiefly from the Parthenon or Temple of Minerva, were bought for the nation for £35,000 in 1816 and deposited in the British Museum.

There have been sporadic controversies ever since as to their artistic value and Lord Elgin's right to remove them from Athens. Lord Byron's protest at the transaction—in

Childe Harold—reflected the feelings of many at the time—and since.

Epicurus of Epicure. Epicurus, from whose name and teaching the familiar words "epicure" and "epicurean" are derived, was a Greek philosopher of Athenian origin, born about 340 B.C.

He founded a school of philosophy at Athens, where he taught in opposition to the Stoics. The three branches of his philosophy were ethics and their handmaids, logic and physics. His teaching has been distorted by his detractors and by some of his disciples into a claim that sensual gratification is the be-all and end-all of life. In physics Epicurus held an atomic theory of the composition of things.

Epicurus was a man of high character and set much store upon happiness, even regarding virtue as of no value in itself, but only in so far as it offers an agreeable life. He did not advocate a sensual or hedonistic philosophy, although that colour is frequently given nowadays to the words derived from his name.

Epicurus died about 270 B.C.

The Epicureans were a flourishing sect of philosophers at the time of Christ, predominant with the Stoics in the world of thought at that time.

Erastus of Erastian. The name applies to the doctrine, attributed to Erastus, of the submission and subordination of ecclesiastical power to the secular power. Erastianism denotes the supremacy of the state in religious causes but does not enter into details of the relations between the church and secular power.

Thomas Erastus (1524–83) was a German-Swiss theologian. The name by which he survives was an adopted one. He was also an eminent physician and held high office in the state. He was for some years excommunicated.

His *Theses* were published in English, under the title *A Treatise on Excommunication*, in 1682. They sought to prove that, on Scriptural evidence, the sins of Christians were to be punished by civil authorities and not by discipline from the Church.

Eros of Erotic. Eros, the Greek equivalent of the Roman Cupid, was the son of Aphrodite (Venus) and Ares. He is presented as a boy of great beauty. His golden bow and arrow are distinguishing marks and his activities do not seem to have

Eros in Piccadilly Circus

altered through the centuries. Even mighty Zeus could not withstand his shafts—an acknowledgment of the omnipotence of love.

Cupid's golden arrow was held to represent the highest virtuous love, but he had a leaden arrow which stirred up sensual passion (see *Psyche* and *Lord Shaftesbury*).

Dr. L. L. Zamenhoff of Esperanto. The name Esperanto, the universal language, derives from Dr. Lazarus Ludovici Zamenhoff. It was so called from the pseudonym which the author and inventor adopted for his first book. The system was launched in 1887.

It spread rapidly in Europe and the first Esperanto Club in Britain was founded at Keighley in 1902. Many thousands of books have appeared in Esperanto, which language received commendation from the League of Nations. It has been used for broadcasting and many International Esperanto Congresses have been held.

Dr. Zamenhoff was born in Grodno, Russia, in 1859, and practised as an oculist in Warsaw. He died in 1917.

Ido, a modification and simplification of Esperanto, was produced in 1907.

Euphuism (Lyly). John Lyly, from whose *Euphues, The Anatomy of Wit* is derived the word euphuism, was a 16th-century author and dramatist (1553–1606). 'The work appeared at a critical period in England's national development and exercised a marked influence upon literature and cultivated speech. Lyly derived much inspiration from Italian tradition and hoped to do away with the barbarities and soften the asperities of our language. In fact he is remembered mainly, and perhaps unfairly, for a consummate artificiality of style which he adopted, making it instantly fashionable and afterwards famous.

Lyly was born in Kent, took his M.A. at Magdalen, Oxford, in 1575, and was incorporated M.A. at Cambridge two years later, after studies at that University.

The first part of his *Euphues* appeared in 1579, to be followed next year by *Euphues and his England*. It brought him to the notice of Lord Burghley, who gave him some employment.

He wrote light plays to be performed at court by the companies of acting children of the Chapel Royal, St. Paul's, London.

For thirteen years, from 1584, he frequented the Court as playwright and wit, striving to secure the part of Master of the Revels. Two earnest petitions to Queen Elizabeth eloquently pleading long service, poverty and domestic claims were unsuccessful. The very human family man, a heavy smoker, was a wit in society with a heart full of seriousness. He was a hungry reader of good books and a hungry waiter at Court, who was fed only with promises.

Sir Philip Sidney might say: "So is that hony-flowing Matron Eloquence apparelled, or rather disguised in a Curtizan-like painted affectation . . . I would this fault [alliteration] were only peculiar to Versifiers and had not as large possession among Prose-printers," but Lyly left his mark. Lyly's continuous straining after antithesis, epigram and high flown phrasing was artificial but could not be ignored.

His best comedies include *Alexander and Campaspe, Midas* and *Endymion*. The plots are loosely fashioned, but many of the lyrics are notable.

He contested Parliamentary elections successfully on four occasions; sitting twice for Aylesbury, in 1593 and 1601.

John Evelyn of the Diary. John Evelyn, one of the most famous diarists in English literature, was born in 1620 of an honourable family. He has been described as a perfect model of the English gentleman of the 17th century.

Evelyn came down from Balliol after two years without a degree and entered the Temple as a law student. He soon relinquished what he calls "the unpolished study" of the law and did not practise as a barrister. He concerned himself with horticulture and brought his father's estates at Wotton, Surrey, "sweetly environed with delicious streams and venerable woods," to a standard of excellence.

Evelyn was a man of means and culture, with leisure to pursue his tastes, and he wrote upon horticulture, engraving and translated allied works, including some on architecture, from the French.

He was at heart a rural economist, a great improver of English gardening with an intense interest in afforestation. It was his love of planting, aided by the knowledge that more timber was needed for the Navy, that prompted his writing *Sylva: a Discourse on Forest Trees.* It was the first book published by the Royal Society and one of the few books in the records of literature that completely achieved its object. Millions of trees were planted as the result of its arguments.

After years of travel on the Continent, Evelyn held a number of minor offices under the Crown and sat on important commissions. He was Secretary of the Royal Society, whose Presidency he declined. He was a man of affairs, in intimate knowledge if not in active participa-tion, and he included many of the important figures of his age among his friends. Pepys was an intimate.

Thus it was that *Evelyn's Diary*, which covers the whole of his active life, is a brilliant and informed picture of his colourful times. The manuscript was accidentally saved from destruction as waste paper. *The Diary*, written in retrospect and not day by day, as was Pepys', was not published until 1818 and then not in its entirety.

Evelyn died in London in 1706 and was buried at Wotton Church.

Fabius of Fabian. Fabian: employing cautious and delaying strategy to wear out an enemy, especially in the matter of policy.

Quintus Fabius Maximus, called Cunctator (the Delayer), was the Roman general who became dictator in Rome in 217 B.C. He baffled Hannibal by avoiding direct encounters and wore out the enemy by marches, counter marches and allied strategic diversions and skirmishes. His policy was one of wariness rather than attack, of gradual erosion in preference to direct assault.

The Fabian Society was formed in 1884 by a group of intellectual Socialists, which included Mr. and Mrs. Sidney Webb (Lord and Lady Passfield) and George Bernard Shaw. The name indicated its strategy. Their aims, as announced in their prospectus, included the reorganization of society by the emancipation of land and industrial capital from individual and class ownership and the vesting of them in the community, and the community owning of industrial capital that could be managed socially. The society's policy was described at the time as one of stealing inches, not grasping leagues.

Washington was called the American Fabius, and the Duc de Montmorency, Grand Constable of France, 16th century, the French Fabius because of their employment of similar strategy and tactics against respectively the English and the Imperial army which invaded Provence.

Gabriel Daniel Fahrenheit of the Thermometer. Gabriel Daniel Fahrenheit (1686–1736) was born at Dantzig but lived mostly in England and Holland. After failing as a merchant, he studied physics, manufactured meteorological instruments and invented several, including a hygrometer. He adopted mercury as a measure of heat instead of alcohol previously used.

In contrast with the Centigrade thermometer, freezing point and boiling point on the Fahrenheit thermometer are 32° and 212°.

Fahrenheit, who died in Holland on September 16, 1736, was elected F.R.S. in 1724.

Celsius, of Stockholm, soon after suggested the more obvious graduation between zero and 100 which is incorporated in the Centigrade thermometer.

The other name associated with thermometers is that of the French scientist, René Réaumur (1683–1757), who has been called the "Pliny of the 18th century." He was a distinguished natural historian. For his thermometer, widely accepted on the continent, he used a mixture of four-fifths alcohol and one-fifth water. Freezing point is 0° and boiling point 80°.

Sir John Falstaff of Falstaffian. The adjective Falstaffian denotes a witty, self-indulgent braggart. Its origin, Sir John Falstaff, is one of Shakespeare's greatest characters.

He is one of the boon companions of Henry, Prince of Wales, has an over-addiction to sack, and is "a tun of a man." When he is detected in his frequent empty boasting he reveals an ingenious artfulness in saving face. Poins, Bardolph and Peto share a riotous life with Sir John. Typical of Falstaff's robust deception is his finding of the body of Hotspur at the Battle of Shrewsbury and his announcement that he has killed him. He is a comic character of superb dimensions. He is an exuberant wit who nourishes his mind with jests and his body with sack and sugar. He is a liar and at times a coward;

he is a glutton and a braggart, but above all he is lovable; a prodigious creation.

The other Falstaff of Shakespeare, who appears in *The Merry Wives of Windsor*, is comparatively an anæmic figure; a sorry designing knave with few redeeming traits.

The character was thought to have been originally named Oldcastle, but renamed on the objection of Lord Cobham, a descendant of the original Sir John Oldcastle, leader of the Lollards, who was declared a heretic and died in 1417, "hung and burnt hanging" in St. Giles' Fields.

Shakespeare in the Epilogue to *II King Henry IV* says: ". . . our humble author will continue the story, with Sir John in it . . . Where, for anything I know, Falstaff shall die of a sweat, unless he be killed with your hard opinions; for Oldcastle died a martyr, and this is not the man."

Frances Eliza Hodgson Burnett

of Little Lord Fauntleroy. Frances Burnett (Mrs. Stephen Townsend), the Anglo-American author, was born at Manchester in 1849, the

Little Lord Fauntleroy

daughter of a house furnisher and decorator who settled in Tennessee.

She married and obtained a divorce from Swan Burnett, a doctor, in 1898, and remarried.

Her most famous book, *Little Lord Fauntleroy*, was published first in America in 1886 and had a prodigious success.

The little, velvet-frocked and over-dressed child became a public figure and the term is still used for an over-dressed, effeminate boy.

The author died in New York in 1924.

St. Fiacre of the cab.

St. Fiacre (or Fiacrach) is thought to have been the son of a 7th-century king of Ireland. He became an anchorite, founding a monastery at Breuil, in France. Miracles were attributed to him and to his shrine.

In the 16th century his remains were removed to the Cathedral of Meaux, northern France.

The Hôtel de St. Fiacre, in Paris, was the site of the first stand of the cabs and coaches which immediately became known as fiacres. They appeared in the middle of the 17th century.

The saint's day is August 30.

François Marie Charles Fourier

of Fourierism. Charles Fourier of Fourierism, or phalanstery, was a French Socialist (1772–1837).

His communistic system provided for the division of the world into phalansteries, consisting of some 400 families, or 1,800 persons. They were to be self-contained units, with their own arts and crafts and only one language. Profits were to be given to communal funds, industry and talent were to be encouraged by incentive and indigence was not to be allowed.

There was to be an over-riding government on the lines of the Swiss canton system or the federated States of America.

The Fourth Estate.

The three estates of the realm are the Lords Spiritual, the Lords Temporal and the Commons.

"The Fourth Estate" has been applied to the Press since the end of the 18th century. The phrase is generally attributed to Edmund Burke (1730–97) but is not to be found in his published writings.

St. Francis of Franciscans. St. Francis of Assisi was born in Umbria, Italy, in the 11th century. After service as a soldier he was converted during illness from a life of extravagant dissipation and devoted himself to poverty, self-denial and good works.

From a growing brotherhood he founded the Franciscan Order, of friars, novices and lay brothers, in 1208. It was confirmed a few years later by the Pope. Its rules required poverty, chastity and much obedient labour. In later centuries the Order relaxed its austerity somewhat. Many eminent figures were associated with it. Their habit was grey, though several allied Orders, which branched from it, wear different coloured habits.

Soon after its inception, the Order established itself in England, at Canterbury and Northampton.

The Franciscans are known as the Minors or Minorites, to mark their humility, and as the Grey Friars, from the original colour of the habit.

The Order of Franciscan Nuns was founded early in the 12th century by St. Clare, virgin and abbess, who was born in Assisi. They are known as the Order of Poor Clares, or the Minoresses.

St. Francis de Sales (1567–1622) was a Bishop of Geneva.

Mary Shelley of Frankenstein. A Frankenstein is an inhuman monster of hideous characteristics. Its creator, or rather the creator of the novel whose title has been applied to the monster, was Mary Wollstonecraft Shelley (1797–1851).

She was the second wife of the poet, and when the Shelleys and Byron occupied a wet summer in Switzerland by reading and telling ghost stories, *Frankenstein* was Mary's contribution. At her husband's sug-gestion it was developed into a long story and appeared with the subtitle *The Modern Prometheus* in 1818.

Frankenstein learns the secret of animating matter and from a collection of bones from charnel houses gives life to a creature of hideous humanity and revolting attributes and appearance. Its supernatural size and strength and its revolting make-up inspire fear and loathing, and in its loneliness it develops hatred for Frankenstein's bride and his brother.

Frankenstein pursues his monstrous creation to murder it but is himself destroyed thereby.

The monster, of which the word Frankenstein has become a synonym, is in fact not named in the book.

Sigmund Freud of Freudian. The founder of psycho-analysis was born, of Jewish extraction, in Moravia in 1856. Most of his life was spent in Vienna, though he moved to London in 1938 after the German assimilation of Austria. His early interests were botany and chemistry. He did not qualify for medicine until 1881.

Freud was compelled by financial restriction to relinquish research work, in which he had studied physiology and cerebral anatomy, to become a clinical neurologist.

Dr. Breuer, of Vienna, described to Freud a remarkable cure in which a patient under hypnosis was persuaded to recollect the origin of the hysteria which was the reason for treatment.

Freud pursued the possibilities of psycho-analysis from that point, studying under the famous neurologist, Charcot, in Paris. There followed the publication of several important works on neurology.

Freud at first developed the use of hypnotism as a means of recalling deleterious memories and emotions which, through the restricting unconscious mind, had an adverse effect on the conscious mind. Later he distrusted hypnotism and was more concerned with the conscious memory of the patient.

Much opposition was met in medical circles, but after ten years Freud was joined by other distinguished workers, including Jung and Adler, who later dissented from some of Freud's principles. His teachings obtained world wide recognition and he was elected F.R.S. in 1936. He died three years later.

Friedrich Froebel of the Educational System. The eminent German educational reformer, Friedrich Wilhelm August Froebel, was born in 1782. After a neglected youth he was apprenticed to a forester and from this work he derived much knowledge of nature's laws. He sought training at Jena in the natural sciences. He practised architecture and held several clerical posts.

After service in the Prussian army, Froebel began his propagation of new ideas in teaching. His school had a precarious existence for many years, but eventually won recognition beyond his own country. He opened the first Kindergarten at Blankenburg in 1837. He wrote, in his notable book, *The Education of Man*, chiefly upon the first seven formative years. He suffered throughout his life, which ended in 1852, from financial restriction, political and sectarian prejudice and active opposition.

His principles of developing natural faculties by creating and stimulating willing interest had a profound effect upon the educational methods of the world.

Jean Froissart of the Chronicles. The famous French chronicler and historian was born in Valenciennes, about 1338. His father was a painter of armorial bearings. Jean was educated for the Church but early revealed a preference for the gay life. He brought arts and graces to its pursuit.

Froissart claimed that the moon ruled the first four years of life, Mercury the next ten, after which Venus took control. Certainly the Chronicler was only of that tender age when he fell in love with a lady *"belle, jone et gente."*

At eighteen, a youth of some accomplishments and charms, Froissart was well received in the English Court, where he wrote ballads and other elegances required of him. He sighed for a return to his first love but she received him not only coldly but antagonistically, seizing him by the hair and pulling out a dainty handful.

When he was twenty, Froissart began his *Chronicles* at the command of Robert of Namur, Lord of Beaufort. They cover the period 1325–1400 and in quest of material the author travelled far and wide, seeking and revelling in the scenes of courtly pageantry and martial splendour. The *Chronicles* deal with the contemporary affairs of Flanders, France, Spain, Portugal, England and Scotland.

Froissart was a born storyteller. His style is racy and delightful and he presents a scene with all the splendid colour of a mediæval painting. He died in 1410. As befits a scholarly troubadour, who, on his confession, rejoiced in dances and minstrels and pricked up his ears at the uncorking of bottles, he left also a considerable body of verse.

Thomas Fuller of the "Worthies." Fuller's "Worthies," or to give the book its original title, *"The History of the Worthies of England.* Endeavoured by Thomas Fuller, D.D.,"* is a landmark in English literature.

The author, Thomas Fuller, was born in the rectory of Aldwinkle St. Peter's, Northants, in 1608. Twenty-three years later Dryden was born in the vicarage of the other section of the village, Aldwinkle All Saints.

Fuller had a distinguished career at Cambridge, which he entered at the age of twelve. As curate of Cambridge he buried Hobson, the famous carrier of "Hobson's choice." He was a prebendary of Salisbury at twenty-three. He was a popular preacher (though Pepys found him dry), and was appointed to the lectureship of the Savoy.

He was a chaplain with the Royal Army during the Civil War, with Sir Ralph Hopton, and at that period wrote *Good Thoughts in Bad Times* for the encouragement of his men. This and its sequels are commended by Coleridge. In 1648 Fuller was given the living of Waltham in Essex, and ten years later went to Cranford in Middlesex.

After the Restoration he returned to his Savoy canonry and lectureship and became Chaplain-in-extraordinary to the King. He wrote a number of books, including histories of the Crusades, the church in Britain up to 1648, and Cambridge University.

The *Worthies* appeared in 1662, the year after Fuller's death; for he had set it aside in his emotion at the King's death. In it he takes the counties of England, describes them and their characteristics and peoples them with short biographies of leading personalities and colourful characters. The work is characterized by much humour, a wry wisdom and deep feeling.

It was dedicated to Charles II, "To his Sacred Majesty, Most Dread Soveraign ... by Your Majesties meanest Subject, The Author's Orphan," who was then a divinity student at Cambridge.

In offering the book to his readers, Fuller writes: "I propound five ends to my self in this Book: First, to gain some glory to God. Secondly, to preserve the memories of the Dead. Thirdly, to present examples to the Living. Fourthly, to entertain the Reader with delight. And lastly (which I am not ashamed publickly to profess) to procure some honest profit to my self. If not so happy to obtain all, I will be joyful to attain some; yea, contented and thankful too, if gaining any (especially the first) of these ends, the motives of my endeavours."

Lamb, in an essay on Fuller's writings, said, "His wit is not always a *lumen siccum*, a dry faculty of surprising; on the contrary, his conceits are oftentimes deeply steeped in human feeling and passion. Above all, his way of telling a story, for its eager liveliness, and the perpetual running commentary of the narrator happily blended with the narration, is perhaps unequalled."

Fuller's baptism is recorded by his father in St. Peter's registers and in the church a memorial describes Thomas as "A scribe instructed into the kingdom of Heaven."

The Furies. The Furies, in mythology, were fearful maidens who resided in the depths of Tartarus. They are generally regarded as three in number; Allecto, Megaera and Tisiphone, though there are references to a chorus of them.

Their purpose was to punish men for crimes such as perjury, murder and lack of hospitality. They were able to order famines and pestilences.

The Furies were said to have been born of the blood of the mutilated Uranus, and they were especially severe upon crimes against the ties and loyalties of kinship.

The name Eumenides, the kindly ones, when applied to them is a propitiatory euphemism.

They were generally represented as winged women, sometimes surrounded by snakes.

The Furies are associated with the story of Orestes who, after killing his mother, Clytemnestra, and her lover, wandered in desolation and near madness until befriended and purified by Apollo. When he was acquitted at the court of Areopagus, on the casting vote of Athene, the Furies threatened the land and its women with barrenness, but were eventually placated by Athene and given a shrine.

In Aeschylus' play, *The Eumenides*, which treats with the story of Orestes, the Furies form the Chorus.

Sir Galahad, the noble knight.
The symbol of the noblest manifestation of knightly chivalry, Sir Galahad was one of the chief heroes of the Arthurian legend.

He was the son of Lancelot and

Sir Galahad

Elaine and at the Round Table occupied the one vacant seat, Siege Perilous, which at the institution had been left vacant for the knight who should succeed in the quest for the Holy Grail.

> *There Galaad sat, with manly grace.*
> *Yet maiden meekness in his face.*
> Scott's *Bridal of Triermain, ii. 13.*

Dr. George Horace Gallup of the Gallup Poll. Dr. George Horace Gallup of the Gallup Poll was born in Iowa in 1902. He was educated at Iowa State University, where he taught, and was Professor of Journalism at North West University.

He first became interested in research through trying to check items read in newspapers and magazines, and his work set a standard in this field.

Dr. Gallup went into market research generally and in 1933 first experimented in the public opinion field. His first releases appeared in 1935, securing nation-wide atten-

tion through his successful forecast of the 1936 U.S. presidential election.

Gallup organizations now cover twelve countries — Great Britain, U.S.A., Canada, Australia, Brazil, Norway, Sweden, Denmark, Finland, France, Holland and Italy. They are affiliated in the International Association of Public Opinion Institutes, but each unit is independent and controlled by its own nationals.

Gallup has also done considerable research in the cinema field, testing the public's reaction to every aspect of film production.

He is married, has two sons and a daughter. He lives on a farm in New Jersey, where he raises beef cattle. His ancestors came from the Dorchester neighbourhood, where the "Gallop Arms" is still an inn sign.

Lewis Carroll of Galumph. Galumph, to go galloping in triumph, is one of the many fascinating "portmanteau" words devised by Lewis Carroll (1832–98).

Lewis Carroll was the pen-name of Charles Lutwidge Dodgson, English mathematician and author, who was born in Cheshire and educated at Rugby and Oxford.

He explains in the Preface of *The Hunting of the Snark, An Agony In Eight Fits,* how two words are packed into one like a portmanteau.

"For instance, take the two words 'fuming' and 'furious.' Make up your mind that you will say both words, but leave it unsettled which you will say first. Now open your mouth and speak. If your thoughts incline ever so little towards 'fuming,' you will say 'fuming-furious'; if they turn, by even a hair's breadth, towards 'furious,' you will say 'furious-fuming'; but if you have that rarest of gifts, a perfectly balanced mind, you will say 'frumious.' "

Carroll, author of the immortal *Alice's Adventures in Wonderland* (1865), was ordained in the Church of England and was Mathematical Lecturer at Christ Church, Oxford, where he had taken a first-class degree in mathematics. He wrote a number of learned mathematical treatises.

Many of his verbal creations, such as Jabberwocky, Snark, Boojum, etc., have passed into common usage. His famous poem, *Jabberwocky*, is written almost completely in an original language, opening with the lines:

> *'Twas brillig, and the lithy toves*
> *Did gyre and gimble n the wabe;*

and includes "He lef it dead, and with its head He went galumphing back."

Luigi Galvani of galvanize.

To galvanize is strictly a scientific electrical process and as such beyond the scope of this book. The word, however, has acquired an even greater non-technical use as implying stimulation, the shocking into greater life. As such it is apparently indispensable to writers of thrillers and detective novels.

Galvani was an Italian physiologist (1737–98), a lecturer in anatomy. The development of his theories of animal electricity led to his invention of the metallic arc.

It is perhaps some justification for the wider use that Galvani, in his experiments, shocked frogs by constructing the arc of two different metals, one placed in contact with the frog's nerve and the other with a muscle. The result was added involuntary activity.

Sarah Gamp of the Gamp.

Sarah is the character in Dickens' *Martin Chuzzlewit*. This voluble and disreputable monthly nurse is invariably accompanied by her bulky, cotton umbrella. She is also famous for her continual reference to the imaginary Mrs. Harris, whose opinions always conveniently endorse her own.

The use of the word "gamp" to describe a midwife has the same derivation.

Ganymede, the cup-bearer, or, facetiously, waiter or pot-boy.

Ganymede, a youth of great beauty, was cup-bearer to Zeus. The office was originally held, according to earlier Greek legends, by Hebe. The name Hebe is often facetiously used for a waitress.

Ganymede was a Trojan youth of royal descent who was taken up by the gods to Olympus and made an immortal. Other accounts say that he was conveyed by the eagles to Zeus himself, on account of his beauty.

Gargantua of Gargantuan.

"Gargantuan: enormous, gigantic" —*O.E.D.*

The word derives from the hero of Rabelais' *Gargantua and Pantagruel*.

The name was originally that of a benign giant in French folk-lore.

Gargantua is represented by Rabelais as a prince of gigantic stature and prodigious appetite who is also studious, athletic and full of a comical peace-loving kindliness. He was "carried eleven months in his mother's belly," and delivered after she had eaten "sixteen quarters, two bushels, three pecks and a pipkin full" of tripe.

When he was hit in the temple by a cannon-ball he reprimanded the enemy for throwing grape-kernels. When he combed his hair, cannonballs fell out, and when he was hungry he thought nothing of eating six pilgrims in a salad.

He lived for several centuries and begot a son, Pantagruel, as wonderful as himself. He is a character unapproached in literature.

(See also *Rabelais*.)

Giuseppi Garibaldi of the red blouse.

A type of blouse, for women or children. was long known as a

Garibaldi. Originally it was red, from the red shirts of the great Italian patriot, Giuseppi Garibaldi (1807–82). He was at first a sailor, but soon allied himself with the Young Italy movement. He was several times obliged to flee the country, or was exiled. He fought for Sardinia against Austria and protested against the ceding of Nice and Savoy to Napoleon III.

He led an expedition against the Sicilies, became dictator of Sicily and crossed to Italy to expel Francis II from Naples. He handed over the city to the King of Italy.

Garibaldi is regarded as one of the creators of modern Italy.

In addition to the blouses which perpetuated his fame, a currant biscuit was named Garibaldi and was widely popular for generations.

David Garrick of the Garrick Theatre.

David Garrick, the famous English actor and playwright, was born in 1716, descended on his father's side from Huguenot refugees.

He was educated at Lichfield Grammar School and partly under Dr. Samuel Johnson, with whom he came penniless to London.

The *Life* of Johnson gives a remarkable portrait of the actor, for whom the great doctor had a profound respect and admiration.

Garrick gave up legal study and experience in the wine trade to follow a theatrical career. His first public appearance was at Ipswich in 1741.

Garrick was joint manager at Drury Lane and at Dublin shared managership with Sheridan. Dissension among the members of his company at Drury Lane led to the famous rivalry between Drury Lane and Covent Garden.

Garrick made a brilliant success in many parts and did much to popularize Shakespeare, in whose honour he conducted a notable jubilee at Stratford-on-Avon in 1769. He introduced many theatrical reforms, including the exclusion of spectators from the stage itself.

Johnson, who had told Garrick's mother, "Madam, David will either be hanged or become a great man," said later that his pupil "deserves everything he has acquired for having seized the very soul of Shakespeare, for having embodied it in himself and for having expended its glory over the world."

Garrick was a member of the famous Literary Club, sharing the friendship of such notable contemporaries as Goldsmith, Burke and Reynolds.

Johnson, who said of Garrick that "he has long reigned the unequalled favourite of the public," declared at the actor's death in 1769 that the event eclipsed the gaiety of nations. He was buried, amid manifestations of great public regard, in Westminster Abbey.

The Garrick Theatre, in Charing Cross Road, was opened by Sir John Hare in April, 1889, with Sir Arthur Pinero's *The Profligate.* There was an earlier Garrick Theatre, opened in 1830 in Whitechapel.

King George VI of the George Cross and Medal.

King George VI instituted the George Cross in September, 1940, as "a new mark of honour for men and women in all walks of life." It ranks immediately after the Victoria Cross, the premier decoration. It may be awarded posthumously and there is a military division to permit its award to members of the fighting services.

The George Medal is awarded for civilian bravery.

The Cross is of plain silver with four equal limbs, and in the centre is a design showing St. George and the Dragon, with the inscription "For Gallantry." The ribbon is dark blue, threaded through a bar adorned with laurel leaves.

John Gerard of the Herball.

John Gerard, author of the celebrated

Herball, or Generall Historie of Plantes, 1597, was born at Nantwich, Cheshire, in 1545. He settled in London and superintended Lord Burghley's gardens for twenty years. He also practised as a barber-surgeon, planned and tended a large physic garden in Holborn, and was Master of the Company of Barber-Surgeons in 1608. Gerard did much to promote the study of botany, particularly in its relation to medicine.

His exhaustive work gave detailed descriptions of plants, their localities, their medical significance and it discussed nomenclature and disposed of certain allied superstitions. The book was illustrated by notable woodcuts.

The *Herball* was in part adapted from Dodoens' *Pemptades,* published fourteen years before. An enlarged edition of the *Herball* was published in 1653. The author died in 1612.

Elbridge Gerry of Gerrymander.
To gerrymander, or jerrymander, is to arrange election boundaries so that representation shall favour the party in power or occasion disproportionate representation.

The word arose from the action of Elbridge Gerry (1744–1814), who, as Governor of Massachusetts, enacted a law which divided the territory into new senatorial voting districts. The fresh boundaries were so irregular and elongated that, tradition says, an observer remarked that they looked like a salamander. To which the astute governor retorted, "Gerrymander, rather."

The word became proverbial and was absorbed into the language.

Gerry, who took a Harvard degree, was elected vice-president of the United States in 1812.

Sir William Schwenck Gilbert of Gilbertian. Gilbertian: characterized by the humorous topsy-turvy absurdity of the famous operas.

Gilbert, the English humorist and playwright, was born in 1836, son of a novelist. He graduated from London University and endured four years as a clerk in the education department of the Privy Council. He decided to follow law and was called to the Bar in 1864. Then began his extensive literary activities, though he found time to serve as a magistrate for Middlesex and to hold a commission in the volunteers.

His *Bab Ballads* brought him fame but he did much dramatic criticism and wrote several plays before he began his incomparable partnership with Sir Arthur Sullivan in 1871. Then followed the stream of outstanding light operas presented at the Royalty and the Savoy under the management of Richard D'Oyly Carte.

They offer invariably "a logical tupsy-turveydom," animated by a rich humour expressed in rhyme of remarkable facility and felicity.

Gilbert tilted at the follies and foibles of his age; in *Patience,* for instance, against the æstheticism that followed Victorian over-decoration; in *H.M.S. Pinafore* against absurd Victorian Admiralty methods. *Ruddigore,* a delicious parody on the old-time melodramas, is typical of Gilbert's unrivalled gift for satire. His witty text, with its spontaneous humour and its shrewd topicality, has a perennial freshness.

The association of Gilbert with Sir Arthur Sullivan, despite the occasional conflict of their pronounced individualities, was a success unparalleled in the history of music. Indeed Gilbert could write with truth to his partner: "We are world-known, and as much an institution as Westminster Abbey."

Gilbert died in 1911.

Gilderoy of "Higher than Gilderoy's Kite." Gilderoy was the nickname of a notorious cattle thief and highwayman of Perthshire. His real name was Patrick Macgregor and he was hanged at Edinburgh in 1636. The height of the gibbet was increased in relation to the immensity of the victim's crimes. Gilderoy flew high and his record would appear to be justification, though there was a certain audacity about his exploits that won the sneaking admiration of many.

He is said to have robbed Richelieu in the Royal presence, to have made Cromwell a victim of his pickpocketing, and to have hanged a judge.

To be hung higher than Gilderoy's Kite is to be punished more severely than the worst criminal.

Gilderoy is mentioned in Percy's *Reliques*, and a ballad by Campbell (1777–1844), put into the mouth of the highwayman's widow, includes the lines:

> *The last, the fatal hour is come*
> *That bears my love from me:*
> *I hear the dead note of the drum,*
> *I mark the gallows' tree!*

> *The bell has toll'd; it shakes my heart;"*
> *The trumpet speaks thy name;*
> *And must my Gilderoy depart*
> *To bear a death of shame?*

She talks of "when first in Roslin's lovely glen, you triumph'd o'er my heart" and claims that "every mean and cruel eye regards my woe with scorn."

John Gilpin. Cowper's *Diverting History of John Gilpin* was first published anonymously in *The Public Advertiser*, reprinted in cheap book form and included in a volume in 1785.

The story of John Gilpin, "a citizen of credit and renown" and "a linen-draper bold" of Cheapside, is said to have been told to the poet by Lady Austen to divert one of his frequent fits of melancholy.

Gilpin and his wife decide to celebrate their twentieth wedding anniversary by a trip to the Bell at Edmonton, "all in a chaise and pair." The chaise drew up three doors away, lest neighbours should say Mrs. Gilpin was proud. "Six precious souls, and all agog, To dash through thick and thin."

Gilpin, on his horse, loses control,

and the ballad describes his headlong career to Edmonton and indeed beyond to Ware. The horse was returning to the place of its owner. Gilpin turns round and races madly back, "nor stopped till where he had got up. He did again set down.".

The story, which Lady Austen recalled from her childhood, is said

John Gilpin's Ride

to have been based upon the parallel adventures of one Beyer, linen draper of Paternoster Row where it meets Cheapside. Beyer died in May 1791 at the age of 98.

There is a similarity between Gilpin's adventures and the marriage escapade of Commodore Trunnion in Smollett's *Peregrine Pickle*, published much earlier, in 1751.

William Ewart Gladstone of the Gladstone Bag. The light portmanteau or travelling bag was named after the great British statesman and Prime Minister, William Ewart Gladstone (1809–98).

The famous politician and orator found his name used for a number of articles which he favoured or were introduced during his long term of office.

Certain cheap French wines were long referred to as "Gladstone," because their importation was largely increased owing to the reduction in Customs duty made while Gladstone was Chancellor of the Exchequer.

Johann Rudolph Glauber of the Salts. The German alchemist and physician, born in Franconia in 1604, appears to have been a scientist of contradictory traits. He combined a belief in the philosopher's stone and the elixir of life with a distinguished record in the advancement of scientific chemical knowledge. He was called the "Paracelsus of his age" and made several notable discoveries, including hydrochloric acid. He was among the earliest users of nitric acid. He discovered his salt in 1658 but appears not to have utilized its purgative properties to remove from his mind a somewhat eccentric contempt for mankind and criticism of its perversity, which hindered his work.

The doctor lived in Vienna, Salzburg and elsewhere and died in Amsterdam in 1668.

Gobelin of the Tapestries. The

Gobelin family, of whom Jehan was the most noted, originated in Belgium, probably in Rheims. They settled in Paris about 1450 and made their reputation as dyers, offering a secret scarlet dye which was without equal. The business flourished and soon the manufacture of tapestries was added to the original business.

Out of the profits of the works at Faubourg St. Marcel there was built by Jehan an establishment of such extravagance that it was known as "La Folie Gobelin."

Later the works were purchased for the throne and famous artists were commissioned to design tapestries made there for the royal household.

Jehan Gobelin died in 1467, but the family was associated with the works until the end of the 17th century. Some members purchased titles of nobility and held distinguished offices in the State.

Apart from a period during the French Revolution the Gobelin works have continued as a state-supported industry.

Johann Wolfgang von Goethe of

Goethian. The great German poet and philosopher, Johann Wolfgang von Goethe, who has given his name not only to his followers but to all associations with his writings and views, was born in Frankfort in 1749.

He was the son of an imperial chancellor married to a daughter of a chief city magistrate. He is regarded as one of the greatest and most balanced minds in recent centuries. His philosophy combines scientific scepticism with supreme faith in spiritual values.

Carlyle, one of his deepest admirers, did much to spread Goethe's fame in this country. There were, he said, some ten pages of Goethe's *Meister* that, "if ambition had been my object, I would rather have written than all the literature of my time."

The chief works of Goethe, who died in 1832, are *Goetz, Werter, Faust* and *Wilhelm Meister.*

Gog and Magog of the famous

Guildhall giants. The famous London statues of Gog and Magog have an interesting, if somewhat confused, history.

The Gog and Magog effigies

Gog and Magog are mentioned several times in the Bible. In *Gen. x. 2*, Magog is the son of Japhet. In *Ezek. xxxviii. and xxxix.* Gog is the chief prince of Meshech and Magog is his territory.

In the Apocalypse (*Rev. xx. 7–9*)

Gog and Magog appear to represent the nations of the earth who are deceived by Satan or all future enemies of the Kingdom of God.

There are varying accounts of the origin of the famous Guildhall effigies. Some claim that they are the images of the last two survivors of a race of giants who inhabited Britain. Diocletian, after murdering the husbands of his notorious thirty-three daughters, left the women at sea and eventually they reached Britain. Here they consorted with demons and the race of giants was the result. The last two survivors were said to have been kept as door-keepers at the palace gates in London, on the site of the Guildhall.

Other authorities consider they represent Gogmagog and his British vanquisher, Corineus. There is a Gogmagog Hill to the south-east of Cambridge.

The famous effigies appear to have been part of London's civic ceremonial since the reign of Henry V. The originals, which were probably of pasteboard and wicker, were destroyed in the Great Fire of London. They were replaced by images, fourteen feet high, carved by Richard Saunders in 1708–9.

Gog and Magog were destroyed in the blitz of 1940 and it is not the intention of the City authorities to replace them.

Goliath, the prototype of giant strength—and its vulnerability. Goliath, the Philistine giant of Gath, defied the armies of Israel for forty days. His height was "six cubits and a span [10 feet and 6 inches], and he had a helmet of brass upon his head and he was clad with a coat of mail; and the weight of the coat was five thousand shekels of brass" (*1 Sam. xvii. 5*).

The staff of his spear was like a weaver's beam and his spearhead weighed six hundred shekels of iron.

Goliath issued a challenge to single combat and the stripling David slew him with a stone from his sling, beheading the senseless giant with his own sword "as there was no sword in the hand of David" (*1 Sam. xvii. 49–51*). The sword was exhibited at Nob as a trophy and was taken again by David: "There is none like that; give it me" (*1 Sam. xxi. 9*).

Another giant, Goliath the Giffite, whose spear was also "like a weaver's beam" is mentioned in *2 Sam. xxi. 19–20*. He had six fingers on each hand and six toes on each foot. "Jonathan the son of Shimei David's brother slew him" (*verse 21*).

De Goncourt of the Prix Goncourt. The name de Goncourt is famous in French literary history for the collaboration of the brothers Edmond Huot de Goncourt (1822–96) and Jules Huot de Goncourt (1830–70).

Their works, both histories and novels, were approached from an intimate angle and presented a new literary technique. They were remarkable for their detail and their sensitivity.

The will of the elder brother provided for the endowment of an academy with which many names famous in French literature were subsequently associated.

The annual award of the academy of 5,000 francs for the best imaginative work in prose is named *Prix Goncourt.*

Don Luis de Gongora y Argote of Gongorism. Gongorism is an affected type of diction or style, of which the nearest counterpart in English literature is the euphuism of Lyly.

The Spanish lyric poet, Don Luis de Gongora y Argote, was born in Cordova in 1561 of a distinguished family. He entered the priesthood in 1599 and resided in Madrid until his memory failed and he retired to Cordova.

He wrote poems in many forms, songs and several dramatic works. Not all his work reflected the strained, tortuous style which was responsible for the addition of his name to the vocabulary of literature. Although he was essentially a lyrical poet, and one of genius, he had also a satirical pen and was quick to pillory contemporary activities and personalities.

Gongora became a prebendary of Cordova (where he died in 1627) and a chaplain to Philip III.

His chief poetic works are the *Soledades* and the *Polifemo* and a play entitled *Las Firmezas de Isabel.*

None of his works, which were praised by Cervantes, was published until after the author's death.

B. J. T. Bosanquet of the Googly.

A googly, the off-break ball in cricket ‘bowled with a leg-break action, has a dubious etymology, but the introduction of the name into the English language was due to its inventor and brilliant exponent, B. J. T. Bosanquet.

Bosanquet, who played for Middlesex, introduced it with sensational effect during the 1904–5 Test tour in Australia.

When the South Africans visited England in 1907 Schwartz and A. E. Vogler revealed that they had mastered the new bowling art.

Gordius of the Gordian Knot.

A Gordian Knot is the symbol of an intricate difficulty or task. To cut it is to solve an oppressive problem by a single stroke.

Gordius, father of Midas, was a Phrygian peasant. The Phrygians had been told by an oracle that in the time of sedition their troubles would be dissolved if they made king the first man approaching the temple of Jupiter with a wagon.

On Gordius the choice fell, and he dedicated the wagon to Jupiter, but the knot of the yoke was found to be tied with such cunning that it was said the man who could untie it would gain the empire of Asia.

The conqueror, Alexander, said he would perform the task and cut the knot in twain with his sword.

> *Turn him to any cause of policy,*
> *The Gordian Knot of it he will unloose,*
> *Familiar as his garter.*
> > *Henry V, i. 1.*

Gorgon, a terribly ugly and repellent woman.

The Gorgons were three terrifying women of mythology, with staring eyes and heads bearing serpents in the place of hair. There were serpents also in their girdles.

They were thought by some to typify the terrors and dangers of the deep.

Medusa (Queen), the chief Gorgon, was a mortal. Her sisters were Sthenno (Mighty) and Euryale (wide-wanderer).

The Gorgons' heads were embodied in shields and their glance was said to turn spectators and objects into stone. They retained such powers even after the monsters' death. The figures were thus used as protective symbols.

Perseus was ordered to secure the head of Medusa, which he acquired by means of the protective mirror-like shield and the sickle of Hermes. This manœuvre prevented his being turned to stone and his helmet rendered him invisible when the other Gorgons awakened.

Medusa was loved by Poseidon (Neptune), and when she was decapitated his child, Pegasus, sprang from her trunk.

Goshen, a place of light and plenty.

The derivation is Biblical. It was the place where Jacob and his family settled — it was "the best of the land" *(Gen. xlvii. 6, 11)*. It escaped pestilences *(Exod. ix. 26)*.

The Three Graces.

The Three Graces in mythology (called Charites by the Greeks) were the daughters of Zeus. They generally appear in a subordinate position, as attendants upon the greater gods. They presided over physical exercises, dancing and festivals and were linked with the Muses through their patronage of the arts.

Their names were Euphrosyne (Mirth), Aglaia (Brilliance) and Thalia (Luxury).

They are generally depicted in art as beautiful nude maidens, holding each other by the hand.

Sir Charles Grandison of Grandisonian. Sir Charles Grandison, of Samuel Richardson's novel of that name (1754), is one of the many famous literary creations whose characteristics have made their name an adjective.

Grandison is a man of high character and splendid appearance.

It was his coach that stopped the abduction of Harriet Byron, the heroine of the novel, when the arrogant Sir Hargrave Pollexfen attempted to carry her off to the country.

Sir Charles is eventually united to Harriet and the name survives to suggest stately courtesy and high-minded magnanimity.

The Rev. James Granger of Grangerize. In 1769 James Granger, an English clergyman and print collector (1723–76), published a *Biographical History of England* "adapted to a methodical catalogue of engraved British heads." Blank leaves were left for the addition of the portraits and extra illustration of the text. The filling up of the Granger became a popular pastime and later other books were treated similarly. The term to grangerize signifies the extra illustration of any book, especially by pictures from other volumes.

Grey of Gray's Inn. The site of the Inn passed in 1294 to the Dean and Chapter of St. Paul's Cathedral, who let it to Reginald de Grey, Chief Justice of Chester and first Lord Grey of Wilton. In its mansion Grey appears to have lived with his legal officers and it remained in the possession of the family for several generations.

Law students occupied the premises in the 14th century and in 1733 the Benchers of the Inn acquired the freehold.

Shakespeare's *Comedy of Errors* was performed in the Hall of Gray's Inn in December, 1594.

Bacon, Laud and Robert Southey were students there and Tonson (see *Cat of Kit-cat*) lived there.

Catherine (Kate) Greenaway of the child fashions. Catherine Greenaway, known as Kate, was born at Hoxton, London, in 1846. She was among the most noted illustrators of children's books. She was the daughter of an engraver.

Her collection of fifty child drawings entitled *Under the Window*, which appeared in 1878, had a remarkable success, and her five little sisters,

Greenaway child fashions

with their muffs and large hats, became one of the most familiar child illustrations of the generation. Her place in the nursery was, and is, assured and her drawings had an enormous influence on the children's fashions of her time. Their characteristics still appear in fashion descriptions of to-day.

Though Ruskin claimed that she sometimes drew feet like boats and her knowledge of perspective is open to criticism, Kate Greenaway achieved fame by her sincerity and freshness. Ruskin devoted one of his Slade Lectures at Oxford entirely to her work. Though critical of details, he was among the first to praise the unaffected beauty and exquisite delicacy of her art.

There were some things she knew she could not draw and on one occasion, after fruitless attempts, a donkey had to be placed in one of her designs by another hand.

There was something of spring-time freshness in the artist and her work, and the long, high-waisted frocks of her children and their quaint bonnets were widely copied.

She trained at the Slade School.

The title, *Under the Window*, was taken from the first line of one of her verses. The book was widely translated.

She paid little attention to money and was the centre of a host of friends, which included Royalty.

She died in 1901.

St. Gregory of Gregorian.

Gregory I, the Great, was first Bishop of Rome and Pope from 590–604. He was a zealous, evangelizing Christian and a reformer, born in 544. He it was who sent St. Augustine to England. The inspiration for this journey was said to have been the famous incident that occurred after Gregory, a man of noble family and inherited wealth, had taken deacon's orders. His attention being drawn to Anglo-Saxon children on sale in the slave market, Gregory said: "Not *Angli* but *Angeli*, if they were Christians."

Gregory took an intense interest in the music of the church, established a school of music and taught in it.

The Gregorian, or plain song system, characterized by free rhythm and a limited scale, is founded on the *antiphonarium*, of which Pope Gregory I is assumed to be the compiler. The use of the system spread widely in the Western Church in his time and is to-day a dominant feature of ecclesiastical and ritual music.

Admiral Vernon of "Grog."

Grog: any spirits (but especially rum), diluted with water, took its name from Admiral Edward Vernon, 1684–1757. He sat in Parliament from 1722–34 and insistently urged war against Spain. He made a spectacular capture of Porto Bello in the West Indies with negligible losses. He attacked Carthagena without success. At the height of his fame his popularity was such that London pageants depicting his humbling of the Spaniards were presented on his birthday in 1740. His command ordering the issue of diluted rum in August, 1740, is still extant.

The name is thought to derive from the grogram cloak which he invariably wore at sea. Grogram is a coarse fabric of silk, mohair and wool, often stiffened by gum.

The Admiral eventually quarrelled with the authorities, was removed from the Navy List and sat as M.P. for Ipswich.

Jean Grolier, Vicomte D'Auigsy of the Grolier binding.

The term Grolier for a magnificent and ornate book binding arose from the library of Jean Grolier (1479–1565), a famous French bibliophile, born at Lyons.

He was prominent in court and diplomatic circles and it was his habit to acquire the best contemporary works and to have them superlatively bound. Each bore the inscription *Grolieri et Amicorum*.

His library, which was dispersed in 1675, had become world-famous and Groliers are now among the most sought collectors' items and examples of the highest manifestations of the bookbinders' art.

Jan Groot of John o' Groats.

Tradition says that Jan Groot came from Holland to Scotland in the reign of James IV of Scotland (1488–1513). Groot purchased lands on the north-east tip of Scotland and the family tree flourished, so that in time there were eight families proudly bearing the name. Once a year they all met in the house of their founder and there, on one occasion, pride prompted the question of precedence. The patriarch promised to prevent a recurrence of the problem and built an octagonal room with eight doors and placed therein an octagonal table. The site of the house was near Duncansby Head.

The expression "from Land's End to John o' Groats" grew naturally from the linking of the extremities of the Kingdom.

Burns refers to the place in the lines:

Frae Maidenkirk to Johnny Groat's . . .
A chield's amang you takin' notes.

Mrs. Grundy.

Mrs. Grundy, the personification of local opinion and respectability, was a character in *Speed the Plough*, by Thomas Morton, a five act comedy produced at Covent Garden on February 8, 1800.

Mrs. Grundy is never seen on the stage, but she is a continual criterion and is perhaps the first recognition of the Victorian respectability which quickly seized upon the character.

"Dame Grundy's butter was quite the crack of the market."

"Be quiet, woolye? Aleways ding, dinging Dame Grundy into my ears. What will Mrs. Grundy zay? What will Mrs. Grundy think?—Casn't thee be quiet, lev ur alone, and behave thyzel pratty?"

Guillotin of the Guillotine.

Joseph Ignace ɩGuillotin (1738–1814) was not the inventor of the instrument which bears his name. The basic process had been employed for execution in several eastern countries many centuries before.

He was a French physician and inventor of several surgical instruments. As a member of the Constituent Assembly he suggested the guillotine's use on humanitarian grounds. It was introduced in Paris on April 25, 1792, for the execution of a highwayman.

Dr. Guillotin died in his bed and not, as is sometimes suggested, by the instrument which bears his name.

In English Parliamentary procedure "to apply the guillotine" means to curtail a debate by fixing previously when the vote on various parts of the Bill must be taken.

Guy Fawkes of Guy.

The use of the word guy to describe an effigy and, by attenuation, any grotesque or unusual figure, comes from Guy Fawkes.

When Roman Catholics planned to destroy James the First, with the Lords and Commons in assembly, Guy Fawkes undertook to fire the gunpowder in the vaults. The date was November 5, 1605, when the King was expected to open Parliament in person. The plot, in which Robert Catesby was prominently implicated, was betrayed and Guy Fawkes was arrested before he had time to carry out his Parliamentary reform.

Since then, November the Fifth has been marked with the burning of effigies and the display of fireworks. Other personalities held in derision are similarly presented and burnt from time to time.

In U.S. slang the word "guy" is synonymous with "fellow" and implies no ridicule.

The "guy" of guy-rope is not associated, deriving from an old French word, *guis* to guide.

Thomas Guy of Guy's Hospital.

The donor of one of London's most famous hospitals was born in 1644, the son of a lighterman and coal dealer of Southwark.

For eight years he was apprenticed to a bookseller, and in 1688 he started business on his own at the corner of Cornhill and Lombard Street. He dealt largely in Bibles which, then poorly printed in England, were supplemented by better editions from Holland.

Subsequently Guy obtained the privilege of printing Bibles from Oxford University, 1679–92. He was a member of the Stationers' Company. Guy, who lived penuriously and was of shabby and melancholy mien, made a considerable fortune from sale of South Sea stock, supplemented by trading in seamen's tickets often paid in lieu of wages. These bills were redeemable at a date ahead for which the improvident could not wait and were prepared to trade at a discount.

It is possible that Guy's munificent gifts were the result of his housemaid's indiscretion. After a long period of careful service, the bookseller decided to make Sally his wife. Among the wedding preparations Guy ordered the repair of the pavement in front of his door. Sally, directing operations, ordered the workmen to repair an adjoining piece of pavement which in fact was beyond the boundary of her husband's property.

Guy, alarmed at this assumption of authority before marriage and fearful of the future, renounced the marriage and began his benefactions.

In 1707 he built three wards of St. Thomas's Hospital and made benefactions to Tamworth, his mother's native town, which he represented in Parliament from 1695–1707.

Guy laid the first stone of the hospital whose foundation he had financed, but died in 1724, a few months before its completion, leaving a fund for its endowment of over £200,000 besides bequests to many other charities. He is commemorated by a bronze statue in the quadrangle and a marble statue in the hospital's chapel.

Sir Charles Hallé of the Orchestra. The eminent pianist and conductor was born Karl Hallé at Hagen, in Westphalia, in 1819. After study at Darmstadt, he went to Paris as a young man and became the associate of Chopin, Liszt, Cherubini and literary celebrities. He started a notable series of chamber concerts, but when the revolution of 1848 drove him from Paris he settled with his family in London. His piano recitals, given at first from his own house, were a focus of London's musical life. He was mainly instrumental in introducing Beethoven's sonatas to the British public.

In 1853 Hallé was made director of the Gentlemen's Concerts in Manchester, and four years later he instituted the famous Hallé concerts. He raised the standard of orchestral playing to new levels and was an outstanding musical influence throughout the country.

In 1888 Hallé married the violinist, Madame Norman Neruda, one of the most brilliant artistes of her day, who shared with the great Joachim the leadership of the famous Popular Concerts. Queen Alexandra gave her the title of "Violinist to the Queen."

Hallé was made LL.D. of Edinburgh in 1884 and knighted in 1888. He died in Manchester in 1895, after a life devoted to the highest ideals in music. The Hallé Orchestra continues to enjoy an eminent position in music and to secure the services of the most brilliant conductors of our time, including Dr. James Richter, Sir Thomas Beecham, Sir Hamilton Harty and John Barbirolli.

Hansom of the Cab. Joseph Aloysius Hansom, inventor of the cab in which a beautiful woman looked like a jewel in a velvet-lined casket, was born in 1803, the son of a joiner. Joseph was first apprenticed to this trade but soon revealed an aptitude for invention. He became an architect, after serving as an assistant in York. He designed many buildings, including Birmingham Town Hall and a number of prominent Roman Catholic churches.

The Hansom cab

In 1834 he registered a "Patent Safety Cab" but received only £300 for the invention. The eventual hansoms differed in some details from the original design but retained the fundamental principles of a low-slung cabriolet with the driver in a high dickey at the back.

Hansom died in 1882.

Harvard and Yale. John Harvard (1607–38), of humble origin, migrated as a Puritan minister to Charlestown, Massachusetts, after taking his M.A. at Emmanuel College, Cambridge.

In 1636 the General Court of the colony voted £400 towards "a schoale or colledge" in memory of Cambridge, where some sixty or seventy of the leading men of the settlement had been educated. For similar reasons the township was to be called Cambridge.

Harvard left to this wilderness seminary half his estate, some £780, and his library of 260 books.

The college took his name; the first building was erected in 1637 and the first graduating class was established seven years later.

In England Harvard is commemorated by the Harvard Chapel at St. Saviour's, Southwark, where he was baptized.

Yale. Elihu Yale, its patron, was born in New Haven, Connecticut, in 1648, the site of the University which was eventually to bear his name. He came to England, entered the service of the East India Company, and became Governor of Fort St. George, Madras.

He sent to the college of the colony, whose charter was granted in 1701, a cargo of gifts, including books, and East India goods that were sold for several hundreds of pounds. This was in 1718, when it was finally decided to establish the college in New Haven. Yale died in 1721.

Sir Christopher Hatton of Hatton Garden. Hatton was one of the many talented and ambitious figures of the romantic Elizabethan age. He was born in 1540, son of a Northampton squire, and was admitted to the Inner Temple.

As a result of playing in a masque in which Leicester had a prominent part, Hatton was ushered into Court circles. He was part author of the tragedy, *Tancred and Gismund*, performed before Her Majesty. Hatton's graceful dancing and general courtliness attracted the Queen even more. Sheridan makes reference to it in his farce, *The Critic*. Hatton made love to his mistress, who called him by the pet name of Liddes. Hatton, however, with characteristic acumen, was careful to see that material advancement accompanied his pleasures. He entered Parliament and also became Captain of the Queen's Guard.

He held the high office of Lord Chancellor, 1587–91, but, doubtless wisely, putting more faith in his courtly accomplishments than in his legal profundity, required the aid of four Masters in Chancery when he sat in Court and two when sitting at home.

Many royal favours were bestowed upon him, including, during a vacancy in the see, Ely Place, Holborn, the province of the Bishop of that diocese. It had a magnificent garden attached, to which Shakespeare makes reference in *Richard III*, *iii. 4*, when Gloucester says to the Bishop:

My Lord of Ely, when I was last in Holborn, I saw good strawberries in your garden there; I do beseech you, send for some of them.

Gray, in *A Long Story*, writes:

His bushy beard, and shoestrings green, His high-crowned hat and satin doublet, Moved the stout heart of England's queen, Though Pope and Spaniard could not trouble it.

A later occupant of the see of Ely, Matthew Wren, uncle of Sir Christopher, made unsuccessful efforts to recover his garden from Hatton's widow.

Hatton Garden has for many years been the centre of the diamond and allied trades in London.

Uriah Heep, the abject, malignant sycophant. The allusion is to the Dickens' character in *David Copperfield* who is always wringing his hands and protesting his 'umble birth, his 'umble calling, etc.

George Heppelwhite of the furniture style. George Heppelwhite was a noted 18th-century furniture designer who had a business at St. Giles's, Cripplegate, London. In 1788 A. Heppelwhite and Company, cabinet-makers, produced *The Cabinet-Maker and Upholsterer's Guide or Repository of Designs for every article of household furniture in the plainest and most enriched styles.*

The style of Heppelwhite's furniture is essentially English and its name is particularly associated with the beautifully proportioned chairs with shield-shaped backs and finely carved wheat-ear decorations.

He received much favour from George the Fourth, when he was Prince of Wales, and this patronage is reflected in the frequent use of the Three Feathers in Heppelwhite's designs. The newly imported satin-wood from India was notably utilized by this maker.

Like Sheraton, he was alive to the personal needs of furniture users and included many adjustable stools for those suffering with the prevalent gout. He made notable and graceful use of painting and inlay work.

Hercules of Herculean. Hercules, the hero of ancient Greek mythology, is still in demand as an adjective for the handsome hero of romantic novels. The users of his name make capital of his massive strength and huge proportions, but not necessarily of his bull-neck.

The fame of Hercules (Heracles) rests upon his triumphant achievement of the tasks imposed upon him by Eurystheus. The Argive set him twelve tasks to accomplish in twelve years, thus securing immortality.

The tasks were:

1. *To slay the Nemean lion.* After driving it into a cave, Hercules strangled it.

2. *To Kill the Lernean Hydra.* After cornering the great water-serpent, Hercules seized it with his hands and struck off its heads with his sword. In place of each head, two sprang up, so he seared the throats of the serpents with fire-brands, then dipped his arrows in the gall, thus rendering wounds inflicted by them incurable.

3. *To slay the Erymanthian Boar.* Hercules caught it alive and carried it on his back.

4. *To capture the Hynd of Cerynea.* This animal, with golden horns and brazen hoofs, was the symbol of untiring fleetness. Hercules pursued it relentlessly for a year and eventually returned with it in triumph.

5. *To kill the Stymphalian Birds.* These fierce feeders upon human flesh were able to shoot out their feathers like arrows. They were not too much for Hercules.

6. *To cleanse the Augean Stables.* This was a one day task, though the stables of King Augeus contained 3,000 oxen. Hercules turned the course of two rivers through the stalls.

7. *To capture the Cretan Bull.* A restful day.

8. *To capture the Mares of Diomedes.* They fed on human flesh—but not on Hercules.

9. *To obtain the Girdle of Hippolyte,* Queen of the Amazons. There was every prospect of the girdle's being unhitched willingly, until reports were spread that Hercules intended to carry off the Queen. So he had to fight for it, but the issue was never in doubt. The Queen it was that died.

10. *To capture the Oxen of Geryones.* Hercules disposed of the herdsman and his dog, but then the three-headed winged giant owner gave battle. The hero's arrows did not fail.

11. *To secure the Golden Apples of Hesperides.* This was more difficult because, like Adam, he did not know his way about the garden. But Hercules had what Adam lacked and made light of the fierce adventures necessary to achieve his end.

12. *To bring up Cerberus from the infernal regions.* Hades consented to his taking the three-headed monster, on condition that he mastered him without the aid of weapons. He managed.

The triumphant completion of these labours released Hercules from his servitude. Later he did many other mighty deeds but the first twelve labours are sufficient to justify his appropriation of a mere adjective.

A "Hercules choice" means the choosing of the immortal spiritual reward of toil in preference to present pleasure. The "labour of Hercules" implies a prodigious task and "The Pillars of Hercules" are opposite rocks in Spain and Africa at the gateway of the Mediterranean. They were said to have been bound together until Hercules parted them on his way to Cadiz.

Hermaphroditus of Hermaphrodite.

A hermaphrodite, a human being or an animal which combines characteristics of both sexes, is named after Hermaphroditus, in Greek mythology the son of Hermes and Aphrodite.

He was beloved by a nymph, Salmacis, but the love was not returned. Salmacis, however, pursued Hermaphroditus and, embracing him, prayed to the gods that they would make the two one body. The gods granted her prayer.

Hippocrates of the Hippocratic Oath.

Hippocrates, who lived about 460–357 B.C., was the most celebrated physician of antiquity. He was born on the island of Cos, off the coast of Asia Minor, and is recognized as "The Father of Medicine." He is said to have travelled and practised widely and to have died at a very advanced age. The Hippocratic Collection, the corpus of Greek medical thought and practice, is not all attributable to Hippocrates. The *Aphorisms*, one of the sections most probably attributable to Hippocrates, contains many pithy principles that would be readily endorsed by modern medicine.

The Hippocratic Oath, still taken at some universities by graduates in medicine, reads:

I swear by Apollo physician, by Asclepius, by health, by panacea and by all the gods and goddesses, making them my witnesses, that I will carry out, according to my ability and judgment, this oath and this indenture to hold my teacher in this art equal to my own parents; to make him partner in my livelihood; when he is in need of money to share mine with him; to consider his family as my own brothers, and to teach them this art, if they want to learn it, without fee or indenture; to impart precept, oral instruction, and all other instruction to my own sons, the sons of my teacher, and to indentured pupils who have taken the physician's oath, but to nobody else. I will use treatment to help the sick according to my ability and judgment, but never with a view to injury and wrongdoing, neither will I administer a poison to anybody when asked to do so, nor will I suggest such a course. Similarly I will not give to a woman a pessary to cause abortion, but I will keep pure and holy both my life and my art. I will not use the knife, not even, verily, on sufferers from stone, but I will give place to such as are craftsmen therein. Into whatsoever houses I enter, I will enter to help the sick, and I will abstain from all intentional wrongdoing and harm, especially from abusing the bodies of man or woman, bond or free. And whatsoever I shall see or hear in the course of my profession, as well as outside my profession in my intercourse with men, if it be what should not be published abroad, I will never divulge, holding such things to be holy secrets. Now if I carry out this oath, and break it not, may I gain for ever reputation among all men for my life and for my art; but if I transgress it and forswear myself, may the opposite befall me.

Hobson of "Hobson's Choice."

Tobias Hobson, the University carrier between London and Cambridge, was the origin of the expression which, as *The Spectator* of October 14, 1712, explains, is by vulgar error taken and used "when a man is reduced to an extremity . . . The propriety of the maxim is to use it when you would say there is plenty, but you must make such a choice as not to hurt another who is to come after you."

At Cambridge, in the 17th century, Hobson erected a handsome stone conduit and left sufficient land for its maintenance for ever.

He inherited from his carrier father "the team ware, with which he now goeth." He carried letters by licence from the University, before the introduction of the post-office system, and this traffic added considerably to the returns from his carriage of passengers and luggage. He plied monthly between Cambridge and the Bull Inn in Bishopsgate Street, London.

The "very honourable man, for I shall ever call the man so who gets an estate honestly," says *The Spectator*, "was the first in this island who let out hackney-horses . . . Observing that scholars rid hard, his manner was to keep a large stable of horses, with boots, bridles, and whips, to furnish the gentlemen at once, without going from college to college to borrow, as they have done since the death of this worthy man. I say, Mr. Hobson kept a stable of forty good cattle, always ready and fit for

Hobson, the carrier

travelling; but, when a man came for a horse, he was led into the stable, where there was great choice; but he obliged him to take the horse which stood next to the stable-door; so that every customer was alike well served according to his chance, and every horse ridden with the same justice . . ."

His business flourished; he became possessed of several manors and contributed generously to the welfare of Cambridge, the University and the poor. He enjoyed a wide popularity and was respected as a shrewd and honest business man. His standing was endorsed by the publication, in 1617, of a quarto tract entitled *Hobson's Horseload of Letters, or Precedent for Epistles of Business, etc.*

He was twice married and had

eight children by his first wife. He died during the plague, 1630, when his journeys to London were suspended by the authorities. The great Milton, in one of his two punning epitaphs upon Hobson, suggests that if the courier had been allowed to continue his journeying, death might have missed him.

In the other Milton says:

Rest, that gives all men life, gave him his death,
And too much breathing put him out of breath;
Nor were it contradiction to affirm
Too long vacation hastened on his term.
Merely to drive the time away he sickened,
Fainted, and died, nor would with all be quickened.
Ease was his chief disease; and, to judge right,
He died for weariness that his cart went light:
His leisure told him that his time was come,
And lack of load made his life burdensome:.
Obedient to the Moon, he spent his date
In course reciprocal, and had his fate
Linked to the mutual flowing of the seas;
Yet, strange to think, his wain *was his* increase.
His letters are delivered all and gone,
Only remains this superscription.

Hobson was buried in the chancel of St. Benedict's, with no monument nor inscription.

William Hogarth of Hogarthian.

A Hogarthian figure is characterized by the robustness, vigour and integrity of the great artist's work.

Hogarth was born in London in 1697. He was apprenticed to a silver engraver and progressed to engraving on copper. His engravings for Butler's *Hudibras* first brought him fame, but it was the strength and vigour of his series of sketches entitled *A Harlot's Progress* that set the seal upon his reputation. He portrayed the enticement of his heroine into vice, her St. Martin's Summer as the mistress of a rich Jew, her descent to Bridewell and final disease and death. It was followed by *A Rake's Progress* and other subjects of a similar satirical character.

Hogarth then concentrated on

"history-painting," stage subjects and portraits.

In 1745 he produced *Marriage à la Mode*, which is in the National Gallery.

He was regarded as the founder of the British School of Painting. As an engraver he has few equals as a satirist, with uncanny observation and acute knowledge of character presented with remarkable strength and vigour. He was a great pictorial moralist and historian of the contemporary scene.

His humour was of a typical frank robustness.

When an ugly peer refused to accept his portrait, which he had commissioned Hogarth to paint, the artist followed several requests for settlement by the threat that if it were not collected in three days the portrait would be sent, with the addition of a tail and other appendages, to "Mr. Hare, the famous wild-beast man."

The threat succeeded, the debt was settled, but the picture was destroyed.

Thackeray pays warm tribute to Hogarth's genius in his *English Humorists*.

The artist died in 1764.

Homer of "Sometimes Homer nods." The phrase, which is common usage to excuse a mistake in the best of us, is taken from Horace, who makes the point that in a long work a drowsy interval is allowable.

Homer, the great epic poet of Greece, is credited with the authorship of the *Iliad* and the *Odyssey*. He is said to have lived about 900 B.C., and in his old age, afflicted by blindness, to have wandered from city to city reciting his verses.

His birthplace is unknown and according to tradition seven cities— Smyrna, Rhodes, Colophon, Salamis, Chios, Argos and Athens—contended for the honour.

The adjective "Homeric" is in frequent use to denote the majestic qualities associated with his work.

Milton was sometimes called "The English Homer."

Robin Hood, the spirited, chivalrous outlaw. Robin Hood, the traditional outlaw hero of many tales and ballads, is placed in several centuries and according to Stow lived in the reign of Richard I (1157–99).

He and his merry men epitomize the spirit of knightly chivalry outside the law. His exploits are particularly associated with Sherwood Forest.

Among his company the names of Little John, Friar Tuck and Maid Marian are still remembered and used as symbols of their respective types.

A Robin Hood wind is a cold-thaw wind, so named because the outlaw confessed his dislike of such conditions.

Edmond Hoyle of "According to Hoyle." The phrase "according to Hoyle" was in use for several centuries and is still heard to-day as a yard-stick against which to measure any games rule or query.

The author, Edmond or Edmund Hoyle, was born in 1672. He was the first to systematize the rules of whist and to assume an accepted jurisdiction over the game. He wrote a treatise upon it and his rules were accepted as authoritative for many generations.

Hoyle gave instruction in whist and gradually extended his authority to many other card and indoor games. Books of Hoyle's games have continued in publication to this day, and his jurisdiction became so widely accepted that "according to Hoyle" had general proverbial use as a synonym of correctness.

It is generally agreed that Hoyle was a barrister and held official legal office for a period in Ireland.

He died in Cavendish Square, London, in 1769, at the age of ninety-seven.

Samuel Butler of Hudibrastic. Hudibrastic: in the metre or manner of *Hudibras*, the mock-heroic poem of Samuel Butler (1612–80). It is in octosyllabic couplets and in three parts, each containing three cantos.

Butler was a farmer's son who, after service as page in the household of the Countess of Kent, became clerk to several Puritan justices of the peace. One of these, Sir Samuel Luke, is thought to be the original of *Hudibras*. Hudibras, or Huddibras, was taken from Spenser's *Faerie Queene*, where he appears as the lover of Elissa. Another character of the same name appears in the poem as a legendary king of Britain.

The satire, reminiscent of *Don Quixote* and of Rabelais, holds up to ridicule the hypocrisy and vain greed of the Presbyterians and Independents. It is notable for its wit and rhyme and its mastery of epigram and revealing conversation.

Hudibras was published in three parts in 1663, 1664 and 1668. It is said to have been relished by Charles II and many characters were identified with contemporary personalities. In it the pedantic Presbyterian, amply provisioned but with rusty arms, is accompanied by his squire, Ralpho, and much of the poem is occupied with their lively sectarian quarrels.

The author of *Hudibras* is not to be confused with a later Samuel Butler (1835–1902), painter and author, who is noted chiefly for *Erewhon* and *Erewhon Revisited*, two Utopian romances full of wit and irony and shrewd comment upon the modes and manners of the world.

Hygieia of Hygiene. Hygieia was the Goddess of Health in Greek mythology. She was credited with the supply of beneficial atmosphere and an ability to ward off pestilence and to promote growth and health, particularly in the young. She was the daughter of Æsculapius, the God of Medicine and Healing. The legend of his assuming the form of a serpent is still met with in symbol form in medicine, i.e. the R.A.M.C. badge.

The symbol of Hygieia was a serpent drinking from a cup in her hand, and she is generally presented as a virgin in a long robe.

Jacob of Jacob's Ladder. Jacob, the younger of the twin sons of Isaac and Rebekah, was a shepherd. His twin, Esau, was "a cunning hunter."

Jacob, fleeing from his brother's threats, went to Paddanaram, to his uncle Laban, the Syrian.

On the way, lying down to sleep, he beheld "a ladder set up on the

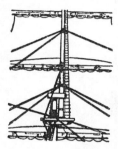

The Jacob's Ladder

earth, and the top of it reached to heaven: and behold the angels of God ascending and descending on it" (*Gen. xxviii. 12*).

The Lord stood above it and offered Jacob and his seed the land whereon he stood. Jacob made a vow, promising that if he returned in peace to his father's house "then shall the Lord be my God . . . and of all that thou shall give me I will surely give the tenth unto thee" (*xxviii. 21–22*).

James II of Jacobite. The name Jacobites was given, after the revolution of 1688, to the adherents of the exiled English King, James II, then to his descendants and later to the descendants of Charles I, of the exiled Stuart House.

They were recruited primarily among Roman Catholics and there were Jacobite Risings in 1715 and 1745.

The Jacobite tradition, which remained for centuries, particularly in the Scottish Highlands, was responsible for a curious custom. Until early in this century, finger-bowls were absent from British royal dining tables because of the former practice of secret Jacobite sympathizers of drinking to "the king over the water."

There were many Jacobite songs and ballads which have survived.

Lord Baden-Powell of Jamboree. "B.-P.," the founder of Boy Scouting, was widely said to have coined the word Jamboree, but it is, in fact, found in 19th-century U.S. literature. He was, however, certainly the first to popularize it in this country and it is immediately associated with his name. It is now widely used to describe any festive gathering, far beyond the limits of Scouting, to which activity it was first applied.

Robert S. Baden-Powell was born in London in 1857, the sixth son of an Oxford professor.

A brilliant military career culminated in his famous defence of Mafeking (1899–1900). He organized the South African Constabulary and in 1908 founded the now world-wide Scouting movement, with its ancillary Girl Guides and Brownies, Wolf Cubs and Rovers.

The international gatherings of Scouts, the first of which was announced as a Jamboree, are held periodically in different countries.

"B.-P.," when asked why he called the first conference by this name, is said to have replied, "What else could I call it?"

Baden-Powell, who was made Chief Scout of all the world and first Baron of Gilwell (the Scout Camp training centre in Essex) in 1929, was an able author, artist and sculptor. He created and inspired the greatest youth movement the world has seen. He died in 1941.

Janus of January. Janus, to whom the Romans dedicated the month, was one of their principal gods. He took precedence in prayer and the offering of sacrifice. Some accounts say that he was an immigrant from Greece. He is connected with the door (*janua*) and is often nominated as the controller of the universe and the opener and closer of all things, including the gates of heaven. January is the door of the year. According to some accounts, King Numa, who increased the year's previous ten divisions by two, decreed that the first month should be called after Janus.

The god is frequently represented as a man with two faces, one looking backward and one forward. He knew the past and foresaw the future.

The shrine of Janus had doors on its eastern and western sides. These were closed in times of peace and open during war.

February, the second of the months added by Numa, derives from *Februare*, to expiate or purify. Candlemas, the feast of Purification of the Virgin Mary, is celebrated on February 2.

De Jarnac of "Coup de Jarnac." In a duel fought in 1547 before Henri II and the French Court, Guy Chabot, Sieur de Jarnac, fought a duel with another young noble, La Châtaigneraie. De Jarnac, by an unexpected and unorthodox stroke, hamstrung his opponent and then killed him. The blow has been named after him and the expression is used as descriptive of any unforeseen and vital stroke.

Pelham Grenville Wodehouse of Jeeves. The name of Jeeves, one of the most famous characters in contemporary humorous fiction, is now accepted as a synonym for the perfect "gentleman's gentleman," shrewd, droll and undefeatable. He is the greatest of the many creations of P. G. Wodehouse, novelist and playwright (b. 1881).

The Inimitable Jeeves was published in 1924.

R. L. Stevenson of Jekyll and Hyde. The phrase Jekyll and Hyde is in universal use to describe a person in whom two personalities alternate, a schizophrenic, or even a person who leads a dual life.

The origin is in Robert Louis Stevenson's novel, *The Strange Case of Dr. Jekyll and Mr. Hyde*, published in 1886.

Dr. Jekyll, sensing the possibilities of the duality of his nature, discovers a drug that enables him to create a separate personality within himself which allows the development of all his evil instincts and desires. This, the Hyde part of him, is essentially evil and repulsive in appearance. It gradually gets the upper hand and, as Hyde, Dr. Jekyll commits a murder. The Jekyll personality is now gradually overwhelmed by the evil and the drug loses its power to restore the doctor's real character and appearance.

He anticipates approaching arrest by taking his life.

Stevenson was born in Edinburgh in 1850 and died in Samoa in 1894.

Jeremiah of the doleful prophet or jeremiad. The allusion is to the Lamentations of Jeremiah, the Hebrew prophet of the Old Testament *Lamentations*. His prophecy was one long protest against the sins and follies of his countrymen and he wailed over the ruin of his country and witnessed the captivity of its people, though he was spared its rigours by the conqueror.

"I am the man that hath seen affliction by the rod of his wrath . . . He hath caused the shafts of his quiver to enter into my reins . . . He hath also broken my teeth with gravel stones, he hath covered me with ashes" (*Lam. iii.*).

Jeremiah, who lived in the 6th

century B.C., is thought to have died in Egypt. He is credited by some authorities with the authorship of certain of the Psalms.

Jeroboam and Rehoboam of the wine measures.

The diverting names for wine bottles or flagons of a certain size derive, curiously, from Biblical personalities.

The table runs thus:

2 quarts	=	1 magnum
2 magnums	=	1 tappit hen
2 tappit hens	=	1 jeroboam
2 jeroboams	=	1 rehoboam

The capacity of the jeroboam varies in practice from 8 to 12 quarts.

Jeroboam, son of Nebat, was a "mighty man of valour" who, Solomon said, "was industrious, and he gave him charge over all the labour of the house of Joseph" (*1 Kings xi. 28*). He sinned, and caused Israel to sin (*1 Kings xiv. 16*).

Rehoboam, Solomon's successor and his only named son, if he did not inherit all his father's wisdom, certainly carried on his lustiness. Rehoboam had eighteen wives, sixty concubines and begat twenty-eight sons and sixtyd aughters (*2 Chron. xi. 21*).

A tappit hen is apparently a Scots term, also applied to a hen with a crest or hackle.

Jezebel.

A woman of flaunting spirit and loose morals, from Jezebel, daughter of Ethbaal, King of Zidon, who became wife of Ahab (*1 Kings xvi. 31*). Her wickedness brought evil upon the Kingdom of Israel and the Lord said (through Elijah), "The dogs shall eat Jezebel by the rampart of Jezreel" (*1 Kings xxi. 23*).

When Jehu entered Jezreel Jezebel "painted her eyes, and tired her head," but she was thrown from the window whence she watched and when they came to bury her they "found no more of her than the skull, and the feet and the palms of her hands" (*2 Kings ix. 30–35*).

Her wickedness is recorded in *Rev. ii. 20*.

Job of the Patience.

The patriarch who lived in the land of Uz, and whose story is presented in the Old Testament, is the personification of poverty and patience.

He enjoyed great prosperity and had a large family, but was suddenly overwhelmed by a spate of misfortunes ascribed to the direct agency of Satan (*Job i. 6–19*). Three friends came to condole with him and sat "upon the ground seven days and seven nights, and none spake a word unto him: for they saw that his grief was very great." He cursed his day and recorded that "man is born unto trouble, as the sparks fly upward" (*v. 7*).

His Book contains much magnificent poetry and many phrases that have passed into universal usage, though few rightly attribute their source: "The Lord gave, and the Lord hath taken away; blessed be the name of the Lord" (*i. 21*). "I am escaped with the skin of my teeth" (*xix. 20*), etc.

I am as poor as Job, my lord, but not so patient.

2 Henry IV, i. 2.

A "Job's comforter" is one who, while sympathizing with you in your grief, implies that it is self-induced and increases rather than diminishes your burden.

Jonah.

A jonah is a person who brings, or is sacrificed lest he bring, ill luck or disaster.

The allusion is to Jonah, the son of Amittai of Zebulun. He prophesied in the reign of Jeroboam II. He was sent to preach to the men of Nineveh, but "rose up to flee unto Tarshish from the presence of the Lord." He went to Joppa and found a boat going to Tarshish, "so he paid the fare thereof, and went down into it."

The Lord sent a mighty tempest,

so "that the ship was like to be broken." The mariners were afraid, and after calling upon their Gods, threw the cargo overboard to lighten the ship. Then they cast lots to decide who was the responsible evil influence. The lot fell on Jonah, who agreed to be cast forth to calm the sea.

Jonah was jettisoned, was swallowed by a whale, and the tempest abated. After three days and nights Jonah was "vomited out upon dry land" (*Jonah i.*).

There is a reference to Jonah's ordeal in *Matthew xii. 40*.

Paul Jones of the Dance.

John Paul Jones (1747–92) was born |in Kircudbrightshire. He made several voyages to America on a slave ship. When war broke out between England and America in 1775 Paul Jones was given a commission in the American Navy. He was, beyond dispute, one of the Service's earliest heroes and a brilliant and ruthless seaman and commander.

He met the British Captain Pearson in command of the *Seraphis* and *Scarborough* off Flamborough Head, and after a desperate, night-long battle, was asked on running close to the *Seraphis* whether he had struck his colours. Jones replied, "I have not yet begun to fight!" The *Seraphis* surrendered when sinking and Jones's ship sank next day.

He completed a distinguished naval career by acting as agent for America in Paris for the collection of prize money. He subsequently joined the Russian Navy for a short but brilliantly active and successful period.

The dance, with its frequent "plundering" of fresh partners, may have been a tribute to his nationwide popularity, to his piratical tendencies (as they were described by the opposition), or to his many real or traditional love affairs. If the latter, it seems a little arbitrary that Paul Jones's name alone should be chosen to typify a habit shared by many naval adventurers of his—and other—days.

Judas, the supreme traitor.

The name of Christ's betrayer, Judas Iscariot, has become the personal synonym for the infamous traitor. At the Passover "Satan entered into him" and he betrayed Jesus to the chief priests by a kiss. When Christ was condemned, Judas repented, cast down the thirty pieces of silver in the temple and hanged himself (*Matt. xxvii. 3–5*). The treachery of Judas had been foretold by David (*Ps. xli. 9*) and anticipated by Christ.

The term "Judas Kiss" has passed into common usage to denote the outward courtesy which cloaks deceit.

A Judas slit or hole is an aperture whereby a prison guard may observe his charge.

A Judas tree is a leguminous tree of southern Europe which flowers before the leaves appear. Tradition says that it was upon such a tree that the traitor hanged himself.

Judas hair or beard is of a red colour, said to have been a characteristic of the apostle.

Shakespeare mentions it in *As You Like It*. A similar colour is attributed by tradition to Cain.

Julius Cæsar of July.

Julius Cæsar restored July to thirty-one days. It was originally the fifth month of the year, named *Quintilis*, and having thirty-six days in the Alban calendar. Romulus reduced its length to thirty-one days and King Numa to thirty. It was the birth month of Cæsar. After his death, Mark Antony changed its name in honour of Cæsar's family name.

Cæsar, 102–44 B.C., was of patrician descent and of democratic interests. He was one of the greatest Roman soldiers and statesmen. He was a noted mathematician, orator and jurist.

Until the end of the 18th century the name of the month was accented on the first syllable, to rhyme with "newly."

Juno, the woman of stately beauty.
Juno, the Roman Goddess, wife of

Juno

Jupiter, was the queen of heaven. She was the impersonation of womanhood and the special protectress of its rights and privileges. The names

Virginalis and *Matrona* were bestowed upon her and she was patron of domestic and even civic economy.

Juno is identified with the Greek Hera and is regarded as the special guardian of the sanctity of the marriage bond. As such she bestowed protection in childbirth and watched over the children.

She is depicted in art as a woman of notable beauty and nobility. A sceptre and a diadem are often distinguishing symbols and the pomegranate appears as a symbol of love.

The peacock, seen in some representations of Juno, is dedicated to the goddess.

Legend says that Juno set Argus, of the hundred eyes, to watch Io, of whom she was jealous. Mercury, however, charmed Argus to sleep and killed him. Juno changed the delinquent into a peacock in the tail of which the characteristic "eyes" can still be seen.

Kim of Kim's game. Kim's game, used to train visual memory, is part of the Boy Scouts' official training and is widely popular as a party diversion.

It is named after Rudyard Kipling's *Kim*, published in 1901.

Kim, whose full name is Kimball O'Hara, is the orphan of a sergeant in an Irish regiment. The boy is a vagabond in Lahore but meets a Tibetan lama and accompanies him on many travels. Kim is adopted by his father's old regiment and continues to indulge his wanderlust in his holidays.

The boy reveals a remarkable observation, knowledge of people and naturecraft.

Charles I of "King Charles's Head." The phrase so frequently employed to describe a constantly intruding and totally irrelevant topic or person is taken from Dickens.

It refers to Mr. Dick, the amiable lunatic in *David Copperfield*, the author's favourite book.

The passage is in Chapter XV: "Mr. Dick and I soon became the best of friends, and very often, when his day's work was done, went out together to fly the great kite. Every day of his life he had a long sitting at the Memorial, which never made the least progress, however hard he laboured, for King Charles the First always strayed into it, sooner or later, and then it was thrown aside, and another one begun. The patience and hope with which he bore these perpetual disappointments, the mild perception he had that there was something wrong about King Charles the First, the feeble efforts he made to keep him out, and the certainty with which he came in, and tumbled the Memorial out of all shape, made a deep impression on me. What Mr. Dick supposed would come of the Memorial, if it were completed; where he thought it was to go, or 'what he thought it was to do; he knew no more than anybody else, I believe. Nor was it at all necessary that he should trouble himself with such questions, for if anything were certain under the sun, it was certain that the Memorial never would be finished."

Christopher Cat of the Kit-Cat Club. Christopher Cat (or Catling), pastry-cook of King Street, Westminster and Shire Lane, north of Temple Bar, was keeper of the 17th-century tavern where the famous Kit-Cat Club met.

Its members included the most prominent Whigs of the day. Their portraits were painted by the famous Sir Godfrey Kneller for the club's secretary, Jacob Tonson (1656(?)–1736), who was a noted publisher and intimate of Addison, Steele, Pope, Wycherley, etc.

Owing to the lowness of the club's dining-room, in which the portraits were to be hung, they had to be confined to less than half length. The term kit-cat is still used for such portraits, reduced in length but including the hands.

Cat's mutton pies were also called kit-cats and are mentioned in *The Spectator* (No. 9).

Kneller of Kneller Hall. Godfrey Kneller, born at Lubeck in 1646, first studied for the army but later became a pupil of Rembrandt. He came to London at the age of twenty-eight and quickly secured a remarkable reputation as a portrait painter. He made a fortune and lived magnificently. "I paint the living, and they make me live," he declared.

He painted portraits of ten crowned heads and most of the celebrities of his day.

King James was sitting to Kneller for a portrait for Pepys when news reached him of the arrival of William of Orange.

Kneller was knighted in 1692 and

Kneller Hall

made a baronet in 1715. Some years previously he had settled at Whitton House, near Hounslow, which is now known as Kneller Hall and is the headquarters of the Royal Military School of Music.

Several of Kneller's portraits are to be seen in the National Gallery. He died in 1723.

The artist suffered from an overweening vanity upon which his friend, Pope, frequently chided him. It was typical that Kneller left a sum of money towards the cost of his Abbey Memorial. He declined to be buried in the Abbey as "they do bury fools there," and was interred in his garden at Whitton. An entry was made in the register in the neighbouring church of Twickenham.

The Abbey monument was designed by Kneller and the bust was executed by Rysbrack.

Kreutzer of the Beethoven Sonata.

Rudolphe Kreutzer (1766–1831) was a French violinist of German extraction, born at Versailles. His father was a musician in the Royal Chapel. He studied in Vienna and was a friend of Haydn's.

Kreutzer was appointed by the Emperor director of the Conservatoire and conductor at the Imperial Theatre, Vienna. He was a prolific composer, his works including several operas. He appeared as a violinist with brilliant success in many capitals.

In 1803 Beethoven dedicated the famous sonata to him. Tolstoy wrote a novel, *The Kreutzer Sonata*, in 1890.

Adrien Lamourette of Lamourette's Kiss. Lamourette (1742–94) was Bishop of Lyons and a member of the Legislative Assembly during the French Revolution. He brought about a temporary reconciliation between the parties which was superficial and soon forgotten.

Annie Laurie of the Ballad. Annie Laurie, "whose face it was the fairest that e'er the sun shone on," was the eldest of three daughters of Sir Robert Laurie, of Maxwelton, Dumfriesshire.

She was born in 1682 and married, in 1709, Alexander Fergusson. The lovely ballad was written by her rejected suitor, William Douglas of Fingland, and published in 1824. Annie Laurie died in 1764.

The ballad, as it is now known, is the revision by Lady John Scott in 1835.

Douglas's original song had only two verses, the second of which was:

> She's backit like the peacock,
> Her breast is like the swan;
> She's jimp aroun' the middle,
> Her waist ye weel micht span—
> Her waist ye weel micht span;
> And she has a rollin' e'e.
> And for bonnie Annie Laurie
> I would lay me doon and die.

Anthony St. Leger of the St. Leger. The famous annual race for three-year-olds, run at Doncaster, was instituted by Anthony St. Leger, of Park Hill, near Doncaster, in 1776. It was not known by the name of its founder until two years afterwards.

The St. Leger was the first founded of the five Classic horse races. The others are the Derby, the Oaks and the Two Thousand and Thousand Guineas.

The Waters of Lethe. The waters of Lethe, together with such allied words as lethal and lethargy, are in frequent literary use.

In Greek mythology Lethe was one of the rivers of Hades which the souls of the dead were required to taste in order to secure oblivion and the obliteration of all recollections.

Pope, in *The Dunciad*, refers to the waters of Lethe, where old Bavius sits to dip poetic souls and blunt the sense.

Jonathan Swift of Lilliput and Lilliputian. Lilliputian, an adjective applied to any diminutive person or object, derives from Jonathan Swift's *Gulliver's Travels* (1726).

In this brilliant and fierce political and social satire, Lemuel Gulliver, "first a surgeon, and then a Captain of several ships," travels in Lilliput, the country of pigmies to whom Lemuel is a giant.

The book has added other words to the English language, notably Brobdingnag (another country of huge giants to whom Gulliver was a pigmy "not half so big as a round little worm plucked from the lazy finger of a maid"), and Houyhnhnyms, the intelligent flying horses met in the narrative.

Brobdingnagian is used as an adjective to imply colossal or gigantic and Houyhnhnyms was coined by the author from the characteristic "whinny" of a horse. It is pronounced "whinms" or "whin-hims."

Jonathan Swift (1667–1745) was born in Dublin, the posthumous son of well-connected parents. He was an unorthodox student at Trinity College, Dublin, receiving his B.A. only "by special grace."

He came to London and took a master's degree at Oxford. After a sojourn in Ireland as Canon of Kilroot, he resumed London activities and became immersed in politics and political propaganda. As a journalist he was among the greatest figures in history, the foremost political writer of his age. He ended his life, which in the closing years was marred by brain disease, as Dean of St. Patrick's Cathedral, Dublin.

Swift's *Journal* to Stella (Hester Johnson), whom he had met as a child while he was amanuensis to Sir William Temple, is one of the greatest diaries in the records of English literature. The other woman who figured largely in his life and writings was "Vanessa," Esther Vanhomrigh.

Lincoln of Lincoln's Inn. In

Edward II's reign the Earl of Lincoln brought professors to study in the buildings occupying the site. He was well versed in law. At that time one of the mansions appears to have been the town house of the Bishop of Chichester and it continued so until 1442.

There is also record of one Thomas de Lincoln, the King's Sergeant who, early in the 14th century, acquired properties on this site which, after passing through other hands, became the property of the Abbot and Convent of Malmesbury.

Edward Lloyd of Lloyd's. Lloyd's,

the Corporation of shipowners, mer-

Lloyd's to-day

chants and underwriters, is synonymous with almost all forms of in-surance, especially marine risks. It derives its name from Edward Lloyd, keeper of a City coffee house in Tower Street, and afterwards in Lombard Street, in the 17th century.

It became the recognized meeting place of business men willing to subscribe policies insuring against sea risks. At this time—the earliest records of Edward Lloyd go back to 1692—the coffee house clientèle was the only organization for placing marine insurance.

Thomas Lord of Lord's. The

Mecca of cricket lovers, which has been the headquarters of the M.C.C. (Marylebone Cricket Club) since its inception in 1787, owes its name to Thomas Lord.

This Yorkshire man, who inherited a keen cricket tradition, rented the first ground, in Dorset Square, from the Portman family, in what was then a rural area.

Threatened with an increase in rent, he moved to St. John's Wood, and four years later, when the ground was in danger from the Regent's Canal plans, he moved to the present site. That was in 1814. There he built the pavilion and tavern which are characteristics of the ground to-day.

At each move Lord took with him to the new site the famous original turf of Dorset Square.

Lothario, the gay libertine. The

term derives from the "haughty, gallant, gay Lothario," a character in *The Fair Penitent*, by Nicholas Rowe (1674–1718), which was first acted at Lincoln's Inn Fields, 1703. He boasts of his triumphs:

Oh 'twas great.
I found the Fond, Believing, Love-sick Maid,
Loose, unattir'd, warm, tender, full of
  Wishes;
Fierceness and Pride, the Guardians of her
  Honour,
Were charm'd to Rest, and Love alone was
  waking . . .
I snatch'd the glorious, golden Opportunity,
And with prevailing, youthful Ardour prest her,

'Till with short Sighs, and murmuring Reluc-
tance,
The yielding Fair one gave me perfect Happi-
ness.

On another occasion Lothario claims [that "The driving Storm of Passion will have way, and I must yield before it." Finally, wounded in the fight and near tó death, he says: "In Love I Triumph'd: Those joys are lodg'd beyond the reach of Fate . . ."

The name appears, with similar characteristics, in even earlier plays.

Lucretia, the model of female chastity. Lucretia was the Roman matron, wife of Collatinus. Her rape by Tarquinius Sextus led to the expulsion of the Tarquins from Rome and the establishment of the Roman Republic. She is referred to by Livy, and Shakespeare, in *The Rape of Lucrece*, says in the Argument of the poem that in the tent of Sextus, after supper one night, everyone commended the virtues of his own wife. Among them Collatinus extolled the incomparable chastity of Lucretia. Arriving at Rome they all sought to vindicate their beliefs, but only Collatinus found his wife occupied in sober diligence; the others were revelling. Collatinus was therefore awarded the victory and his wife the fame.

Tarquinius, inflamed by the extolling of Lucrece's virtues and beauty, treacherously steals into her chamber, ravishes her, and flees.

60

What could he see but mightily he noted?
What did he note but strongly he desired?
What he beheld, on that he firmly doted,
And in his will his wilful eye he tired.
With more than admiration he admired
Her azure veins, her alabaster skin,
Her coral lips, her snow-white dimpled chin.

99

But she hath lost a dearer thing than life,
And he hath won what he would lose again;
This forced league doth force a further strife;
This momentary joy breeds months of pain;

This hot desire converts to cold disdain:
Pure chastity is rifled of her store,
And lust, the thief, far poorer than before.

Lucullus of Lucullan. Lucius Licinius Lucullus was a Roman general, born about 110 B.C. He was later a consul. A brilliantly successful career, which included several victories over Mithridates VI of Pontus, later waned, and when Lucullus eventually returned to Rome he met some disfavour.

He acquired immense wealth and lived in splendid luxury, surrounded by artists, poets and philosophers, whose arts he patronized. He was a well-read author and entertained on such a sumptuous scale, often spending a small fortune on a single meal, that his name became the basis of the adjective to describe a banquet of unparalleled luxury and elegance.

Horace records that he had five thousand rich purple robes. His retort when asked to name the guest for a magnificent banquet led to the phrase "Lucullus will sup with Lucullus" to describe a gormand who gormandizes alone.

Ned Ludd of the Luddites. The Luddites were bands of English mechanics who destroyed machinery in the Midlands and North as a protest against the disastrous econ-omic disturbances caused by its introduction. They operated first in Nottingham about 1811.

The origin of the name is thought to have been Ned Ludd, a half-wit who, some few years previously in a fit of insanity, had wrecked the newly introduced stocking frames in his Leicestershire working place. The Luddites' leader was known as "General Ludd," which title was passed to several men.

The Luddites protested not only against the unemployment due to the introduction of machinery, but against worsening conditions of labour from competition and reduced quality in the product. They worked by night and were masked.

They won much public support and refrained from personal violence until a group of Luddites was shot down by the military at the command of a threatened employer who was subsequently murdered.

The Luddites were eventually suppressed by vigorous legislation and preventive measures and in part diminished by the gradually improving industrial conditions. There were sporadic outbreaks over an appreciable period, particularly in difficult winters.

Lord Byron spoke against the repressive legislation in the House of Lords and wrote *The Song of the Luddites*, which was published in 1830, but had been written fourteen years before. The movement is the background of Charlotte Brontë's *Shirley* (1849).

Sally Lunn of the Teacake. Accounts of the 18th-century Bath pastry-cook who gave her name to the teacake are indefinite in their details. She is said, in some accounts, to have sold her particular cake in the streets, offering them in the morning and evening from a basket covered with a white cloth.

So popular was the Sally Lunn that W. Dalmer, a respected baker and musician of Bath, bought her business and exploited the popularity of the cake. He extended its publicity by writing a song about the Sally Lunn and setting it to music. He had special barrows made to distribute the delicacy. Certainly it is featured in many of his advertisements.

In one, which appeared in the *Bath Chronicle* of December 19, 1799, he announces himself as a "Large Bread and Biscuit Baker, nearly opposite Walcot Church, Bath." Most of his cakes are offered at threepence per dozen and the "SALLY LUNNS" are "sent out warm every morning in a portable oven, constructed for the purpose, by which means the public will have them in the greatest perfection." They should, Dalmer states, "be cut with a sharp knife, and the butter either melted or cut in thin slices."

The advertisement ends with the offer of a reward of a guinea for the apprehension of a baker's boy who, on the previous night, had tried to set fire to one of the Sally Lunn barrows.

Captain Gronow, whose reminiscences were published in 1863, gives a very different setting to the pastry-cook. He claims that a French Madame de Narbonne opened a shop in Chelsea, "not far from the then fashionable balls of Ranelagh." The fame of her cakes spread through the West End and she received many orders from the houses in St. James's. Madame de Narbonne employed a Scottish maid to execute her orders. Her name was Sally Lunn, and it was swiftly associated with the particular type of teacake she delivered.

Gilbert refers to the cake in *The Sorcerer*:

> *Now for the tea of our host,*
> *Now for the rollicking bun,*
> *Now for the muffin and toast,*
> *Now for the gay Sally Lunn!*

A florid poetic recipe for the delicacy appeared in the *Bath Chronicle* in 1796. It was written by a Major Drewe, of Exeter, and its quaint instructions, in themselves a tribute to the cake's popularity, are as follows:

> *Nor more I heed the muffin's zest,*
> *The Yorkshire cake or bun,*
> *Sweet Muse of Pastry! teach me how*
> *To make a Sally Lunn.*

> *Take thou of luscious wholesome cream*
> *What the full pint contains,*
> *Warm as the native blood which flows*
> *In youthful virgins' veins.*

> *Hast thou not seen in olive rind,*
> *The wall-tree's rounded nut?*
> *Of juicy butter just its size*
> *In thy clean pastry put.*

> *Hast thou not seen the golden yolk,*
> *In crystal shrine immur'd;*
> *Whence brooded o'er by fostering wing,*
> *Forth springs the warrior bird?*

*Oh! save three birds from savage man
And combat's sanguine hour;
Crush in three yolks the seeds of life
And on the butter pour.*

*Take then a cup that holds the juice
Fam'd China's fairest pride:
Let foaming yeast its concave fill,
And froth adown its side.*

*But seek thou, first, for neatness' sake
The Naiad's crystal stream:
Swift let it round the concave play,
And o'er the surface gleam.*

*Of salt, more keen than that of Greece,
Which cooks, not poets use,
Sprinkle thou them with sparing hand,
And thro' the mass diffuse.*

*Then let it rest, disturb'd no more,
Safe in its steady seat,
Till thrice Time's warning bell hath
   struck
Nor yet the hour compleat.*

*And let Fancy revel free,
By no stern rule confin'd,
On glitt'ring tin, in varied form,
Each Sally Lunn be twin'd.*

*But heed thou well to lift thy thought
To me thy power divine;
Then to the oven's glowing mouth
The wondrous work consign.*

Martin Luther of Lutheran.

Martin Luther, the great Protestant reformer (1483–1546), was born in Prussian Saxony, in conditions of hardship.

He became a monk and was appointed preacher and professor at Wittenberg by the Elector of Saxony.

Luther quarrelled with some of the practices of Rome and eventually the Pope issued a decree condemning Luther's writings to the flames. Luther responded by the famous burning of the decree at the Elster Gate of Wittenberg and already world attention was centred upon his actions.

He was summoned to the Diet of Worms and there made his great declaration: "Here stand I; I can do no other: so help me God."

He wrote voluminously and with vast influence and Carlyle has described his spiritual and intellectual pre-eminence as "great as an Alpine mountain." He maintained the doctrines of salvation by faith alone, universal depravity, vicarious atonement and the use of the Bible as well

Martin Luther

as of the Sacraments as a means of Grace.

The acceptance of Luther's doctrines gave rise to the Lutheran branch of the Protestant church. It spread widely in Europe and Scandinavia and was one of the most potent forces in the history of religious development and practice.

Lynch of Lynching.

Lynching, or the practice of inflicting summary punishment without trial by a properly constituted court, is credited with several derivations.

The name is generally attributed to Charles Lynch, Judge of Virginia, who, in 1782, was indemnified by the act of the Virginian Assembly for hanging certain Tories illegally fined and imprisoned two years previously.

Another tradition associates the name with Lynch Creek, in North Carolina, where a form of court martial and execution was carried out on the corpse of a Tory who had already been hanged to prevent rescue.

Machiavelli of Machiavellian. Niccolo Machiavelli (1469–1530) was born in Florence of a distinguished family. He was Secretary of the Florentine Republic from 1498–1512. He achieved remarkable diplomatic and political success and was sent to many embassies. He opposed the restoration of the Medici family and on its return to power suffered imprisonment and torture. When he regained his liberty he devoted himself to literary works, the most famous or notorious of which is *Il Principe* (*The Prince*).

Its general purport is the assertion that rulers may resort to any artifice or treachery to gain their ends and to uphold their absolute power. Any dishonourable acts of rulers are fully set off by the insubordination of their subjects. Rulers are too precious an institution to be endangered by any considerations of justice and humanity.

His name gave birth to the adjective which signifies complete unscrupulousness and brilliant dissembling, particularly in affairs of state.

Charles MacIntosh of Mackintosh. Charles MacIntosh (1766–1843) was a Glasgow chemist whose research led to the production of waterproof fabrics on the principle of two or more layers of cloth cemented together with india-rubber. The process was patented in 1823, in which year the inventor was elected F.R.S.

Mæcenas, the patron of the Arts. The name for a generous patron of Letters derives from the Roman statesman of the reign of Augustus who was notable for such patronage. Mæcenas kept open house for men of letters, was the friend and adviser of Augustus Cæsar, and the patron of Virgil and Horace. The former undertook the *Georgics* at Mæcenas' request. He claimed descent from the Etruscan Kings, and left most of his property, when he died in 8 B.C., to Augustus.

The Earl of Halifax called Nicholas Rowe, dramatist and Poet Laureate, Mæcenas when he was admitted to the Order of the Garter, four years before his death in 1718.

Samuel Rogers (1763–1855), poet and banker, was called "The Last English Mæcenas."

The Magdalene. A Magdalene is a reformed prostitute. The derivation is from Mary Magdalene, or of Magdala, a town on the shore of the Sea of Galilee. She is first mentioned as having had seven devils cast out of her (*Luke viii. 2*) and as ministering to Christ of her substance. She, with other women, is said to have followed Christ, but Mary Magdalene is not specifically named again until the Crucifixion. Then she and Mary, the wife of Cleophas, watch beside the cross, attend Christ's burial and anoint the body.

They go together to the Apostles to tell them that they have found the sepulchre empty and guarded by angels.

Mary Magdalene returns and is the first to see the risen Saviour. She supposes Him to be the gardener, but He speaks to her by name (*John xx. 11–18*).

Authorities are divided on the question whether Mary Magdalene should be identified with the woman who was "a sinner" referred to in *Luke vii. 37–50*, the incident of the alabaster box of spikenard.

The word "maudlin" derives from the same source; probably in particular reference to the frequent portrayals in early art of the Magdalene as a weeping figure.

André Maginot of the Maginot Line. Though the Maginot family came from Lorraine, André was born in Paris in 1877. During the 1914–18 war, in which he served as a sergeant, Maginot determined that never again should his native fields suffer the desolation of war. He was in fact Under-Secretary for War in 1913, but at the outbreak of war he insisted on enlisting as a private, despite the protestations of his friend M. Briand. He was severely wounded in 1916 in the defence of Verdun.

Maginot left the Army with the Cross of the Legion of Honour and the Medaille Militaire. He became Minister for the Colonies in 1917 and, after the war, Minister of Pensions. He served in various ministries before going to the Ministry of War in 1929 under M. Tardieu. There, with the aid of technicians and generals, he was able to develop his Maginot Line. Its cost was immense and Maginot, dying in 1932 from typhoid contracted from eating his favourite oysters, did not live to see its completion. He was spared the agony of realizing its inability to achieve the impregnability he so passionately desired.

Maginot was a man of great height and possessed of a vigorous, colourful personality. He was a brilliant administrator who might have been expected to take a leading part in the reshaping of France.

Mrs. Malaprop of Malapropism. Malapropism: the ludicrous misuse of a word, especially in mistake for one resembling it. It was the habit of Mrs. Malaprop, a character in Sheridan's *The Rivals*, originally acted at Covent Garden Theatre, 1775. She delivers her errors with great aplomb:

Examples are:

"Don't attempt to extirpate yourself from the matter . . ."

"I would by no means wish a daughter of mine to be a progeny of learning."

"A supercilious knowledge in ac- counts . . . and something of the contagious countries . . ."

"He is the very pineapple of politeness."

"She's as headstrong as an allegory on the banks of Nile."

Mammon of Mammon. "Ye cannot serve God and Mammon" (*Matt. vi. 24*) is an expression in universal use, but few realize its derivation.

Mammon was the Syrian or Chaldean god of riches and worldly possessions, to describe which the word is now the most familiar general term.

In addition to the Biblical references (including its use to describe money in "The Mammon of unrighteousness," *Luke xvi. 9*), Spenser and Milton refer to Mammon in *The Faerie Queene* and *Paradise Lost*. The latter identifies Mammon with Vulcan, "the least erected Spirit that fell." Even in Heaven, Mammon's thoughts and looks "were always downward bent, admiring more the riches of Heaven's pavement, trodden gold, than aught divine or holy."

The accent in the use of the word is always upon inherent dangers of wealth and allied worldliness.

Ben Jonson has a character named Sir Epicure Mammon in *The Alchemist*.

Mars of March. March is named from Mars, the Roman god of war. It was originally the first month of the year. Previously Mars had been regarded as a spirit of vegetation, but it is his warlike attributes and patronage that figure chiefly in history.

The wolf, a raiding animal, was sacred to him and during the month the Salii, the priests of Mars paraded the city with the god's sacred shields. Chariot races were held in honour of Mars, and in one, held in October, the right-hand horse of the winning team was sacrificed to the god.

A temple of Mars stood on the Appian Way and later a magnificent temple of Mars Ultor (Mars th：

Avenger) was built by Augustus in fulfilment of a vow when he avenged the murder of Julius Cæsar.

The French Republicans called the month Ventôse, the windy month.

The name April is commonly supposed to have derived from the Latin, *aperio* (I open), as marking the time of the burgeoning of nature.

The origin of the name of the month of May is undefined. Some associate it with the month assigned in honour of the *Majores*, or *Maiores*, the senate in the original constitution of Rome. Other accounts link the month with Maia, the goddess of growth and increase.

June is said to be named in honour of the *Juniores*, the lesser branch of the Roman legislature. Ovid attributes the name to Juno, goddess of the moon, and guardian of the female sex. From this association probably comes the superstition that June is the luckiest month for marriages.

Giambattista Marini of Marinism.
The word Marinism, to denote a literary style of excessive affectation and elaboration, derives from the writings of the Neapolitan poet, Giambattista Marini (1569–1625).

It was full of excessive "conceits" and over-written, whimsical descriptions.

Marplot, the officious meddler.
The name is taken from a character so called in *The Busybody* (1710), a comedy by Susannah Centlivre (1667–1723). He is an inquisitive, senseless meddler.

Other writers, including Shakespeare, have used the word "mar" in its literal sense to indicate a character, i.e. Sir Oliver Martext in *As You Like It*.

Martha, the domestically pre-occupied woman. Martha was the sister of Lazarus and Mary at Bethany. When Lazarus died and Christ was sent for, Martha revealed strong faith in His power to help.

The association of Martha with domestic preoccupation is drawn from the passage in *Luke x. 39–42.* Mary sat at Christ's feet and heard His word. But Martha was cumbered about much serving and protested to Christ, saying, "Lord, dost thou not care that my sister did leave me to serve alone? bid her therefore that she help me."

Christ replied: "Martha, Martha, thou art anxious and troubled about many things: but one thing is needful: for Mary hath chosen the good part, which shall not be taken away from her."

Colonel Martinet of Martinet.
The term martinet, for a punctilious disciplinarian, derives from Jean Martinet, who was a lieutenant-colonel of the King's regiment of foot and Inspector General of Infantry in the reign of Louis XIV.

He was an autocratic disciplinarian whose name became synonymous with sharp, military efficiency. He was also responsible for certain drill systems that bore his name, and for several inventions in military engineering.

Martinet was killed at the siege of Duisberg in 1672, accidentally shot by his own artillery while leading the infantry assault.

The term martinet became common usage throughout military circles and Wycherley, in *The Plain Dealer*, has a line: "What, d'ye find fault with Martinet? . . . 'tis the best exercise in the World."

St. Martin of St. Martin's Summer.
St. Martin, Bishop of Tours in the 4th century, was previously an unwilling soldier.

The most familiar story associated with his name is the incident of his dividing his cloak, during his military days, with a naked beggar found dying from cold at the gate of Amiens. The cloak was miraculously preserved and became a venerated relic over which many legal disputes were raised.

He is the patron of tavern keepers, which association finds confirmation in the records and representations of the Vintners' Company.

The saint's day is November 11 and as a result his name has been given to the welcome short period of mild genial weather which is not infrequently enjoyed at that time. Shakespeare refers to its "halcyon days" in *1 Henry VI, i. 2.*

L. von Sacher-Masoch of Masochism. Masochism, a form of sexual perversion in which the sufferer derives pleasure from his or her own pain or humiliation; the opposite of sadism.

The word derives from the Austrian novelist, Leopold von Sacher-Masoch (1835–95), who made a sufferer from this perversion the central character of one of his novels in 1893.

Mausolus of Mausoleum. The name for a sepulchral monument, generally of considerable dimensions, is derived from Mausolus, King of Caria. His tomb, erected at Halicarnassus by his widow, Artemisia, in

The Tomb of Mausolus

353 B.C., was accounted one of the Seven Wonders of the World. The tomb, which was over 100 feet high, was surmounted by a group of statuary which included Mausolus and his wife.

The Mausoleum survived in good condition until the 12th century. Remains of the monument were brought to England in 1859 by Sir Charles Newton and placed in the British Museum.

Dame Nellie Melba of Peach Melba. The famous British soprano was born Nellie Porter Mitchell at Burnley, Australia, in 1861.

She took her professional name from her association with Melbourne, Australia.

She studied in Paris, making her operatic début at Brussels in 1887. She was hailed in many countries as the successor of Patti.

Melba was created Dame of the British Empire in 1918 and died in 1931.

Mephistopheles, a fiend, the incarnation of evil. The devil, so named, first appeared in the late mediæval Faust legend and as such appears in Goethe's *Faust.*

Mephistopheles epitomized universal scoffing and scepticism. He is incapable of seeing good in anything and no evil in sin and ugliness. He is a sneering, malicious tempter.

The character appears frequently in literature, notably in Marlow's *Faustus,* and is mentioned by Fletcher and Shakespeare.

The origin of the Faust legend is said to have been a Dr. Johann Faust, or Faustus, a vicious magician and astrologer who flourished with devilish results in Germany in the 15th/16th centuries. He became the magnet of many legends associated with contemporary astrologers and necromancers, and figured in books of the time.

Gerardus Mercator of the Projection. The name Mercator is a latinized form of Gerhard Kremer, a Flemish mathematician and geographer of German extraction who was born in 1512.

In early projections the conical principal was employed, but Mercator's chart, a cylindrical projection, gave all the meridians as straight lines perpendicular to the equator and all the parallels of latitude as straight lines parallel to the equator. It presents an unnatural view of the earth, with some distortion, but it offers an unbroken view of the earth's surface. It was and is of great value in the study of maps and in navigation because it represents any compass course or bearing as a straight line. It was the basis of maps as they are known to-day.

Mercator founded a Geographical establishment at Louvain and was soon in the employment of Charles V. He built several historical globes.

In 1534 he published his great map of Europe, which revealed his departure from the then reigning principles or "tyranny" of Ptolemy. He is one of the greatest figures in the history of cartography.

Mercator died in 1594 in Duisburg, where he had accepted the Chair of Cosmography many years previously.

Mercury of Mercurial. Mercury, the Roman counterpart of the Greek Hermes, was the son of Maia and Jupiter, to whom he acted as messenger. He was regarded also as the deity presiding over commerce. The two associations are doubtless the reason why the name Mercury is incorporated in many newspaper titles, not the fact that Mercury was the patron of rogues and vagabonds.

Mercury was generally presented as a young man with wings upon his helmet and upon his heels. Some statues include a herald's staff or caduceus, a white wand carried when they sued for peace. Others show Mercury holding a well-filled purse, a reference to his patronage of commerce.

Mesmer of Mesmerism. Dr. Franz Mesmer, who was born in 1733, graduated M.D. at Vienna at the age of thirty-three. Six years later he began research upon the curative properties of the magnet and developed the theory that a power similar to magnetism could exercise a profound influence upon the human body.

Animal magnetism, or mesmerism, is another facet of hypnotism which has had many names and varying manifestations through the centuries.

Dr. Mesmer's methods achieved outstanding success, the details of which he published. He first used magnets in his cures, but later confined himself to the use of his hands to convey the animal magnetism.

He secured much support from the medical profession in Paris, but refused munificent offers to reveal his secrets. He visited London with somewhat spectacular results.

A French government commission reported unfavourably on Mesmer's activities, though admitting surprising results, and the doctor's prominence declined into obscurity. He died in 1815.

Methuselah, the yardstick of old age. "As old as Methuselah" refers to the Biblical patriarch, son of Enoch and father of Lamech. Methuselah inherited his longevity and virility from his father who, after Methuselah's birth, "walked with God ... three hundred years, and begat sons and daughters" (*Gen. v. 22*). But Enoch's three hundred and sixty-five years before "he was not," are eclipsed by his son, whose days "were nine hundred sixty and nine years" (*v. 27*). He is the oldest man mentioned in the Bible and he died in the year of the Deluge.

Wilkins Micawber, the hopeful idler who hopes something will turn up. Micawber is a character in Dickens' *David Copperfield* (1849–50), a novel that has added several names to our language.

Copperfield meets Micawber in London and is enlivened by the poor but mercurial idler who is always trusting that something good will turn up.

Eventually, relieved of his debts,

he appears as a respected magistrate in Australia.

Midas of "the Midas touch."

Midas, the mythical founder and king of Phrygia, developed an increasing appetite for gold as he grew richer.

After entertaining the drunken Silenus, the god rewarded his host by promising the fulfilment of any wish he might make. Midas wished that everything he touched might be turned to gold. The wish was granted, but eating, among other things, became a problem and Midas was only saved from disaster by washing, at the god's command, in the river Pactolus, which has ever since brought gold down in its sands.

A later legend makes Midas judge in a musical contest between Apollo and Pan. He decided in favour of Pan and the god, in contempt, gave Midas the ears of an ass. Though the gold-digger hid the blemish under his Phrygian cap, his barber discovered it. The man was afraid to reveal his knowledge but anxious to relieve his mind, so he dug a hole in the ground, whispered his secret in it, and then filled in the hole.

The action would appear to have much to commend it.

Joe Miller of the Stale Jest.

A "Joe Miller" is used in the profession to designate a "chestnut" by many who do not know its derivation.

Joe Miller, born in 1684, was a comic actor of excellence. He was a permanent star at Drury Lane. When the Theatre Royal was closed he established himself as a popular booth-theatre manager. At his benefit at the Lane in 1717 the tickets were designed by Hogarth.

Miller was a prime favourite in the profession, but despite his eminence as a comic actor he was said to be so grave in his demeanour off the stage that he never uttered a joke. Even so the wits gathered round him and it was the custom to ascribe every new joke to Joe Miller. In consequence, soon after his death, his name was seized upon as the title for a joke book which achieved immense popularity. So great, in fact, was its success that *Joe Miller's Jests: or, the Wit's Vade Mecum* was swiftly followed by fraudulent imitations, all of which included the comedian's name in the title.

Joe Miller

It was a contemporary custom for party guests to memorize a selection of jokes and to repeat them. As the *Joe Miller* joke book was the most obvious source, its jokes were constantly repeated—hence the association with the "chestnut," or stale joke.

Miller died in 1738 at the age of fifty-four. His tombstone in the burial ground of St. Clement Danes, Strand, bore testimony to a tender husband, a facetious companion and an excellent comedian.

Mithridates VI of Mithridatize.

To mithridatize is to render proof against poison by gradually increasing the doses thereof.

In old pharmacy a mithridate was a universal antidote to or preservative against poison.

There were many Kings of Pontus, a district in Asia Minor bordering on the Black Sea, whose names were Mithridates. The name is also spelt Mithradates.

Mithridates VI, called The Great, lived in the first century B.C. and was only a boy when he succeeded his father. He was credited with great physical powers and courage, a remarkable intellect and the mastery of more than twenty languages. He is said to have been the centre of cultural life and to have had a weakness for good trenchermen, whom he lavishly rewarded. He spent much time in the practice of magic.

He trusted no one and is reputed to have so steeped his system in poison that none had deleterious effects—hence the word that has survived him through two thousand years.

Mithridates was a fierce and persistent enemy of Rome and when, on the revolt of his troops, poison failed, he ordered a hired soldier to kill him.

The king was a wholesale murderer disposing by poison of his mother, sons and his wife, who was his sister. When the enemy threatened his harem he liquidated them also.

Mnemosyne of Mnemonics. Mnemonics, the art of memory aid, generally by design or pattern, is associated with Mnemosyne, Greek goddess of memory. An instance of a mnemonic aid is the memorizing of the word "Clip" to recall the types of wounds—Contused, Lacerated, Incised and Punctured.

Mnemosyne was one of the six female Titans. By her Zeus became father of the Muses.

Mohammed of Mohammedanism. Mohammed (or Mahomet) was the great prophet of the Arabs and founder of Islamism, or Mohammedanism. He was born about 570 in Mecca and died in Medina in 631. He was given to meditation and claimed to have received divine revelations. For many years his converts were few. Mecca is the place of holy pilgrimage to millions of Mohammedans and their "Bible" is the Koran. It is said to have been communicated to Mohammed by the angel Gabriel. The Mohammedan religion has much similarity with the Jewish faith, with some Christian elements.

The familiar phrase, "If the mountain will not come to Mohammed, Mohammed must go to the moun-

tain," is said to derive from the early demands of the Arabs for miraculous proof of the prophet's claims.

When he ordered a mountain to move and it did not, he pointed out to the unbelievers that God was merciful as a literal answer to his command would have involved the destruction of them all. He therefore went to the mountain to give thanks for God's mercy upon the doubters.

From the towers of the mosques the muezzins chant five times a day the call to prayer, "There is no God but Allah and Mohammed is His prophet. Come to prayer. Come to salvation."

Moloch, the inexorable, all demanding God. Moloch, or Molech, was the god of the Ammonites, who burnt their children in his honour (*Lev. xviii. 21* and *2 Kings xiii. 10*).

Milton, in *Paradise Lost*, says that Moloch was worshipped in Rabba, Argob and Basan.

David took the crown from the head of the idol (*2 Sam. xii. 30*) and Solomon built a high place for him (*1 Kings xi. 7*).

The name is continually applied to any fiercely destructive person or state, such as personal tyrants, war, mob rule, the guillotine, etc.

The Mona Lisa. The immortal Mona Lisa, the "smiling woman," was painted by Leonardo da Vinci (1452–1519). In France it is known also as "La Joconde" and in Italy as "La Giocondo."

Leonardo's father was an obscure Florentine lawyer; his mother of humble birth and unmarried. His model for the great portrait, which was finished in 1504, was the wife of Giocondo. Francis I bought the Mona Lisa for 4,000 golden florins and it was placed in the Louvre. It was mysteriously stolen in 1912 but was later recovered and restored.

Dr. Maria Montessori of the Montessori System. The distinguished Italian educationalist was born in 1869 and was the first woman in Italy to graduate in medicine. That was at Rome in 1894.

She investigated the educational problems of the defective child and from her experience evolved methods which she considered could be equally fruitful when applied to normal children.

Dr. Montessori met some opposition from orthodox educationalists to her imaginative methods, but they succeeded and were embodied in the creator's book, *The Montessori System* (1912). This was translated into many languages. The author received state recognition in Italy and became Government Inspector of Schools.

Montessori schools became famous in many countries and her principle of freedom of movement among the children and the encouragement of individuality and imagination was adopted by many other authorities.

Dr. Montessori spent much time in London, where she held Training Courses, and visited many other countries. Durham University conferred an Hon. D.Litt. upon her in 1923. As a Roman Catholic she applied her principles to the production of a number of religious instructional books.

Francis Moore of "Old Moore."

At one time there was a doubt whether Francis Moore of the *Almanac* was a real person or a pseudonym. *Notes and Queries, vol. III, page 466,* however, states categorically that he was a physician and one of the many quack doctors who duped the credulous in the latter part of the 17th century. It claims that he practised in Westminster.

His *Almanac* for 1711, however, is issued from the Sign of the Old Lilly, near the Old Barge House, in Christ Church Parish, Southwark, July 19, 1710. There follows an advertisement in which he undertakes to cure diseases.

Moore's *Almanac* follows closely on the lines of Tanner's, which appeared in 1656, forty-two years before the publication of the first "Old Moore." He is described under a contemporary portrait accepted as genuine as having been born in Bridgenorth, Salop, in January, 1656. Moore's *Vox Stellarum* was the most successful of the predicting almanacs and its author apparently practised, with considerable success, as astrologer, physician and schoolmaster.

The family grave at Bexley, Kent, which covers the father of Francis, records "Old Moore" as dying on February 5, 1714, at the age of seventy-nine.

Morpheus of Morphia. Morpheus
was the Greek god of dreams and sleep, hence the expression "in the arms of Morpheus," and such derivative words as morphia, which is an alkaloid narcotic principle of opium, used to deaden pain. In many accounts Sleep and Death were presented as twin brothers, the children of Night.

Homer describes two Gates in the House of Dreams, one of ivory, through which false, flattering dreams issued and one of horn through which good dreams proceeded.

Samuel Finley Breese Morse of
the Morse Code. The American inventor of the telegraphic code which is in universal usage under his name was born at Charlestown, Mass., in 1791.

His first leanings were towards art, during the study of which he visited England.

At the age of thirty-four he was one of the founders of the U.S. National Academy of Design and became its first president in 1826.

Shortly afterwards he renewed his early student interest in electricity, although he continued his study of the Old Masters in Europe. On his return he devoted himself to designing and executing models of the telegraph. He met with delay of recognition in his own country and opposition elsewhere, but in 1843 a telegraph between Baltimore and Washington was used for the first time, financed by Congress.

Morse patented other inventions, including a marble cutting machine (he gained some distinction as a sculptor), and explored the possibilities of marine telegraphy.

He lived to see his system adopted in many countries, some of which eventually recognized its inventor, financially and with honours. A substantial international present was given to him at the instance of Napoleon III.

Morse died in New York in 1872, where there is a bronze statue to his memory.

Moses of the Moses' cradle. The term "Moses' cradle" applied to a shallow cradle (as distinct from the wooden cradle on rockers), generally made of wicker, derives from the finding of the great law-giver as a child. The Biblical reference is *Exod. ii.*

When the Israelites were oppressed by the Egyptians, they were ordered to drown all their male children. Therefore Moses was hidden by his mother for three months "and when she could no longer hide him, she took for him an ark of bulrushes, and daubed it with slime and with pitch; and she put the child therein, and laid it in the flags by the river's brink."

Pharaoh's daughter found the baby. She said: "This is one of the Hebrews' children," took compassion on it and arranged for the child's mother to nurse it.

Pharaoh's daughter called the child Moses, "because I drew him out of the water."

Baron Karl von Munchausen, the prodigious, mendacious story-teller. The use of the word Munchausen to denote a story-teller of fantastic exaggeration derives from Baron von Munchausen (1720–97), who is said to have served in the Russian cavalry against the Turks. His capacity for incredible story-telling became notorious.

The collection of his fantastic yarns, in which the Baron was the heroic traveller, was published in English in 1785 at the instance of Erich Raspe, an expatriated countryman of the Baron's. Raspe, who was escaping the consequences of a theft, sought to implement his finances by the publication of the book which, in fact, was a swift success. The title was, *Baron Munchausen's Narrative of his Marvellous Travels and Campaigns in Russia.* A German edition appeared several years later.

Many of the stories were derivative but the collection achieved a new level of preposterousness and became a criterion of fantastic, mendacious story-telling.

The Muses. The Nine Muses are frequently alluded to and several adjectives derive from individual names. They can conveniently be referred to together.

They were the children of Zeus and Mnemosyne (Memory) and were originally goddesses of memory, later to be identified with particular sciences and arts.

According to Pindar, the celestials prayed to Zeus to create beings who would perpetuate in song the valorous deeds of the gods. They appear originally to have been fountain nymphs and the music of the streams led to a belief in their existence. They were originally venerated on Mount Olympus, but later their activities centred upon Mount Helicon where the Castalian fountain sacred to them had its source. At first they were regarded as a company or chorus but gradually specific functions and patronage were ascribed to each. The paintings of Herculaneum depicted the Muses with their particular attributes.

Calliope was the chief of the Muses

and was associated with epic poetry and science generally. A pen and a scroll of parchment were often used in representations of her.

Clio, often similarly depicted, was the Muse of history and heroic exploits.

Euterpe was the patron of lyric poetry and is distinguished by her double flute.

Thalia, associated with gaiety, comedy and pastoral life, was marked by a comic mask, a garland of ivy, a crook and a tambourine.

Melpemone, the Muse of tragedy, song and harmony, was differentiated by a tragic mask, a sword and a garland of vine leaves.

Terpsichore, the Muse of dancing, was depicted with a lyre.

Erato, associated with erotic poetry, miming and geometry, carries a large stringed instrument.

Polyhymnia, the goddess of the chant and the inspired hymn, is depicted as grave in mien and countenance and closely wrapped in her long, flowing garments. She has no symbol.

Urania, the Muse of astronomy and celestial phenomena, holds a globe in one hand and a small wand in the other.

The word museum is literally the home or seat of the Muses. The first building so named was erected by Ptolemy at Alexandria about 300 B.C.

Alexandre Dumas of the Three Musketeers. Athos, Porthos and Aramis, the immortal trio of Alexandre Dumas' *The Three Musketeers*, have given their names to any three inseparable adventurers.

The story, with its sequels, *Twenty Years After* and *The Vicomte de Bragelonne*, is concerned with the impoverished Gascon gentleman, d'Artagnan, who, joining the King's musketeers in the reign of Louis XIII, links up with the famed trio and shares their heroic adventures.

Alexandre Dumas (1803–70) was a clerk in the service of the Duc d'Orleans. He wrote plays and first achieved varied success in that field. He was a man of prodigiously fertile imagination and remarkable industry. He wrote on the grand scale and received high praise from most of his literary contemporaries. Thackeray was one of his greatest admirers.

Dumas employed a number of collaborators and research workers, but the unique creative talent and the ability to vitalize everything he wrote were gifts entirely Dumas' own.

His natural son, Alexandre Dumas (1824–95), was one of the most distinguished French dramatists of his age. He is best known in this country for the famous *La Dame aux Camélias*.

Many of the romances of Dumas, *père*, were derivative and the sources of *The Three Musketeers* (8 vols., 1844) are known. The two above-named sequels, published in 1845 and 1848–50 respectively, occupied 10 and 26 volumes—striking evidence of the author's brilliant fecundity.

The chief source of *The Three Musketeers* was a book published at The Hague in 1700. It was *Mémoires de Monsieur d'Artagnan*, by Courtilz de Sandraz. In it appeared Athos, Porthos and Aramis and several subsidiary characters represented by Dumas, but not before they had been invested with his incomparable vitality and personality.

They had, in fact, an even earlier origin, for Sandraz drew his characters from real people in French life. d'Artagnan was Charles de Batz-Castelmore, fifth son of Bertrand de Batz, seigneur de Castelmore. Athos was a Béarnese, named Armand de Sillègue d'Athos. Porthos was drawn from Isaac de Portau, from Pau in Switzerland, and Aramis had his original in Henri d'Aramitz, a squire and lay abbot of Béarn.

Dumas was writing six books simultaneously with the creation of *The Three Musketeers*.

Naboth of "Naboth's vineyard," a possession to be secured at any cost. The reference is taken from *1 Kings xxi*.

Naboth, the Jezreelite, had a vineyard in Jezreel, hard by the palace of Ahab, King of Samaria.

Ahab coveted the vineyard owing to its contiguity and offered Naboth a better vineyard in exchange for his ground, which Ahab intended to make into a garden of herbs. Alternatively, he offered its value in money.

Naboth replied: "The Lord forbid it me, that I should give the inheritance of my fathers unto thee" (*verse 3*).

And Ahab was displeased and fasted until Jezebel, his wife, taunted him for accepting refusal, and promised to give him the vineyard.

So she wrote letters in Ahab's name, sealed them with his seal, and sent them to the elders and nobles that dwelt with Naboth in the city. The letters instructed them to set Naboth on high among the people when two sons of Belial were to bear witness against Naboth, saying that he did curse God and the King. They were then to stone him to death. This was done and Jezebel was informed of Naboth's death.

She told her husband and at her instruction arose and took possession of the coveted vineyard (*verses 8-16*).

Elijah heard of the crime and denounced Ahab, and said: "Behold, I will bring evil upon thee, and will utterly sweep thee away, and will cut off from Ahab every man child . . ." He also said of Ahab's wife, "The dogs shall eat Jezebel by the rampart of Jezreel" (*verses 17-23*).

Ahab humbled himself and the punishment was deferred until his son's days.

When Jehu slew Joram he cast his body in Naboth's vineyard (*1 Kings xxi. and 2 Kings ix. 21-6*).

Jezebel was later devoured by dogs (*2 Kings ix. 30-7*).

Ambrose Philips of **Namby-Pamby.** This synonym of wishy-washy, insipid and offensively sentimental has, alas, been particularly associated with authors. It was originally bestowed on Ambrose Philips (1678-1749), a minor poet, pastoral writer and friend of Addison and Steele.

When he wrote some insipidly pretty verses for the children of Lord Cartaret, Henry Carey (the dramatist and ballad writer who wrote "Sally in our Alley") dubbed Philips "namby-pamby." The term was eagerly utilized by Alexander Pope, which was not surprising as Johnson describes the quarrel between Pope and Philips as a "perpetual reciprocation of malevolence."

Anne Oldfield of "Miss Nancy." The term "nancy," as applied to an effeminate, foppish youth, derives from the nickname of Anne Oldfield.

Born in London in 1683, the daughter of a soldier, she worked as a sempstress, but attracted the notice of George Farquhar by reciting lines from one of his plays. She was mistress of both comedy and tragedy. She appeared at Drury Lane in 1692 and was soon generally acknowledged to be the leading actress of her time. Anne Oldfield was a woman of beauty and conspicuous generosity, which did not fail to find its detractors. She appeared in plays by the leading contemporary dramatists, including Cibber and Rowe. She is said to have befriended the wayward poet, Savage.

Pope wrote of Anne in *Sober Advice from Horace*:

Engaging Oldfield, who, with grace and ease,
Could join the arts to ruin and to please.

She was the Narcissa of his *Moral Essays.*

The actress died in 1730 and was buried with pomp in Westminster Abbey.

Narcissus was a beautiful youth in Greek mythology who saw his reflection in a spring. This son of the river-god, Cephisus, wooed by Echo, fell in love with his own image, but finding it unattainable, pined away. Other accounts say that he died in trying to reach his reflection. When the nymphs came to take away the body they found only a flower.

Colonel Francis Negus of Negus, the hot, sweetened wine. The name derives from the inventor of the drink, Colonel Francis Negus, who died in 1732.

Negus is hot, sweetened wine and water. Port or sherry were the ingredients most favoured.

Walpole, Peacock and other literary men make reference to it.

Nemesis, the overtaker. Nemesis: retribution or retributive justice.

The Greek Goddess, Nemesis, was the personification of divine retribution. She watched over the equilibrium of the universe. As is human, her name was more particularly associated with adverse judgments and punishments which, however well deserved, were not well received.

In art, Nemesis is reflected in both aspects. Sometimes she is a kindly, gentle goddess, contemplating her instruments of assessment and control (cubit, bridle and rudder). At others she is the unrelenting avenger of human faults, descending upon mankind in a fearsome chariot and fully armed to flay the offenders.

Neptune of the deep. Neptune was the Roman god of the sea, the counterpart of the Greek Poseidon.

He is represented in art as a man of fine stature, like his brother, Zeus, with dark waving hair, a beard and a grave, dominating expression. He is distinguished by a trident, though

Neptune

in some cases this is displaced by a tiller.

Shakespeare, in *Macbeth,* says:

Will all great Neptune's ocean wash this blood
Clean from my hand?

Nereids, the sea nymphs. The original sea nymphs were the many daughters of Nereus, the kindly spirit of the sea and particular spirit of the Aegean Sea.

The Nereids were gay, benevolent creatures, to be relied upon in danger and ever ready to charm the sailors. The best known were Amphitrite, Galatea and Thetis.

Nero, the bloody-minded tyrant. Nero, the ferocious tyrant and Roman emperor A.D. 54–68, was born in Antium. He seized the throne to the exclusion of the rightful heir, Britannicus.

The first years of his reign revealed a sage administration, but thereafter his inordinate lust for power and his inherent vice led to many murders and the massacre of Christians after torture and on false charges of which Nero himself was suspected.

Many suffered death for alleged responsibility in the burning of Rome, which conflagration the Emperor is said to have started for the fiendish pleasure of seeing what Troy would have looked like when it was burning.

He regarded the spectacle with cynical detachment and amusement, hence the phrase, "Nero fiddled while Rome burned."

Nero kicked his pregnant wife, Poppæa, to death and sought the hand of Octavia. Her refusal brought death and many subsequent infamous crimes resulted in rebellion. Nero fled from Rome and committed suicide.

Christian II of Denmark was called "The Nero of the North" owing to his massacre of Swedish nobility at Stockholm in 1520.

Nessus of the Shirt of Nessus. The phrase "a shirt of Nessus" describes the source of an inescapable misfortune or a fatal gift.

The mythological story is that Hercules ordered Nessus the Centaur (half human, half horse) to carry his wife Deianira across a swollen stream while Hercules waded through.

Nessus, succumbing to the charms of the lady, attempted to make off with his fair burden, only to be shot by Hercules with a poisoned arrow.

Nessus, in revenge, gave Deianira his shirt, falsely telling her that it would preserve her husband's love.

Later, Deianira, suspicious of Hercules' attentions to Iole, thought it was high time to utilize the magic shirt. Hercules donned it dutifully and at once the flames of the altar drew forth the poison contained therein. Some accounts imply that it was the poison remaining from Hercules' own arrow, others that Deianira had anointed the shirt with an ointment prepared from the blood of the Centaur who died for his sin.

The effect was fatal, for Hercules strove vainly to tear the shirt from his flesh. It tore pieces from his body and in agony he was brought to Trachis, where he found his wife had taken her life in remorse at her action.

He threw himself upon a funeral pyre and amid thunderous manifestations from the heavens, the hero was borne aloft to Olympus, where he became reconciled to Hera and found solace in the beauty of her daughter Hebe.

Sir Roger Newdigate of the Newdigate Prize. The founder of the famous Newdigate Prize at Oxford for English Verse, which has had so many distinguished winners, was Sir Roger Newdigate, born 1719 and educated at Westminster and University College, Oxford.

He was the fifth baronet of Harefield in Middlesex and Arbury in Warwickshire. He had an active political career, sitting as member for Middlesex and his University. As a collector of antiquities he made many gifts to Oxford. The prize, which is open to undergraduates, was first awarded in the year of his death, 1806.

He was the author of a treatise on the harmony of the four gospels.

Friedrich Wilhelm Nietzsche of Nietzschean. Friedrich Nietzsche (1844–1900), the brilliant German philosopher and ethical writer, was born in Saxony, the son of a Protestant pastor. He was profoundly influenced by Schopenhauer and Wagner and was a considerable musician.

Nietzsche fought against romanticism, revealed art and religion. He denied the ruling values of beauty, truth and goodness and would supersede them by the will to power and a higher existence, producing a superman of ruthless domination.

Nietzsche was antagonistic to Christianity, with its accent on compassion and humility. Christ he regarded as the most telling temptation to diversion from his own ruthless moral and ethical conception.

His best known work translated into English is *Thus Spake Zarathustra* (1883–91).

His doctrines met with profound opposition and he became a solitary figure whose later years were afflicted by madness. Afterwards the more creative aspects of his ethics were appreciated and his place as a brilliant, if mainly destructive, philosopher is assured.

Nimrod, the great hunter or sportsman. The source of the expression is Nimrod, the Biblical character, son of Cush and founder of Babel. "He began to be a mighty one in the earth. He was a mighty hunter before the Lord" (*Gen. x. 8–9*).

The "land of Nimrod" (*Mic. v. 6*) is Babylonia or Shinar.

Niobe of Niobean. Niobe: an inconsolable bereaved woman; the personification of maternal sorrow.

All seemed set fair for Niobe, daughter of the Phrygian King, Tantalus (*q.v.*). Her marriage with Amphion was auspicious. The gods showered blessings and soon Niobe's quiver was full of lovely children. In her ecstasy she committed her father's sin and went too far with the gods. In Niobe's case she boasted of her glorious children, even preferring them to Latona's family, which was only two. She claimed the honour of sacrifices, which were Latona's right for herself.

In one day, all Niobe's children were slain by the arrows of Apollo and his sister, Diana, children of Latona.

Amphion slew himself, and Niobe, stricken with grief, was turned into stone through the clemency of the gods, and for ever the stone wept.

Shakespeare refers to the allusion in *Hamlet, i. 2.*

The legend has been attributed by some to the process of the melting snows before the encroaching sun.

Alfred Nobel of the Nobel Prizes. Alfred Nobel, whose family took the name Nobelius in the 17th century from the town Nöbbelöf, came originally of Swedish peasant stock, but his ancestors had included a barber-surgeon and a "drawing master." Later generations were concerned

with the construction of mines for defensive purposes at sea and on land, and general military engineering.

Alfred was born in 1833 and devoted himself to chemical research. His first great invention was a compound of powder and nitro-glycerine, which notably increased the blasting capacity of gunpowder. He succeeded in causing nitro-glycerine to explode under water. Nobel established factories in several countries, including Britain, and for many years his work and discoveries were revolutionary.

He possessed a brilliant imagination and was, according to his confession, at heart a poet, with a deep

Alfred Nobel

humanitarian interest which found outlet in medical research. He was much influenced by Shelley. His keenest desire was for peace and he hoped that his factories would end war sooner than all the congresses. "The day when two army corps will be able to destroy each other in one second, all civilized nations will recoil from war in horror and disband their armies."

Nobel suffered from incessant ill-health and recorded in a quaint testimony that "his miserable existence should have been terminated at birth by a humane doctor." He recorded his principal virtues as that he kept his nails clean and was a burden to no one. His greatest sin he recorded as "that he does not worship Mammon."

He died in 1896 and left by his will some 31,250,000 kronor for the Nobel Prize Foundation. The prizes were to be awarded to those who had contributed most materially to the benefit of humanity during the previous year. The categories are Physics and Chemistry, Physiology and Medicine, Literature, Peace.

Dr. Matthew Parker of Nosey **Parker.** The familiar term, "Nosey Parker," for an unduly inquisitive and critical person, derives from Dr. Matthew Parker (1504–75). He was Archbishop of Canterbury and as one of marked Protestant persuasion he acquired a reputation for poking his nose into all matters of church ritual and ceremonial.

He was Master of Corpus Christi College, Oxford, and later Dean of Ely.

He was deprived of office by Mary but became Primate under Queen Elizabeth.

Nostradamus, the seer or pre-diction-monger. Nostradamus was the assumed name of an astrologer of Jewish descent, Michel de Notre-dame. He was born in Provence in 1503. He practised as a qualified doctor and was conspicuous for his medical work in the plague at Lyons and Aix.

Later he published at Lyons his *Centuries*, which were predictions in rhymed quatrains, divided into centuries.

He secured the notice of Catharine de Medici, who invited Nostradamus to visit her. Charles IX appointed the prophetic doctor his physician-in-ordinary.

The apparent accuracy of his predictions secured wide fame for the seer and further editions were published. They were condemned by the Papal Court.

Much literature has arisen concerning the prophecies and attempts are made from time to time to link them with the happenings of the present century.

The books were translated into English by Theophilus de Garencieres, who was a doctor of Oxford and a member of the Royal College of Physicians. They received wide attention.

Nostradamus died in 1566.

Œdipus of the Œdipus complex.
The Œdipus complex, a sexual complex held by psycho-analysts of the Freudian school to influence the child in relation to its parent of the opposite sex, derives from the Greek Œdipus.

Laius was told by the oracle to beget no children as he was destined to perish by the hands of his son, who would then marry his mother, Jocasta.

When a child was born, Laius exposed it, with pierced feet, on Mount Cithaeron. The child, so named from its swollen feet, did not die but was brought by shepherds to the King of Corinth.

The King, Polybus, adopted the child, who assumed at first that Polybus and Merope were his parents.

When doubts assailed him he consulted the Delphic Oracle. Œdipus was told not to return to his own country for, if he did, he would kill his father and marry his mother.

Still thinking of Corinth as his own country he resolved not to return thither and set out for Thebes. On the way he met his real father, Laius, though ignorant of his identity. The meeting was at a place too narrow for their chariots to pass. Œdipus killed Laius in a quarrel over the right of way.

At Thebes he succeeded in delivering the country from the Sphinx by solving her riddle which had been the cause of the death of many.

He was rewarded by the crown and the hand of Jocasta. By her he had four incestuous children. When the crime was discovered, Jocasta hanged herself and Œdipus put out his eyes.

Dr. William Oliver of the Bath Oliver. William Oliver, M.D., F.R.S., was born at Kenegie, near Penzance, Cornwall, in 1695. He entered Pembroke College, Cambridge, at the age of nineteen and took his M.D. in 1725. He completed his medical training at Leyden University and subsequently practised, according to some accounts, in Plymouth.

In 1728 he went to Bath with his friend, Rev. William Borlase, the antiquary, whose health, it was thought, would benefit by the waters of the spa. Dr. Oliver practised with success in the city and soon built up a fashionable and influential clientèle. He was a considerable social figure and enjoyed the company of Pope and Warburton. He caused a hamper of Cornish stones to be sent to the poet for his famous Grotto at Twickenham. The relationship was of such cordiality that when Dr. Oliver proposed to erect a monument to his parents, Pope wrote the epitaph and designed the pillar which was subsequently erected in Sithney churchyard.

Dr. Oliver was one of the moving spirits in the erection of the Mineral Water Hospital at Bath and was appointed its first physician. This was in 1740, and at the same time Jeremiah Pierce was appointed first surgeon to the hospital. They both resigned in 1761.

Dr. Oliver invented the biscuit, which still enjoys world popularity, for the benefit of his patients. He had them made in his house, but when the demand for them became too great for domestic production the doctor pensioned off his old coachman, Atkins, and confided to him the secret recipe.

Atkins is said to have been started in business by Oliver with a capital of £100 and ten sacks of the finest wheat flour. He opened a shop in Green Street and made a fortune.

In later years Dr. Oliver purchased

the manor of Weston, near Bath, where he died on March 17, 1764. He was buried in Weston Church, where there is a monument to his memory.

He had one son and five daughters.

His medical skill is mentioned in Mrs. Delany's autobiography and in Mrs. Anne Pitt's *Suffolk Letters*. He wrote some pastoral essays, a treatise on the use and abuse of warm bathing and a sketch of Beau Nash, "King of Bath."

He also composed some elegiac lines on the death of Ralph Thicknesse. Dr. Oliver was standing at Thicknesse's elbow when he fell dead while playing first violin in a work of his own composition at a Bath concert.

Orion of the constellation. Orion, in Greek mythology, was a giant hunter of notable beauty. He was the husband of Eos (Aurora), goddess of the dawn.

He was struck blind for attempting an outrage on Merope, but recovered his sight by exposing his eyes to the dawning sun.

Orion became the hunting companion of Artemis, but fell a victim to the jealousy of Apollo and was transformed into the constellation, where he is depicted as a giant with a girdle and wielding a raised club.

The appearance of Orion is said to be accompanied by stormy weather. Some accounts name Sirius (the Dog Star) as Orion's dog.

Oscar Pierce of the Oscar film trophy. The origin of the Oscar, the golden symbol of fame conferred by the Academy of Motion Picture Arts and Sciences, is little known and confused by elaborate myth. Many erroneously associate it with Oscar Deutsch.

The Oscar was in fact nameless when it became an award symbol in the year in which the Academy was founded, 1927. It remained "the statuette" for four years.

The idea for a statuette originated at a meeting of the first board of governors of the Academy. Cedric Gibbons urged that the awards should be represented by a figure of dignity and individual character which recipients would be proud to display. While he talked he sketched a figure and design—Oscar's first representation. The drawing was adopted and sent for modelling to George Stanley, a Los Angeles sculptor.

The golden figure was nameless

The Oscar Film Trophy

until 1931, when Mrs. Margaret Herrick, later secretary of the Academy, reported as librarian. A copy of the statuette stood on an executive's desk and she was formally introduced to it as the foremost member of the organization.

"He reminds me," she observed, "of my Uncle Oscar."

Nearby sat a newspaper columnist who subsequently wrote that "Employees have affectionately dubbed their famous statuette 'Oscar.'" The name stuck.

Mrs. Herrick's "Uncle Oscar" in fact was a second cousin.

Mr. Oscar Pierce, of a wealthy western pioneer family, formerly lived in Texas. He did well in wheat and fruit and retired to California.

The Academy's Oscar is ten inches high and weighs seven pounds. The inside is bronze and the exterior gold plate. Each statuette costs about a hundred dollars.

On May 6, 1929, eleven first year awards were presented—for achievements of 1927-8. Since that day the number of statuettes given the annual "choice few" has increased, until in 1947 thirty-six were presented. During the intervening years a total of three hundred and eighty golden knights have gone to persons contributing "best achievements" in motion pictures.

To date, writers have captured the greatest number of trophies—sixty-seven—with their closest competitors the art directors and cinematographers with thirty-six each. Cedric Gibbons, designer of the trophy, had in 1947 been voted "best art director of the year" six times and had acquired six Oscars.

Cleisthenes of Ostracism. Cleisthenes, the founder of Athenian democracy, of 500 B.C., completely reorganized the State and placed supreme authority in the hands of the *Ecclesia*, or the assembly of all the citizens.

It was to safeguard his civic constitution, which had enemies among the influential whom he had overthrown, that he instituted the practice of ostracism. The name derived from the Greek word ostracon (plural, ostraca), a piece of pottery, or potsherd, which it was common practice to use as material for writing upon.

The system devised by Cleisthenes was designed to suppress any attempts against established order in Athens. The *Ecclesia* met annually to decide if it was necessary to apply ostracism. If an affirmative decision was reached by the assembly, each member inscribed on a potsherd the name of the person whose withdrawal from the State appeared expedient in the public's interest. Any person whose name was thus recorded by a certain number of votes was required to leave Athens for ten years. His property was not confiscated.

Very few citizens were ostracized, but the inscribing of their names, even if the required number of votes was not forthcoming, had a salutary effect. Among those suffering ostracism was Aristides, a great Athenian, known as "The Just."

A number of these ostraca have been found, bearing their inscriptions. Several were discovered as recently as 1932, on the site of the Agora, the meeting place of the people's assembly, as opposed to the Council. It was the civic focus of the day, adorned with statues and temples and accepted as a social and commercial centre.

Pan of the pipes, pantheism, panic, etc. Pan was the very ancient Greek rural god, the spirit of nature and paganism. He is, in some accounts, the son of Hermes and Penelope. His mother was a little startled at his birth to find that he was hairy all over and had the horns and the feet of a goat. His father bore him to Olympus but the gods were not alarmed, and were rather pleased with the appearance of the wood sprite.

The Greek shepherds regarded Pan as their special protector and many caves which gave sanctuary at

Pan and his pipes

night were sacred to him. He is also associated with the patronage of fishing and bee-keeping. He was fond of music and in the evening would play upon his pipes (Syrinx) while the Oreads danced to his tune.

The pipes received their name from the legend which says that Syrinx was a nymph with whom Pan fell in love. She fled from him and caused herself to be transformed into a reed. The device failed her, for Pan cut the reed into seven pieces, making from them his familiar pipes, or Syrinx.

Pan was also a keen dancer and is often thus depicted. He is full of mischief and fun. The startling noises that Pan made, particularly by night, are the basis of his association with the word panic.

A later legend records that at the time of the Crucifixion, when the veil of the Temple was rent in twain, a cry, "Great Pan is dead," swept across the universe and silenced the Oracles for ever. Elizabeth Barrett Browning has a poem on this theme.

St. Pancras of the London borough. St. Pancras is recorded as the son of a heathen noble of Phrygia. He was taken to Rome as a child after he had lost both his parents. He was baptized but slain in A.D. 304, when a youth of fourteen, during the Diocletian persecutions.

It is stated that the first pagan temple consecrated for Christian worship in England by St. Augustine was named in honour of St. Pancras. It was at Canterbury.

St. Pancras is regarded as a patron saint of children, and churches abroad are frequently ascribed to his patronage. His day is May 12, and he is usually depicted as bearing a sword and a palm branch.

Pandora of Pandora's Box. Pandora's Box is the box in which only hope remained when by its ill-judged opening many ills were released to play havoc among mankind. It typifies a present which, while seemingly valuable, is in fact a curse.

The originating legend in mythology is associated with the creation and primitive condition of mankind. With the name of Prometheus is linked the first civilizing influence due to the introduction of fire, which he stole from heaven.

Zeus, in revenge, determined to leave mankind in possession of Prometheus' gift, and he ordered the creation of the image of a beautiful woman, which the Gods endowed with life and many gifts, hence the name Pandora. She was taught every art and artifice and then sent to the foolish Epimetheus, who in spite of the warning not to accept any gift from Zeus, received Pandora and married her.

In his house was a closed box, which he had been forbidden to open as it contained all kinds of ills and diseases. Pandora opened the box and all the ills which flesh is heir to, escaped—to the detriment of mankind.

She closed the lid just in time to retain the last ingredient, which was Hope.

Another version implies that the box contained blessings, all of which, except hope, were dissipated at the opening. There is a basic similarity to the story of Adam and Eve and the tree of knowledge of good and evil.

Sam Foote of Panjandrum. The word was coined by the noted English actor, Samuel Foote (1720–77). Foote, who was born in Cornwall, passed through a ruinous gaming period after Oxford and the law, but became a successful lessee of the Haymarket Theatre. There he had remarkable success in comedies, revealing inimitable powers of wit and mimicry. Johnson found him "irresistible."

The Panjandrum owed its creation to the boast of the veteran actor, Charles Macklin, at a lecture, that he could remember any passage by reading it over once.

According to the *Quarterly Review* of 1854, Foote composed as a test the familiar nonsense passage which includes, "So she went into the garden to cut a cabbage leaf to make an apple-pie . . . And there were present the Picninnies, the Joblillies, the Garyulies, and the Great Panjandrum himself, with the little red button a-top, and they all fell to playing the game of catch-as-catch-can till the gunpowder ran out at the heels of their shoes."

Macklin didn't play.

San Pantaleone of Pantaloon. The word pantaloon for baggy trousers or, originally, full trousers, or breeches and stockings in one piece, is believed to originate, via the stage, from San Pantaleone, a favourite saint of Venice.

He was a popular and persistent character in Italian comedy and generally an old, lovable but simple-minded type.

The term is also used for a dotard and this is largely his presentation as a stock character in the Harlequinade.

Shakespeare refers to Pantaloon in *As You Like It, ii. 7*.

The word "pants" derives from the same source.

Paris of "the Judgment of Paris." The term is used continually in application to a treacherous problem whose solution courts disaster.

Paris, also known as Alexander, was the son of Priam and Hecuba. The Trojan king, hearing from the soothsayers that the child would bring destruction upon his people, ordered his death. The slave responsible for carrying out the sentence exposed the child upon Mount Ida, where he was reared by shepherds.

Paris lived happily with the nymph, Œnone, until, at the marriage of Peleus and Thetis, Eris (Strife) threw down the golden apple with its inscription, "For the Fairest." Three claimed it, Hera, Athene and Aphrodite, and it was given to Paris, the handsomest mortal, to make the award.

Hera offered him greatness, Athene success at arms, and Aphrodite the most beautiful of women for his wife.

Paris awarded the golden apple to Aphrodite and soon after, with her aid, he carried off Helen, the wife of Menelaus and the fairest woman of her time. This abduction led to the expedition of the Greek princes against Troy in the Trojan war. So were the soothsayers justified.

Paris was mortally wounded by an arrow during the course of the fighting and had himself transported to the faithful Œnone. But it was too late and the nymph took her life when her lover died.

Louis Pasteur of Pasteurization.

The distinguished French chemist was born in June in 1822, the son of a tanner. He taught mathematics and the piquant comment "*médiocre*" was put alongside chemistry in his diploma. From the first Pasteur's devotion was to work, which, with will and success, for him filled human existence.

At the age of twenty-six he was Professor of Physics at Dijon, but was soon to become Professor of Chemistry at Strasbourg. There he married Mlle Laurent, who was to become a devoted fellow worker.

He did much research upon fermentation, both lactic and alcoholic, and brewing. He studied and defeated diseases of silkworms that were threatening the industry. He turned his attention to anthrax and chicken cholera with brilliant success. He also did revolutionary research on hydrophobia and rabies. He was indirectly the saviour of millions of lives and fortunes. He received world honours.

The creed of this devout, singleminded man was that "science, in obeying the law of humanity, will always labour to enlarge the frontiers of life."

Pasteur died in 1895.

Paul Pry.

Paul Pry, the inquisitive, meddlesome fellow, the less plebeian "Nosey Parker," derives from the principal character of the play *Paul Pry*, by John Poole (1786(?)–1872).

The farce was first produced at the Haymarket in 1825 and the author's model was said to be one, Thomas Hill, who turned his inquisitiveness to account by writing for the Press.

Poole wrote a number of successful farces, satires and books of a light, humorous nature.

Sir Robert Peel of "Bobby" and "Peeler."

The great British statesman was born near Bury, Lancashire, in 1788, and was a classmate of Byron at Harrow. He was a brilliant politician and noted orator.

As Secretary for Ireland, appointed in 1812, he was a masterly administrator in troublous times. Two years later he instituted the regular

A "Peeler"

Irish Constabulary, which was nicknamed the "Peelers." The name extended to the police in England. The nickname "Bobby" derives from the same source, as Peel, in addition to the Irish police association, was Home Secretary when the new Metropolitan Police Act was passed in 1828.

Peel died in 1850 as the result of being thrown from his horse while riding up Constitution Hill.

John Peel of the song.

Peel, of the famous hunting song, was born at Caldbeck, or Caldreck, in Cumberland, in 1776. For forty years he ran the famous pack that bore his name. He was described as "a man of very limited education outside hunting."

The famous song was written in 1820 by his friend John Woodcock Graves, while the two sportsmen were sitting "in a snug parlour."

In an adjoining room the author's mother was singing "a very old rant called 'Bonnie Annie,' " which incidentally is the march of the Border Regiment.

The author, fitting the words to the overheard air, said, "By jove, Peel, you'll be sung when we're both run to earth!"

Peeping Tom. The allusion comes from the story of Lady Godiva's ride through Coventry.

She was wife of Leofric, Earl of Mercia, one of Edward the Confessor's greatest noblemen. According to tradition her husband proposed a tax upon the people which he agreed to remit if Godiva would ride naked through the streets at noonday.

Lady Godiva accepted the challenge and ordered the inhabitants to remain indoors behind drawn blinds. One man, Peeping Tom, looked out.

According to some accounts he was killed by the irate inhabitants; in others he is struck blind. In subsequent commemorative festivals a sculptured bust of Peeping Tom was placed upon the sill of the window whence he is alleged to have looked out.

The legend appears frequently in literature and is referred to by Drayton, Leigh Hunt, Tennyson and Landor.

Pelagius of Pelagian. Pelagius, a 5th-century monk born in Britain or France, was the subject of a celebrated heresy of the early church. His teaching denied the doctrine of original sin and the power of divine grace as the sustaining power in redemption.

Pelagius suffered ecclesiastical banishment from Rome for this heresy in 418. St. Augustine was one of the fiercest opponents of the monk's teaching.

Later, a modified doctrine, known as Semi-Pelagianism, propounded the view that the first step in conversion was attributable to free will and the subsequent spiritual progress to divine grace.

Aristotle of Peripatetic. The word peripatetic, meaning itinerant or walking from place to place, arose from the custom of Aristotle of walking up and down the Lyceum while teaching there. His school became known as the Peripatetic School.

Thomas Percy of the Reliques. Thomas Percy, born in Bridgnorth, Salop, in 1729, was educated at Christ Church, Oxford, and took Orders. He became Chaplain to the King, Dean of Carlisle and Bishop of Dromore, which see he occupied at the time of his death in 1811. He brought considerable scholarship and antiquarian knowledge to his writing, which included a *Key to the New Testament*, an elegant version of the Song of Solomon and some verse translations.

His fame rests upon his *Reliques of Ancient English Poetry*, published in 1765, a celebrated collection of English ballads, sonnets, historical.songs and romances in verse. The several editions in the author's lifetime each included additional material.

The work did much to revive interest in English poetry and is said to have been a considerable influence in the work of Wordsworth, Coleridge and Scott.

Percy was a poet of distinction and enjoyed the friendship of many eminent literary men, including Johnson, Burke and Goldsmith. He suffered much criticism at the hands of the irascible antiquary, Joseph Ritson, who had a gift for invective unfettered by stringent libel laws.

Ritson, who supported a meticulous accuracy, was critical of Percy for his embellishments and his habit of filling in gaps from his imagination. The charges were not without foundation, but the *Reliques* was a milestone in the development of English poetry and has outlived its critic's detractions.

Sir James Barrie of Peter Pan. Peter Pan, "the Boy who wouldn't grow up," was the creation of Sir James Barrie (1860–1937) in his play of that name, produced in 1904.

The name is generally applied to

one of perennial youthfulness and spiritual questing. "To die would be an awfully big adventure."

The story of the play was published as *Peter and Wendy* in 1911. Many famous actresses have taken the title role in the play, which added also to common usage the name Tinkerbell, the fairy who takes the children, including the motherless Peter, off to the Never-Never Land.

The name clung closely to its creator, who once said that some of his stories petered out altogether and others panned out very well.

The famous Peter Pan statue in Kensington Gardens is by Sir George Frampton, R.A. (1860–1928).

Phaeton of the open carriage. The word phaeton, familiarly used for the open horse-drawn carriage, is named after Phaeton, son of Helios, the sun god.

He undertook to drive his father's chariot across the heavens but lost control of the horses and nearly set the world on fire. As it was, he caused the aridness of Libya and the deserts of Africa. Zeus transfixed the careless driver with a thunderbolt and turned Phaeton's sisters, who had yoked the horses, into poplars and their tears into amber.

The name Phaeton is also given in mythology to one of the horses of Eos, who preceded the sun god to announce the coming of day.

"Phaeton's bird" is the swan. Cygnus, the reckless driver's friend, was so distressed by Phaeton's fate that Apollo changed him into a swan and placed him among the constellations.

> . . . such a waggoner
> As Phaeton would whip you to the west,
> And bring in cloudy night immediately.
> *Romeo and Juliet, iii. 2.*

Philip of Macedon of Philippic. The term philippic, for a bitter invective, arose from the denunciatory oratory of Demosthenes (4th century B.C.) against Philip of Macedon (382–336 B.C.). They were designed over a period of fifteen years, to arouse the Athenians to resist the aggressions of Philip, father of Alexander the Great, and a brilliant if unscrupulous strategist.

The term "Philippics" is also applied to the orations of Cicero against Antony.

Phœnix of Phœnix-like. The frequent allusion in literature to the Phœnix is generally in connection with its unique ability to rise anew from the ashes of its former self. It is thus used to typify regeneration, either of a person, project, or building.

The Phœnix

This mythical Arabian bird, at the close of its life, was said to make a nest, sing a dirge and set fire to the nest by the flapping of its wings. From the ashes of itself and the nest it rose to a fresh life (Shakespeare refers to it as "the Arabian bird" in *Cymbeline*), and it was frequently represented in signs connected with chemistry and pharmaceutical practice.

Samuel Pickwick of Pickwickian. Samuel Pickwick, one of the greatest creations of Dickens, was general chairman of the Pickwick Club which he founded with Tupman, Snodgrass and Winkle as Corresponding Members to report upon their activities and observations.

The *Pickwick Papers*, actually entitled *The Posthumous Papers of the*

Pickwick Club, appeared first in twelve monthly parts and as a volume in 1837.

"In a Pickwickian sense" is applied to uncomplimentary language which should not be taken at its face value. The allusion is to a scene in the first chapter, wherein Pickwick says Blotton has acted in "a vile and calumnious manner," to which Blotton retorts that Pickwick is a humbug. It is eventually decided that both have used the expressions in a Pickwickian sense, which robs them of offence and friendship and esteem are restored.

Baroness Orczy of the Pimpernel. The Baroness Orczy, the Hungarian-born novelist and playwright, created in the Pimpernel a character of such widespread popularity and originality that the term has become common usage for any brilliantly elusive and attractive hero with chivalrous integrity. He has appeared also on stage and screen since his introduction in novel and play form in 1905.

The Pimpernel, brilliantly successful in the setting of the French Revolution, appeared in several of the author's subsequent books, which were translated into many languages. The Baroness died in 1947.

The pimpernel is a small annual found in cornfields and waste grounds of Britain. It has characteristic scarlet (and also blue and white) flowers which close in inclement weather.

Pindar of Pindaric. Pindaric: of, or like the Greek poet. The adjective is most frequently applied to verse of an irregular style, of various metres, favoured by the poet. His odes were noted for magnificent style, colourful imagery and outstanding diction. He was highly praised by Horace.

The great lyric poet of Greece was born of a musical family near Thebes about 522 B.C. He played the flute and competed in music festivals.

He was honoured alike by princes and the populace for his nobility of character. He was pre-eminent in every aspect of lyrical poetry, songs and hymns.

He is said to have been greatly influenced by the Bœotian poet, Corinna, who wrote principally poems on the legends of her native Thebes, and who vanquished Pindar in a famous poetic contest. Much of his verse was devoted to the celebration of Olympic athletic triumphs.

The Pindaric form has been used by English poets, including Gray (*The Bard*, for example), Cowley (*Pindarique Odes*), and Dryden (*Threnodia Augustalis*). It was the last named who greeted Jonathan Swift's attempt to produce the Pindaric form with the comment "Cousin Swift, you will never be a poet."

Pindar is ranked by Ruskin with Homer, Virgil and Dante for the purity and loftiness of his imagination and creative gifts.

He died in 442 B.C., and when Alexander razed Thebes he reflected the honour in which the poet was held by sparing his house.

The name Peter Pindar was made prominent in literature as the *nom de plume* of John Wolcot (1738–1819), who achieved considerable popularity with satires and lampoons, the most noted of which was *Lyric Odes to the Royal Academicians*. He attacked the leading personalities of his day, including George III and Boswell and Mrs. Thrale.

Pindari, Indian mounted marauding bands of the 17th and 18th centuries, have no connection with the poet, but derive their name from a Hindu word.

Sir Isaac Pitman of the Shorthand System. Sir Isaac Pitman, whose name is almost synonymous with shorthand, was born at Trowbridge, Wiltshire, in 1813. His father was a factory overseer and later a cloth manufacturer. He was superintendent in the Sunday School of the English poet, George Crabbe (1754–1832), who was appointed Vicar of Trowbridge in 1814.

This fact gave edge to the later difference when Isaac joined the New (Swedenborgian) Church. He started as a clerk, but after some training he taught in several schools and eventually opened a school at Bath.

In 1837 his *Stenographic Soundhand* was published, deriving in part from a previous system by Samuel Taylor.

Thereafter he devoted his life to developing shorthand and advocating spelling reform. He wrote, lectured and travelled extensively. London premises were secured for the sale of Pitman's publications in 1845. Previously they had been issued from his Phonetic Institute at Bath.

Pitman was knighted in 1894 and died at Bath three years later, but he had already received world recognition of his labours in the almost universal adoption of his system.

His epitaph to his wife, in Lansdowne Cemetery, Bath, is a quaint example of his insistence upon spelling reform. It reads:

In memori ov
MERI PITMAN,
Weif ov Mr. Eizak Pitman,
Fonetik Printer, ov this Site.
Deid 19 Agust 1857 edjed 64
'Preper tu mit thei God'
EMOS 4, 12.

Christophe Plantin, William Caslon and others of the famous type faces. The men behind the names of some of the greatest contributors to the production of literature are little known. They are the designers of type faces which have become classic standards; such men as Plantin, Garamond, Caslon, Baskerville and many others.

Christophe Plantin was born near Tours in 1514. His printing works at Antwerp was one of the largest in Europe. They were famous for their accuracy and excellence of craftsmanship. They secured the patronage of many influential figures. Plantin also opened houses at Leyden and Paris, which were carried on by the family.

Late last century the Antwerp house was purchased by the city and established as the Musée Plantin. The great printer died in 1549.

Claude Garamond, who first substituted Roman for Gothic characters in printing, was a 16th-century typefounder of Paris.

The English William Caslon (1692–1766) was born at Cradley, Worcestershire. He established his business in London and his type was used for, almost all contemporary works of importance.

Giambattista Bodoni, the celebrated Italian printer, was born in 1740, in Piedmont, the son of a printer. In Rome he was a compositor in the printing house of the *Propaganda*. In 1788 he was placed in charge of the ducal printing house in Parma, from which press came many exquisite works now among the classics of the printer's art. Bodoni died in 1813.

John Baskerville, a native of Worcestershire, acquired substantial wealth in a japanning business in Birmingham. He is said to have spent a small fortune in the perfecting of his printing art and in the design of his types. He manufactured all the machinery of his trade, including his inks. He was a man of eccentric habits and each panel of his carriage bore pictorial representations of different aspects of his craft. He died in 1775 and was buried in his garden. It is said that when the coffin was accidentally disturbed and opened fifty years later, the body was found in a remarkable state of preservation and a branch of laurels therein was still complete.

Among modern type designers of eminence may be mentioned Eric Gill and F. W. Goudy, the contemporary U.S. designer. On a visit to London, when asked how he designed his type faces, Goudy playfully replied that he thought of a letter and drew round it.

Eric Gill (1882–1940), brilliant alike as a sculptor and type designer, was born in Brighton. He wrote freely upon his creed as a craftsman.

Type is now estimated on the point system—72 points to the inch—rather than by the old method of naming each size, though the ancient usage persists in many places.

The very minute sizes, such as Diamond and Pearl, are seldom used and for general purposes the range starts at:

Nonpareil . .	6 point
(i.e. 12 unleaded lines to the inch)	
Minion . . .	7 point
Brevier . . .	8 point
Bourgeois . .	9 point
Long Primer . .	10 point
Small Pica . .	11 point
Pica . . .	12 point

Some of the names have unexpected pronunciations and are often misused by laymen. Nonpareil is called Nomprell; Brevier, Breveer; Bourgeois, Burjoice; Primer, Primmer; and Pica, Pieka.

In the early days, when there were seven sizes of types, the first was called "prima." Pica, in France and Germany, was called Cicero, because the works of that author were set in its size. In England it was the type used for the ordinal or service book of the Roman Catholic Church, first called the pica, or more familiarly, pie.

Bourgeois is so named from its French derivation, in which country it was dedicated to the bourgeois printers of Paris.

Brevier was used in the printing of the Breviary. Nonpareil was, at its introduction, regarded as the finest small type then produced.

Such book and printing terms as folio, quarto, octavo, sextodecimo (16mo), etc., are often misunderstood and held to apply to the number of pages. Strictly speaking, they apply to the number of times the original sheet has been folded. In folio the sheet is once folded, in quarto, twice; in octavo, three times; in 16mo four times, etc. A sheet of 20 in. × 15 in. folded thrice (octavo) will give eight leaves or 16 pages, measuring 7½ in. × 5 in.

This original sheet, however frequently folded, constitutes a "signature" and is the integral unit of the book. Its extent can be discovered by examining the actual binding of the book, and the first page of the "signature" bears a small letter or other reference to assist in the correct collation, or assembling, of the book's sections in the right order.

Before about 1850 the size of a sheet was instantly decided by its watermark. The smallest, marked with a jug, was called "pot," the next size watermark was cap and bells—hence our foolscap.

The principal book sizes, untrimmed, are:

	Octavo	*Quarto*
Pot . .	6¼ × 4	8 × 6¼
Foolscap .	6¾ × 4¼	8½ × 6¾
Crown . .	7½ × 5	10 × 7½
Post . .	8 × 5	10 × 8
Demy (*pro.* Dee-my)	8¾ × 5⅝	11¼ × 8¾
Medium .	9½ × 6	12 × 9½
Royal . .	10 × 6¼	12½ × 10
Super Royal .	10¼ × 6¾	13¾ × 10¼
Imperial .	11 × 7½	15 × 11

Plato of Platonic. The great Greek philosopher, Plato (427–348 B.C.), taught a form of Idealism that attributed real Being to general concepts or Ideas, while individual things were but their ephemeral and imperfect imitations. The world of sense was a world of becoming, not of being, only half-real, as opposed to the world of intelligible forms where, for instance, twice three is really, exactly and eternally six. To Plato the world owes almost all of its knowledge of the character and life of Socrates, also the Socratic dialogues and the great *Republic*. Plato is probably the greatest name in the history of philosophy.

Platonic love is spiritual love between opposite sexes, friendship devoid of all sexual significance. The originating phrase is found in the *Symposium*, wherein Plato lauds not the sexless love of a man for a woman, but the love of Socrates for young men, which was pure and therefore particularly noteworthy in those times.

Samuel Richardson, in *Pamela*, says that he is convinced, and always was, that Platonic Love is Platonic nonsense.

The "Platonic Cycle," or great year, was the space of time which, according to ancient astronomers, elapses before all the stars and their constellations return to their former positions in relation to the equinoxes —a period of some 25,800 years.

The Pleiades of the Constellation.
The Pleiades, in Greek mythology, were the seven daughters of Atlas. One of them, Electra, is invisible. Some accounts say that this is to hide her shame because she married a mortal, Dardanus, others that she might spare herself the mortification of seeing the destruction of Troy. Electra is known as "the lost Pleiad."

The Pleiades, a great number of stars of which six are prominent, form the group on the shoulder of Taurus, the bull, in the Zodiac.

They are known as the stars of the mariners because their coming was awaited for the season of safe voyaging. They appear in the last week in May and rise and set with the sun until August, after which they follow the sun and are seen in varying degrees at night until the following May.

The basic seven motif of the Pleiades has led to the names being given to several formations of that number. The Seven Sages of Greece, for instance, were known as the Philosophical Pleiad and the name was applied to the seven French literary men, headed by Ronsard who, in the 16th century, sought to reform the French language and literature on classical lines.

Samuel Plimsoll of the Plimsoll Line.
Plimsoll, "the sailor's friend," was born at Bristol in 1824. He was first a Sheffield brewery clerk and later, after steady promotion, he started his own coal-dealer's business in London.

He began to interest himself in the merchant service and the dangers to which it exposed its members. They were, Plimsoll decided, often unnecessary and inexcusable dangers— the overloading and under-manning of "coffin ships," over-insurance of

The Plimsoll Line

unseaworthy ships in the hope of a profitable wreck.

Plimsoll accumulated extensive and damning data, and when he entered Parliament as a Liberal for Derby, he attempted, unsuccessfully, to secure the passage of a bill preventing such iniquities. He published *Our Seamen*, and it made a profound impression on the country, so that Plimsoll secured the appointment of a Royal Commission and subsequently a government bill which, though inadequate in the reformer's opinion, at least showed progress.

Plimsoll lost his temper in the House when Disraeli announced that the bill would be dropped. He suspected that it had been stifled by vested interests. The country agreed with him and eventually legislation gave wide powers to the Board of Trade to enforce regulations which prevented a continuation of the scandalous conditions. The maximum load line—immediately known as the Plimsoll line—was required to be marked, first by the owner and later at the direction of the Board of Trade (Merchant Shipping Act, 1876).

It was a milestone in the history of mercantile shipping and Plimsoll's victory saved thousands of lives.

He became Président of the Sailors' and Firemen's Union and continued his efforts to improve mercantile conditions, and particularly conditions in cattle ships, until his death in 1898.

Pluto of Plutonic. Plutonic: infernal, pertaining to Pluto.

Pluto (Hades) was the Roman God of the underworld, the most detested and the most feared. Later conceptions were less austere, even to the extent of allying with Pluto the god of riches, Plutus of Greek mythology. He was responsible—etymologically, at least—for plutocrats and such expressions as "Rich as Plutus."

Pluto was the son of Saturn and brother of Jupiter and Neptune. The rape of Proserpine (counterpart of the Greek Persephone) is laid at Pluto's door. She was fated to spend one-third of the year with her seducer in the infernal regions and the rest of the year in the upper world. The myth symbolizes the seasons and the bleakness of nature while Proserpine is languishing in the winter of the nether world.

Pluto's domain, or Hades, represents the place of the dead before they are admitted to higher distinction or lower extinction—Elysium or Tartarus. Homer placed Tartarus as far below Hades as Hades was beneath the earth or the mortals.

Spenser talks of "Pluto's baleful bowers" in *The Faerie Queene*.

The Marquise de Pompadour, the witty, unscrupulous mistress in high places. The Marquise de Pompadour (1721–64) was one of the most famous (or notorious) and influential mistresses of Louis XV of France.

She was born in Paris and was a celebrated wit and beauty. She was already married when she secured the King's favour and, installed at Versailles, she exercised a profound influence upon national and international politics for two decades. It was a corrupting influence and the Pompadour aroused the enmity of an impotent people.

She was preceded in the King's favour by La Châteroux and succeeded by the Du Barri, daughter of a dressmaker, who was eventually guillotined for squandering state funds.

Pompadour as a colour is between claret and purple and the 56th Foot were named the Pompadours from the use of this commemorative colour in their regimental facings.

Pooh-Bah, the holder of many offices simultaneously. The name is taken from the character, Pooh-Bah, in one of the famous Gilbert and Sullivan operas, *The Mikado*, or *The Town of Titipu.*

In the opera, Ko-Ko is nominated as the Lord High Executioner, and Pooh-Bah as "Lord High Everything Else."

This comic opera in two acts was first produced at the Savoy Theatre, London, on March 14, 1885.

Procrustes of Procrustean. Procrustean: tending to produce uniformity by violent methods.

Procrustes was a fabulous brigand of ancient Athens who placed his victims upon a bed. If they were too short, he stretched them: if too long, he amputated the extending limbs.

He was eventually overcome by Theseus, one of the chief heroes of Attic legend, who slew the brigand by means of his own violent malpractices.

Prometheus of Promethean. Promethean: of or like Prometheus in his skill or punishment. Capable of producing fire.

The Titan Prometheus, son of Iapetus and the ocean nymph Clymene, is credited in some accounts with the creation of mankind. It is uncertain whether this was effected before or after the flood of Deucalion. Prometheus made men of clay and water and Athene breathed a soul into them.

In pity for the state of mankind the god is said to have stolen fire from heaven and revealed its uses to man. Fire, when employed by man, lost its celestial elemental purity, which was sacrilege. For causing this sacrilege, Zeus ordered Prometheus to be chained to a rock on Mount Caucasus, where an eagle preyed daily upon his liver (recognized as the seat of evil desires). In order that the torture might be sustained the liver grew again each night.

The legend of Prometheus appears in its most notable form in the play, *Prometheus Bound* by Aeschylus, the father of Greek tragic drama, 524–456 B.C.

The fire aspect of the legend was perpetuated in the name Prometheans, given to sticks used in India for producing fire by friction. It was also used for early "safety" matches, manufactured in France at the beginning of the 19th century.

"Promethean fire" is a phrase for the vital principle; the fire with which the god animated the figures of clay.

He gave man speech, and speech created thought,
Which is the measure of the universe.
Shelley's *Prometheus Unbound, ii. 4.*

Proteus of Protean. Protean: variable, versatile; of or like Proteus; assuming as many shapes as; full of shifts, aliases, disguises, etc.

Proteus was an inferior deity, represented as an old man and servant of Poseidon (Neptune). He lived in the island of Pharos. Some accounts say that after telling over his sea-calves at noon he would sleep and the only way to catch him was then to creep up and bind him. To elude capture he assumed different shapes.

Another tradition is that Menelaus craved the advice of this unerring old man of the sea. Proteus sought to elude the importunings of the hero by changing into a lion, a dragon, a wild boar and other forms.

Proteus is generally depicted as a Triton, with a body ending in a tail, and he is usually distinguished by a crook.

Psyche of Psychology and many other modern manifestations. Psyche is breath; hence life or the soul itself.

The legend of Cupid and Psyche is of comparatively late origin and can be found in the *Golden Ass* of Apuleius, 2nd century A.D.

Cupid visits the beautiful Psyche every night but leaves her at sunrise. He insists that she shall never seek to discover the identity of her lover, but as with many a later counterpart, her prudence is overcome by curiosity. She lights the lamp to look at her fair companion and a drop of hot oil falls on Cupid and wakens him. He is inflamed and flees and the abandoned Psyche searches far and wide for her lover. She becomes the slave of Venus, who is a hard taskmistress, but eventually she is united to her lover and becomes immortal.

Puck, the mischievous sprite. Puck and puckish derive from a traditional sprite or hobgoblin, a Robin Goodfellow, who had malevolent characteristics until Shakespeare's character of the name of Puck, in *Midsummer Night's Dream*, gave it the more attractive gay qualities to-day linked with the name.

In the play Puck, who is described

as "Robin-Goodfellow, a Fairy," is asked:

> . . . *are you not he,*
> *That frights the maidens of the villagery:*
> *Skim milk; and sometimes labour in the quern,*
> *And bootless make the breathless housewife*
> *churn;*
> *And sometimes make the drink to bear no barm;*
> *Mislead night-wanderers, laughing at their*
> *harm?*

To which he replies:

> *Fairy, thou speak'st aright;*
> *I am that merry wanderer of the night.*

It is Puck who speaks the familiar lines, "Lord, what fools these mortals be!" and "I'll put a girdle round about the earth in forty minutes."

A Phooka, or Pooka, is also a hobgoblin of Irish folklore, here presenting the original malevolent characteristics and sometimes appearing in animal or bird form.

A puck is a cattle disease attributed to the nightjar (possibly from the bird-sprite association) and the name given to the rubber disc used for play in ice hockey. In both these cases the etymology of the word is dubious.

George Pullman of the Pullman car.

The name Pullman for a luxuriously fitted railway saloon or sleeping car originally applied only to the products of the Pullman Palace Carriage Works, Illinois, U.S.A., whose president and designer was George Mortimer Pullman (1831–97). He was born near New York and in 1863 produced the "Pioneer," the first car to bear his name. Pullman invented and designed the vestibule car and was a pioneer in enlightened conditions of employ-ment and housing, building a model city near Chicago.

Pygmalion.

Pygmalion, which has become a general literary reference since G. B. Shaw's famous play of that name, was an ancient king of Cyprus who was a sculptor of distinction.

In Greek legend, though the king hated women, he fell in love with the ivory statue he had carved of a woman. Some accounts say that the statue was of Aphrodite. He asked the goddess to breathe life into the statue. The king's request was granted and he married the maiden. By her he was the father of Paphus.

The legend is mentioned by Ovid and is dealt with by W. S. Gilbert in *Pygmalion and Galatea* (1871).

Shaw's *Pygmalion* was published in 1912.

Pyrrhus of a Pyrrhic Victory.

A Pyrrhic victory, one gained at too great a cost, is derived from Pyrrhus, King of Epirus, the kinsman of Alexander the Great. He planned to conquer the Western World and in 280 B.C. invaded Italy with a vast army.

In his victory over the Romans at Asculum in 279 B.C. he lost the flower of his army and is credited with saying that if there were more such victories "Pyrrhus is undone."

His military fortunes waned and the final note of irony (not unique in the records of potential world dominators) was that Pyrrhus was fatally struck by a tile thrown by a woman.

The Marquess of Queensberry of the Queensberry Rules. The 8th Marquess of Queensberry (1844–1900), in association with John G. Chambers, drew up the code of laws for boxing still known by his name. That was in 1867, and the rules, which govern all glove contests in Great Britain, governed in America until the adoption of the boxing rules of the Amateur Athletic Union of America. In the same year Lord Queensberry presented cups for the British amateur championships at the recognized weights.

The Queensberry title (1633) is one of the many with which the Scottish House of Douglas is associated and there have been many famous sporting figures in the line. One of the most picturesque was the fourth Duke, "Old Q," whose romantic escapades were notorious and his patronage of the Turf a byword.

Vidkun Abraham Quisling. Quisling, who gave his name to political traitors with a special sinister significance, was born in Norway in 1887. He was trained for politics, but spent some years in the Army.

In 1933, soon after Hitler became Chancellor of Germany, Quisling organized the Norwegian fascist party. He secured active and passive assistance of the German invasion of Norway. He was made Fuehrer of Norway by Hitler, with orders to reconstruct the country he had betrayed on acceptable Nazi principles. As Prime Minister he instituted typically brutal measures to counter the national opposition he experienced.

Two days before Germany collapsed in May, 1945, Quisling and several members of his Cabinet were arrested by Norwegian resistance officials. He was charged with treason, found guilty of this and other charges and was shot on October 24, 1945.

Don Quixote of Quixotic. Quixotic: enthusiastically visionary, pursuing lofty but impracticable ideals, ignoring material interests in comparison with honour and chivalry.

The word derives from Don Quixote de la Mancha, hero of the satirical romance of the same name by Cervantes (1547–1616).

Don Quixote, a humble man of amiable character, has his wits deranged by the romances of chivalry and feels called to roam the world

Don Quixote

in search of adventure. He is accompanied by his old horse, Rosinante, and his squire, the rustic Sancho Panza. He earnestly conforms to the chivalrous tradition and in consequence is involved in absurd adventures with distressing consequences to himself. The valorous yet tender Quixote, always tilting at windmills, is one of the greatest figures in literature, and it is clear that the author, who started the book as a burlesque of the romances of chivalry, was the first to fall under the spell of the man who "unluckily stumbled upon the oddest fancy that ever entered into a madman's brain." The knight errant is soon scouring his great grandfather's armour and viewing his horse, "whose bones stuck out like the corners of a Spanish Real." Few readers will be surprised that Sancho Panza "forsook his wife and children to be his neighbour's squire." Together they enjoy or suffer fantastic adventures with a spirit that has done far more than merely to add an adjective to our language.

The first part of *Don Quixote* was published in 1605, the second ten years later.

François Rabelais of Rabelaisian. Rabelaisian; marked by exuberant imagination and language and coarse humour and satire.

The word derives from the great French author, François Rabelais (1490(?)–1553). His most famous work is *Gargantua and Pantagruel*, published in five books (the last posthumously), between 1532 and 1552.

He was the youngest son of an obscure family of vine-growers and had an illegitimate child. He appears to have revealed a brilliant facility for learning and scholarship. He took orders, joined the Friars Minor of Fontenay, but left after fifteen years. Probably his wit and gaiety were too much for them.

Rabelais took his degree in medicine and practised and lectured notably in the profession. He secured permission to exchange the Franciscan habit for that of the Benedictines, while continuing a medical career of distinction.

His work is characterized by brilliant scholarship, remarkable gifts of satire and a grossness of humour that could not completely hide a fundamental nobility of character. As Professor Dowden said: "Below his laughter lay wisdom; below his orgy of grossness lay a noble ideality."

The work is gigantic, both in the sweep of its conception and in the prodigious proportions of its characters. "Hearken, jolt-heads, ass-faces, *vietsdazes* . . . Pantagruelism . . . is a certain Jollity of Mind, pickled in the scorn of Fortune."

Rabelais tirades with unassailable power against the immorality of the religious Orders, against the pedantry of the doctors of learning; against the ascetics, the spoil-sports, the prigs and the prudes and the folly of kings. He wrote in an age of lethal intolerance, when criticism of those in high places, however justified, generally met with torture or death. It is a prodigious performance, unequalled in literature. Rabelais was one of the foremost creative minds in history.

The great translation, of the first three Books, is by Sir Thomas Urquhart, a squire of Cromarty. (See also *Gargantua*.)

E. W. Hornung of Raffles. Raffles, the gentleman-burglar whose name has become common usage for that type of criminal, was the creation of E. W. Hornung (1866–1921). He was born in Middlesbrough and spent some years in Australia, which country he used as background for several of his novels. He did much journalism also.

The Amateur Cracksman, published in America and England in 1899, achieved prodigious sales. The Raffles character appeared in the title of several subsequent books. Though he wrote of sensation in what was once called "almost unpardonable gusto," Hornung had a refined style and considerable literary quality. He married a sister of Conan Doyle's.

The name character of his book *Stingaree*, concerned with a monocled Australian bush-ranger with Dundreary whiskers, also passed into general usage at the time.

The uncommon name, Raffles, is known in history through Sir Thomas Stanford Raffles (1781–1826), founder of Singapore.

Raphael of the Pre-Raphaelites. The Pre-Raphaelite Brotherhood was formed about 1848, with Holman Hunt, Millais and Dante Gabriel Rossetti among its leading members. They set forth their creed in *The Germ*, the first of whose four issues appeared on January 1, 1850, with the sub-title: *Thoughts towards nature in Poetry, Literature and Art.*

The aim of the Pre-Raphaelites was to resist contemporary conventions and to return to art forms as they supposed them to exist before the time of the great Raphael. They were determined, by a patient study of nature, to present the faithfulness, sweetness and strength of the old masters. Ruskin supported the movement but pointed out that the name was unwise as the members were on neither pre- nor post-Raphaelite lines. They were endeavouring to paint everlasting values, in fact what they saw in nature presented with the highest possible degree of completion. Their style was by no means the imitation of the style of any past epoch.

Raphael, the great Italian master (1483–1520), is one of the supreme figures in art. He studied under Perugino and received great favour from the Church. Raphael was appointed by Pope Leo X to succeed Bramante as architect of St. Peter's, Rome. Several of the cartoons by Raphael intended for the tapestries of the Sistine Chapel came into the possession of Charles I and are exhibited at the South Kensington Museum.

Grigory Efimovich Rasputin, the malevolent seer.

During the first World War the reputation and mythical achievements of Rasputin, the Russian "monk," achieved such world prominence that his name has received common acceptance to designate a malevolent seer and so-called miracle man.

He appears to have been born about 1870, of peasant stock, and to have received little education. Early in life he became a "holy man" of wandering habits, but his character had a background of licentiousness.

He insinuated himself into the Imperial Court, where his striking personality and hypnotic eyes caused an impression which was further established by his apparent success in restoring to health the heir to the crown. The Tsarevitch was suffering from hæmophilia. After this so-called miracle, Rasputin capitalized his success to such an extent that he superseded Feofan as the Empress Alexandra's confessor. He became the greatest power in the land and the highest in the courts sought his favours and were prepared to bribe heavily to obtain them. Always there was a background of scandalous intrigue and gross immorality, and Rasputin's many enemies made it necessary for him to have his own secret police and to live frequently in heavily guarded seclusion.

Reports of his death vary in detail, but it took place at a planned supper-party at the house of Prince Felix Yusupov, in December, 1916. Some accounts say that he was there half poisoned and then shot by his host; others that he was offered a pistol to end his life, that he fired at and missed another guest, the Grand Duke Dmitri Pavlovitch, and was then shot. The body was thrown into the Neva.

The self-appointed executioners reported their action and there was national rejoicing.

The body was recovered and taken to the Imperial Summer Palace, where it was buried in state by the Empress.

Mrs. Belloc Lowndes, in *A Passing World* (Macmillan, 1948), records that conflicting accounts of the death were received by the Foreign Office from reliable sources.

Baron de Reuter of the international news agency.

Baron Paul Julius de Reuter (1816–99) was born in Germany and as a youth interested himself in experimental telegraphy.

He organized news agencies in Europe, bridging the telegraphic gaps with the then frequently used pigeon post.

He became a naturalized British subject and his organization gradually extended all over the world, so that his service became the backbone of world news-gathering and his name synonymous with news collection and dissemination. His agency was founded in 1849. It developed an unchallenged reputation for speed and accuracy.

The organization was eventually converted into a private trusteeship in which to-day the Press of the country, through elected members, have control.

de Reuter was made a baron by the Duke of Saxe-Coburg and Gotha in 1871, and he received royal permission in this country to enjoy the privileges of this rank in his adopted country of England.

Rhadamanthus of Rhadamanthine. Rhadamanthine, stern and incorruptible, derives from the Judge, Rhadamanthus, of Greek mythology. All souls, on reaching the lower world, had to appear before the triumvirate of which the other members were Minos and Æacus.

Rhadamanthus is said, with Minos, to have been the son of Zeus and Europa. Some accounts place Sarpedon as the third son.

Europa afterwards married Asterion, who brought up her sons by Zeus as his own. At his death he left his kingdom to Minos, who expelled his two brothers. Rhadamanthus found sanctuary in Bœotia. He was distinguished among men for his piety and strict judicial qualities. After his death he was appointed one of the judges of the dead.

Cecil Rhodes of the Rhodes Scholarships. The Rhodes Scholarships are a lasting reflection of the vision and patriotism of a great Empire builder.

Rhodes (1853–1902) went to South Africa first for health reasons, and acquired and developed considerable Kimberley diamond interests.

He planned the federation of South Africa under British rule, and when the British South Africa Company was incorporated to administer the territory north of Bechuanaland it was named Rhodesia.

Rhodes was Prime Minister at the Cape for six years, but subsequent political activities came under censure from the Parliament and the House of Commons. Rhodes resigned and occupied himself with the development of Rhodesia.

His will provided for a gift of £100,000 to his Oxford College, Oriel, and over £6,000,000 for the foundation and endowment of some 200 Rhodes Scholarships to be held at Oxford.

The donor left explicit and unusual instructions with regard to the holders of these Scholarships. He was animated by the desire for world peace, an international outlook and the dissemination of all that was best in the British spirit and administration.

Holders of the Scholarships were to be men picked for character, leadership and athletic prowess. Rhodes was critical of the essentially academic approach. The Rhodes Scholars were to be drawn from every important British colony and from all States in the U.S.A. By a codicil signed just before his death, Rhodes provided for five such Scholarships to be awarded in Germany, but this provision was annulled by Parliament in 1916. It was revived in 1929. Of the eleven German Rhodes Scholars killed in the second World War, eight were executed for treason to the German State.

There is a Rhodes Birthplace Memorial at Bishop's Stortford, Herts, and a Rhodes House at South Parks Road, Oxford, next to Wadham Garden. It was opened in 1929 and the rooms are named after his friends, seven of whom were chosen by Rhodes as first Trustees.

Rip Van Winkle, the person who wakes after a prodigious sleep. The famous character, Rip Van Winkle, was created by Washington Irving (1783–1859), the distinguished American essayist and historian, born of British parentage in New York.

The story appeared in Irving's *Sketch Book* (1819) and describes the adventures of a Dutch colonist in pre-Revolutionary days who was driven from home by a shrewish wife. In a ravine of the Catskill Mountains, Van Winkle meets a strange man and assists him to carry a keg. When they reach the man's destination, Rip sees a crowd of similar strange creatures playing at ninepins in complete silence.

He seizes the opportunity to drink from the keg and falls into a stupor. He sleeps for twenty years and on waking finds his world changed, also his beard. His wife is dead, his daughter married, his village altered and America is independent.

In the *Sketch Book* also, Irving names a quiet old-world village on the Hudson, Sleepy Hollow, which phrase is in common usage to describe a rural backwater.

Daniel Defoe of Robinson Crusoe. Any lonely traveller or a lone traveller in distant isolation is known as a Robinson Crusoe.

The title comes from the best-known work of Daniel Defoe, *The Life and strange surprising adventures of Robinson Crusoe* (1719). It was an immediate and permanent success and was translated into many languages.

Defoe (1660(?)–1731) was the son of a London butcher, James Foe. The author changed his name to Defoe in middle life.

He fought in Monmouth's Rebellion and with William the Third's army. He was a famous pamphleteer and was fined, imprisoned and pilloried. As a journalist he was supreme, adopting many aliases to give plausibility to his work. His brilliant description of the Plague, long thought to be first-hand reporting, was, in fact, fictional detail embodied in a most convincing narrative.

His *Moll Flanders* (1722) is, like

Robinson Crusoe, a classic—and a widely read book still.

The story of *Robinson Crusoe* was based on the adventures of Alexander Selkirk, which attracted other less successful pens. Selkirk, a Scottish shoemaker, ran away to sea and from a privateering expedition was

left, at his own request, upon the uninhabited island of Más-a-Tierra in the Juan Fernandez group, S. Pacific, west of Valparaiso. He was rescued therefrom after some years.

Robinson Crusoe

Defoe's book has given another name to our language—Man Friday.

Crusoe, with his man Friday, revisited his island in *The Farther adventures of Robinson Crusoe* (1719), and the phrase is now continually applied to a lone companion of unswerving loyalty in adverse, isolated conditions.

Heath Robinson of the Absurd Contraption. Heath Robinson, born in London in 1872, gave a new and much used adjective to our vocabulary. It is instinctively employed for the fantastic, improvised contraption, the prototype of which he created and made famous in his drawings.

He came of an artistic line and his talent was transmitted to his colourful family of five, which includes a Roman Catholic monk.

Heath Robinson studied at the Royal Academy School and was by instinct a water-colourist. He was a brilliant draughtsman and illustrated some notable editions of the classics, including *Rabelais* and *Don Quixote*. Kipling thought very highly of his work and used him as an illustrator for his Collected Poems.

Heath Robinson had a singular delicacy of line and grace of conception which made his illustrations of such authors as Hans Andersen collectors' items.

After persuasions from an advertiser, he launched, somewhat reluctantly, into the creation of his inimitable characters and mechanical devices. A grateful public never allowed him to forsake them, though he still painted in water colours and oils for his pleasure. His topical drawings in the 1914–18 war were so famous that they were later incorporated in the official German military handbooks as an example of British humour which did so much to sustain and fortify morale.

Although Heath Robinson had no mechanical or engineering training it was admitted that his most complicated contraptions were mechanically correct and workable. Underlying all of them was a gentle tilt at human absurdity.

Heath Robinson died in 1944. He was portrayed on the West End stage, saw his incredible houses and gadgets erected and painted the murals for the Knickerbocker Bar and Children's Room of the *Empress of Britain*.

Karel Capek of Robot. Robot, indicating a mechanical man, derives from the play, *R.U.R.* (Rossum's Universal Robots), by the contemporary Czech dramatist, Karel Capek, pronounced Sharel Chapek.

He was born in Bohemia in 1890.

The origin of Robot is a Slav word, *robotnik*, meaning a workman.

In the play, society is represented as being dependent upon mechanical men. They ultimately revolt against their employers and destroy them.

Capek's "Insect" play, *The Life of the Insects*, in which he collaborated with his brother, Josef, received considerable attention in London. Karel has also written novels and *Letters from England* (1925), and *Letters from Italy* (1929).

Dr. Peter Mark Roget of the Thesaurus. Although a thesaurus can be any lexicon or encyclopædia, being derived from the Greek for "treasure," the word is almost synonymous with Roget's great literary compilation of *English Words and Phrases*.

Dr. Roget, a distinguished physician, was born in 1779. He was a Doctor of Medicine, Fellow of the Royal College of Physicians, Member of the Senate of London University and of Literary and Philosophical Societies in many cities in several countries.

His great work on words and phrases, "classified and arranged so as to facilitate the expression of ideas and assist in literary composition," was the labour of a long lifetime.

In 1805 he had completed a classified catalogue of words on a small scale and had found this collection, "scanty and imperfect as it was, of much use to me in literary composition." (Dr. Roget wrote a number of medical treatises, notably on physiology in relation to natural theology.)

It was only upon his retirement from the Secretaryship of the Royal Society, of which he was a Fellow, that he found time to develop his vast project to the stage of publication. It appeared in 1852, was immediately successful, and has become one of the outstanding works of literary reference. Roget thought that nothing would conduce more directly to bring about an age of union and harmony among the races of mankind "than the removal of that barrier to the interchange of thought and mutual good understanding between man and man, which is now interposed by the diversity of their respective languages."

His son and his grandson carried on the work of incorporating the material that Dr. Roget had gathered in the last years of his life, which ended in 1869 at the advanced age of ninety.

Roland of "A Roland for an Oliver." A Roland for an Oliver; tit for tat; an effective retort; a reference to the evenly matched combat between the two parties named.

The epic poem, *Chanson de Roland*, dates from the eleventh century, and is probably of Norman origin. There is an early copy in the Bodleian.

Roland is the nephew of Charlemagne, King of the Franks, 742–814. Like Oliver, Roland is one of Charlemagne's paladins; the twelve peers who accompanied the king. After an undecided single combat lasting five days, the two heroes develop a friendship of a David and Jonathan devotion and similarity of action.

The story presented in the *Chanson* is concerned with the battle of Roncevaux, in which the death of Roland is planned. In gallant resistance to the Saracen enemy the two heroes perish. Roland, as the situation becomes desperate, sounds his ivory horn at Oliver's request. Charlemagne, thirty miles away, hears the clarion call and hastens to the scene with his army. He is too late to save the heroes but avenges their death by routing the enemy.

Shakespeare, in *I Henry VI, i. 2*, refers to *England all Olivers and Rolands bred*.

Romeo and Juliet, the prototypes of youthful, loving constancy. The chief characters of Shakespeare's *Romeo and Juliet* (1597) are based upon earlier romances of Verona.

The "star-crossed lovers" are representatives of "two households, both alike in dignity," at feud with one another. Juliet, the fair daughter of Capulet, loves Romeo of the house of Montague. They do, as the Prologue recites, "with their death, bury their parents' strife. The fearful passage of their death-mark'd love, And the continuance of their parents' rage, Which but their children's end, naught could remove, Is now the two hours' traffic of our stage."

The lyrical quality of the young lovers' tragic romance is sung in some of the finest and most often quoted of Shakespeare's lines.

The names Montague and Capulet are still used to describe warring personalities and the balcony scene and the famous Queen Mab speech by Mercutio, Romeo's friend, are universally quoted extracts from the play.

Juliet was a child, "Come Lammaseve at night, shall she be fourteen," declares her nurse.

In supposed solitude Juliet cries: "O Romeo, Romeo! wherefore art thou Romeo? Deny thy father, and refuse thy name, for my sake; or if thou wilt not, be but my sworn love, and I no longer will be Capulet."

They are married secretly in the cell of Friar Lawrence.

Romeo is banished, following recrudescences of the feud in which he slays Juliet's cousin. The lovers spend a night together before Romeo's exile.

Juliet, now faced with another contrived match, undertakes to swallow a liquid that will render her cold and lifeless so that Romeo can recover her seemingly dead body from the family vault. The wedding feast changes into a funeral rite. Banished Romeo, hearing the news of Juliet's assumed death and knowing nothing of the deception, visits the tomb. He there disturbs the prospective husband, Paris, who is slain. Romeo takes poison and Juliet, awaking from her coma, stabs herself, dying by her true lover's side.

Roscius of Roscian. The adjective roscian implies eminence or perfection in acting or allied arts.

The origin of the word was Quintus Roscius, a brilliant comic actor of the 1st century B.C., born in the Sabine territory. He was a friend of Cicero, enjoyed the patronage of the famous and reached such a standard of excellence in his art that the derivative adjective was used as a synonym for perfection in any of the arts.

Rosinante, the worn-out horse or jade. Cervantes' Don Quixote gave this name to his steed, which he regarded as a priceless charger, though in fact its bones stuck out like the corners of a Spanish Real. Don Quixote chose Rosinante as "a name in his opinion, lofty sounding and significant of what he had been before, and also of what he was now; in a word, a horse before or above all the vulgar breed horses in the world."

He commended Rosinante to an innkeeper's especial care, as "there was not a better in the universe; upon which the innkeeper viewed him narrowly."

Lord Rowton of Rowton Houses. Montagu William Lowry-Corry, created first Baron Rowton in 1880, was born in 1838.

He was private secretary for two periods to Disraeli during the latter's Premiership.

At the end of last century he was asked by Sir Edward Guinness (afterwards Lord Iveagh) to advise him in the formation of the Guinness Trust for the provision in London and Dublin of artisan dwellings at low rentals. His researches persuaded him that something should be done for those who could not occupy the accommodation offered by the Guinness Trust and other institutions. He offered to find the £30,000 considered necessary for such a scheme. He did in fact provide this sum for the first Vauxhall site and building.

Lord Rowton took infinite pains to secure the best design and equipment for the lodging-house, which was opened in December, 1892, with 470 cubicles, subsequently increased to 484. The House, which offered accommodation at 6d. a night, was an immediate success. The govern-

ing company, against much opposition from its founder, was named Rowton Houses, Ltd.

Many Houses were later opened, in London and the provinces, and the scheme, which met a profound need, was examined and copied by many overseas authorities.

Lord Rowton died in 1903.

The Rubicon of "Crossing the Rubicon." The Rubicon, though impersonal, is so often encountered in writing that a note is necessary.

The expression "to cross the Rubicon," implying the taking of an irretrievable step, derives from a famous river in Italy which marked the boundary between Roman Italy and Cisalpine Gaul, a province administered by Julius Cæsar.

When Cæsar crossed the river in 49 B.C. it was tantamount to an invasion of the Republic and an automatic declaration of hostilities. It precipitated the Civil War.

Sir Anthony Hope Hawkins of Ruritania. Ruritania, an imaginary Kingdom in Central Europe, was created by Sir Anthony Hope Hawkins who wrote as Anthony Hope. It has since become the accepted word in literary and theatrical usage for a kingdom of make-believe romance and chivalry.

The novelist used it most successfully as the background for *The Prisoner of Zenda* (1894) and its equally popular sequel, *Rupert of Hentzau* (1898).

Hope was born in 1863, the son of a vicar of St. Bride's, Fleet Street. In the vicarage of this church, "the journalists' cathedral," much of his work was written. He took a double First at Oxford and was President of the Oxford Union Society.

His novels enjoyed wide popularity and his *Dolly Dialogues* were the talk of the season.

Hope was a wit, a brilliant talker and a boon companion. He was knighted in 1918 and died in 1933.

Count de Sade of Sadism. The French writer, Count Donatien Alphonse François de Sade (1740–1814), was born in Paris and saw considerable active service in the army. He was addicted to vicious practices and condemned to death for an unnatural crime. He escaped, was re-arrested and sent to the Bastille.

His skill as a playwright and author was marred by a constant obscenity.

The unbalanced author who encouraged his address as "The Marquis de Sade" died in an asylum and himself added to the language the word "sadism" to denote a sexual perversion, marked by love of cruelty and the infliction of pain.

Sadler of Sadler's Wells. The well, near Islington, was accepted as of medicinal value for many centuries. It once belonged to the monks of Clerkenwell.

In the reign of Charles II the house and grounds were in the hands of a surveyor of the highway, named Sadler. The work of his men led to the rediscovery of the well under a stone arch in 1683.

Sadler exploited the occasion by commissioning "T. G., Doctor of Physick," to write *A True and Exact Account of Sadler's Well: or, the New Mineral Waters lately found at Islington.* Therein the virtues of the waters were compared favourably with those of the fashionable Tunbridge Wells.

The enterprising publicity succeeded and Sadler built on the site a "music house" which was highly successful for several years.

Though, during several periods, the Wells had a distinguished theatrical record, there were other less cultural pages in its history. A handbill of 1825, inviting patrons to special Christmas festivities, offers "an amaz-ing quantum of amusement," culminating in the presentation of the "Living Leek, which being served up the last thing before supper, will constitute a most excellent Christmas carminative, preventing the effects of night air on the crowds who will adorn this darling little edifice."

Sadler's Wells to-day

Another advertisement headed "SERIOUS NOTICE, IN PERFECT CONFIDENCE," offers the presentation of "*Enchanted Girdles: or Winki the Witch, and the Ladies of Samarcand,*" also "a most whimsical burletta, which sends people home perfectly exhausted from uninterrupted risibility."

So also, nowadays, would the footnote advertising wine from the Wells at "three shillings and sixpence a full quart."

The Good Samaritan. The use of the word Samaritan to describe a philanthropist or disinterested well-doer derives from the parable of the Good Samaritan, unnamed in the Bible narrative, who assisted the man attacked by robbers on his way to Jericho from Jerusalem.

It was told by Christ in answer to the lawyer's question, "Who is my neighbour?" and is found in *Luke x. 30–7.*

Sir Samuel Browne of the Sam Browne. The distinctive Officers' belt with its cross strap known as the Sam Browne was invented by General Sir Sam Browne, V.C., while on service in India in 1852. He commanded the 2nd Punjab Cavalry. The inventor's son, Brigadier-General S. Browne, wore an identical belt when he received his commission in 1882 and retained it through his long military service.

John Montagu of Sandwich. The word is thought to derive from John Montagu, the fourth Earl of Sandwich (1718–92), who once spent twenty-four hours at the gaming table subsisting only on thick slices of meat placed between slices of toast. Other accounts place the origin of the sandwich during a long day's hunting by the Earl.

He had a notorious reputation in politics and from a pointed reference in Gay's *The Beggar's Opera*, he was generally known as "Jimmy Twitcher."

The Sandwich Islands were named after him (he was at one time First Lord of the Admiralty) by James Cook.

Sandwiches, as such, were known even in Roman times.

St. Nicholas of Santa Claus. St. Nicholas, thought to have been bishop in Myra, Asia Minor, in A.D. 300, was the patron saint of Russia, Aberdeen, children, scholars, pawnbrokers, thieves, etc. Various legends associate the bishop's special services to the classes of people who enjoy his patronage.

The link with pawnbrokers, for instance, is based on a story of the bishop's turning the familiar three brass balls into bags of gold to save the daughters of a poor but honest man from earning their living in dubious ways.

His festival day was December 6, and it was originally the custom for someone to dress up as the bishop and to make the familiar distribution of toys to young friends.

A poor scholar is frequently referred to in literature as a Nicholas clerk, from the bishop's patronage of scholars, and the name is used in *I Henry IV* for a highwayman.

Sardanapalus of Sardanapian. Sardanapian, notorious for effeminate luxury, originated in Sardanapalus, a notorious king of Assyria, 7th century B.C., whose mode of living was a byword. He was also known as Asurbanipal and is mentioned by the name of Osnappa, in *Ezra iv. 10*, as "great and noble."

Byron, in *Sardanapalus* (1821), says:

*And femininely meaneth furiously,
Because all passions in excess are female.*

He makes him a voluptuous tyrant whose effeminate excesses led Arbaces, the Mede, to conspire against him. He was surprised in his luxury by the invaders but was spurred by his favourite concubine, Myrra, to heroic resistance at the head of his army. After a long siege at Nineveh he sacrificed himself on a funeral pyre and Myrra threw herself into its flames and perished with him.

Saturn of Saturnine. Saturnine: of a sluggish, gloomy temperament; grave, phlegmatic, dull.

Saturn was the Roman diety identified with the Greek Kronos. He was associated with agriculture and is said to have devoured all his children except air, water and the grave, which are indestructible. He was ruler in a golden age, undisturbed by trouble and need.

The Roman festival of Saturnalia, held in December, was a time of unrestrained licence, during which all normal business and civic processes ceased.

The god was associated with lead, a dull metal, and astrologers averred that those born under the planet Saturn were miserable wranglers and pessimistic unforgiving enemies.

Pope refers to the association in *The Dunciad, iv. 13.*

The name is seen again in our Saturday.

Despite the god's association with agriculture and the general public's suspicion, all farmers are not born under this baleful planet.

Saturn is generally distinguished in art by a pruning knife and club.

Antoine Joseph Sax of the Saxophone. Antoine Joseph Sax, known as Adolphe Sax, was born in Dinant, Belgium, in 1814. He was one of the eleven children of Charles Joseph Sax, a distinguished musical instrument and cabinet maker.

Adolphe, who was trained in his father's works, showed an early aptitude for music and an unusual craftsmanship. He invented a series of brass instruments giving a new tone

A Saxophone

quality, and these he called saxophones. This was about 1840 and the name and invention were registered six years later. They had already been used by French army bands.

Sax had moved to Paris, where he enjoyed the support of leading musicians, including Berlioz.

He received many awards for his instruments, which included a saxhorn and a saxo-tromba, but experienced periods of acute financial difficulty.

He died in 1894.

Scylla and Charybdis. Between Scylla and Charybdis; between equal difficulties, between the devil and the deep sea.

A sea monster dwelt on the rock Scylla, opposite Charybdis, a whirlpool on the Italian side of the Straits of Messina. Homer says that Scylla had twelve feet and six heads, each armed with ferocious teeth, and that she barked like a dog.

Charybdis, according to the Homeric account, dwelt under a huge fig tree on the rock and three times a day he swallowed the waters of the sea and threw them up again.

Thus when I shun Scylla, your father, I fall into Charybdis, your mother.
Merchant of Venice, iii. 5.

Horace Walpole of Serendipity. Serendipity, that wholly delightful word for the wholly delightful faculty of making pleasing and unexpected discoveries by accident, was coined by Horace Walpole, fourth Earl of Orford (1717–97).

He claimed that he derived it from the title of a fairy story, *The Three Princes of Serendip*, whose heroes possessed the facility for making happily unexpected discoveries. Serendip is the ancient name for Ceylon.

He was the youngest son of Robert Walpole, the great statesman. He made the grand tour and visited France and Italy in company with the poet, Gray. It was from Walpole's printing press that Gray's *Odes* were published.

Walpole's political career is overshadowed by his reputation as one of the great social historians of the 18th century. He was a brilliant letter-writer and published a number of antiquarian works. He lived at Strawberry Hill, Twickenham, which housed a museum and his printing press.

He had an intense interest in people as distinct from position. Thus he wrote, in his *Letters*: "I do not love great folks till they have pulled off their buskins and put on their slippers, because I do not care sixpence for what they would be thought, but for what they are." And again: "I have always rather tried to escape the acquaintance and conversation of authors. An author talking of his own works, or censuring those of others, is to me a dose of ipecacuana."

The Seven Wonders of the World.

Although not essentially personal, this much-needed reference demands inclusion in a literary reference book.

While some places are disputed by different authorities, the generally accepted list is:

The Pyramids of Egypt.
The Hanging Gardens of Babylon.
The Tomb of Mausolus.
The Temple of Diana at Ephesus.
The Colossus of Rhodes.
Jupiter's statue by Phidias at Olympia.
The Pharos (450-feet lighthouse) of Alexandria, built by Ptolemy Philadelphus.

The Seven Wonders of the Middle Ages are generally listed as the Coliseum, the Catacombs, the Great Wall of China, the Leaning Tower of Pisa, the Porcelain Tower of Nanking, the Mosque of St. Sophia, Constantinople, and Stonehenge.

Lord Shaftesbury of the Shaftesbury Homes and Shaftesbury Avenue.

One of the most noted names synonymous with the rescuing and care of children is that of the 7th Earl of Shaftesbury, Anthony Ashley Cooper (1801–85).

In 1843, William Williams, a solicitor's clerk, was a passenger in a London train bound for the West Country. He investigated a commotion in the next compartment and found a gang of handcuffed boys on their way to be transported to a convict settlement. He determined to save others from a similar fate and his efforts resulted in the forming of a Ragged School in a hay-loft, over a cow-shed in Streatham Street, St. Giles. The work flourished and that great philanthropist, the 7th Earl of Shaftesbury, became the Society's first President.

One of his first acts was to invite 300 half-starved youths to supper, when he requested those who would like to be trained for the sea to put up their hands. They all put up both hands and as a result the Earl chartered the frigate *Chichester* to be transformed into a training-ship. That was in 1866. Eight years after it became necessary to fit out another ship on similar lines—the famous *Arethusa*.

Farms, homes, schools and industrial and technical training centres followed naturally, in response to revealed demands.

The Earl, who entered Parliament as a Conservative, took office under Wellington and was a Lord of the Admiralty under Peel. His life work was marked by such social milestones as the Mines and Collieries Act, 1842, which excluded women and boys under thirteen from working in the mines; the Better Treatment of Lunatics Act, 1845, and several factory acts and regulations. He was intimately and actively associated with numerous religious and benevolent movements. He was the close friend and adviser of Queen Victoria and Prince Albert.

Shaftesbury is commemorated by the world-famous statue of Eros in Piccadilly Circus. It was designed by Alfred Gilbert, R.A., executed uncommonly in aluminium, and erected in 1893.

Thomas Sheraton of Sheraton furniture.

Thomas Sheraton, the distinguished furniture designer, was born at Stockton-on-Tees, in 1751, and died in 1806. He can fairly be termed one of the first professional furniture designers. He describes himself as a cabinet-maker, but there is no substantial evidence to show that he was actively engaged in making or selling furniture. Experts are also undecided as to whether he originated the style associated with his name, or whether his published designs were merely a reflection of current styles and taste. For Sheraton was essentially a draughtsman intent upon teaching cabinet-makers and upholsterers how to draw correctly and in perspective.

He lived in humble surroundings, often precariously, and had no part in the social life with which a number of famous names associated with furniture were actively linked.

Sheraton's *The Cabinet Maker and Upholsterer's Drawing Book*, published in 1781, was chiefly devoted to drawing theory and practice and dismissing rococo elaborations and eastern extravagances.

The legs of Sheraton furniture are straight, square wrought and tapered and turned. They are slender to the point of suggested fragility. He was ingenious in construction and favoured many-purpose pieces. In general his curves are of geometric derivation. In beds he recognized fancifulness, which "seems most peculiar to the taste of females." He insisted upon the importance of comfort and convenience in furniture design.

Sheraton published *A Cabinet Dictionary* in 1803, but did not live to complete his *Cabinet Maker's Encyclopædia*, of which only one volume appeared before his death in London. He wrote also on religious subjects.

Sir Arthur Conan Doyle of Sherlock Holmes.

Sherlock Holmes is the title instinctively given to the amateur investigator or detective.

Its origin, one of the classic figures in detective fiction, is the supreme creation of Sir Arthur Conan Doyle (1859–1930).

Holmes, who appears in many of the author's works, was in part suggested by the character of Dr. Joseph Bell, a distinguished Edinburgh Professor of Medicine under whom the author studied.

Holmes was remarkable not only for his powers of deduction but for the eccentricities of his manners and dress. He has been depicted on stage and screen. Scarcely less famous are his assistant and foil, Dr. Watson, and the famous Baker Street consulting rooms.

Conan Doyle, whose first book appeared while he was practising as a doctor at Southsea, served in the medical forces in the field during the Boer War.

The Sherlock Holmes stories first appeared in *The Strand Magazine*.

Doyle wrote several non-detective novels, plays (in one of which, *The Story of Waterloo* (1894), Irving appeared), and several war histories. *Rodney Stone* (a boxing novel), *The White Company* and *The Fortunes of Nigel* are also famous.

In his later years Conan Doyle became a leading spiritualist and writer and lecturer on the subject.

Shylock.

This synonym for a hard-hearted money-lender, or, in fact, for anyone grasping in financial affairs, derives from the rich Jew in Shakespeare's *The Merchant of Venice*, "a stony adversary, an inhuman wretch uncapable of pity, void and empty from any dram of mercy."

He lends three thousand ducats to Antonio, as an enemy, and counts on the opportunity to get even with a generous Christian merchant who has often reviled Shylock for his covetous methods.

The bond is signed with the proviso that if it is not honoured, Shylock shall claim "in merry sport . . . a pound of your fair flesh, to be cut off and taken in what part of your body pleaseth me."

At the trial of this infamous action, before the Duke of Venice, Portia appears (in the guise of a counsellor and under the name of the young doctor Balthasar) to plead Antonio's cause in the absence of the learned Bellario.

The scales are produced, the knife is sharpened and Shylock prepares to take his pound of flesh from the breast of Antonio.

The Jew resists appeals for clemency with, "I swear there is no power in the tongue of man to alter me." He brushes aside Portia's appeal that he should have "some surgeon by, lest he bleed to death."

"It is not in the bond," he cries, eager for the kill and praising the "wise and upright judge,"

Then the masquerading Portia plays her last and triumphant card against the exulting Shylock:

Tarry a little: there is something else.
This bond doth give thee here no jot of blood;
The words expressly are "a pound of flesh":
Then take thy bond, take thou thy pound of flesh;
But, in the cutting it, if thou dost shed
One drop of Christian blood, thy lands and goods
Are, by the laws of Venice, confiscate
Unto the state of Venice.

Shylock counters with "pay the bond thrice, and let the Christian go," but Portia insists upon the operation, and if the pound of flesh taken differs from the exact amount by the "twentieth part of one poor scruple" or the scale turn "in the estimation of a hair," Shylock "shall die and all his goods be confiscate."

Chang and Eng of "Siamese Twins."
Twins, physically joined, are occasionally born to-day, but the phenomenon was called "Siamese twins" because of Chang and Eng.

They were discovered in Mekong, near Bangkok, Siam, in 1829. They were then eighteen and their parents were thought to have been a Chinese father and a half-Chinese mother.

They were joined by a flexible band between the breast-bones.

A visiting sea captain exploited the twins on a world tour exhibition which included inspection by leading medical authorities in the countries visited. The twins do not appear to have benefited financially by the tour as the organizer decamped with the proceeds.

The twins, who at one time adopted the name of Chang-Eng Bunker, after a New York benefactress, led normal lives and played games. They suffered the usual childish ailments.

The great Barnum exhibited them and they accumulated a substantial fortune. They farmed a large property.

They had several suitors and eventually married two sisters, Adelaide and Sarah Ann Yeats. The wedding day was April 1, 1843, and the grooms were already U.S. citizens by a special Act. Between them they had twenty-two children, all intelligent and normal physically, with the exception of two deaf mutes.

At the age of sixty-three, Chang died of what the *post mortem* revealed was a clot on the brain. No physical cause could be diagnosed for the death of Eng, who expired two hours later.

A number of Siamese twins have lived normal and long lives and there have been several instances of Siamese twins being separated successfully, either at birth or later from their living or dead partner.

Sibyl, the seductive fortune-teller.
The Sibyls, in classical legend, were the mouthpieces of the gods who gave forth the divine utterances at the oracles or shrines. The name is now applied to any female fortune-teller.

The Sibyls were named in many places and were consulted before great undertakings. They are mentioned frequently in contemporary literature.

The Sibylline Books were a collection of oracles of supernatural origin which were consulted by the Roman senate in times of grave emergency. There were reputed to be nine originally and they were offered for sale to Tarquin by Amalthea, the Sibyl. She burnt three of the books on Tarquin's refusal and offered the remaining six at the same price.

She was again refused and subsequently burnt another three of the books and secured her first price for the balance. The legend gives its particular significance to the term "a sibylline bargain."

Silenus, the rollicking, bloated old drunkard. Silenus was the drunken companion of Dionysus (Bacchus) in Greek mythology. He was the son of Pan and an inveterate, lazy wanton. He was bald-headed and jovial, with a taste for music. The old satyr is said to have brought up Dionysus and to have become his constant companion.

Silenus is used as the symbol of elderly lasciviousness and he is often depicted as bald, squat-nosed, pot-bellied and riding upon an ass in the company of Dionysus. Satyrs often support his drunken frame.

Within his car, aloft, young Bacchus stood . . .
And near him rode Silenus on his ass.
Keats, *Endymion.*

Etienne de Silhouette of Silhouette. A silhouette is a profile or shadow-outline filled in with a dark colour. Such pictures were frequently cut in black paper and the best examples reveal a remarkable delicacy and skill.

A Silhouette

The name is derived from Etienne de Silhouette (1708–67), French author and politician. He was French Minister of Finance for a few months in 1759 and his short régime was marked by parsimony and some capricious reforms. His name became a byword for anything plain and cheap. It was *à la Silhouette*. Some writers attribute the phrase to the brevity of his tenure of office and others credit him with the hobby of shadowgraphy and claim that his chateau at Bry-sur-Marne was decorated with many examples of this art.

Silvanus of Silvan. Silvanus, in Roman mythology, was akin to Pan. He was a god of the forest, wherein he dwelt, protecting the trees and woodland dwellers. Like Pan, he played tricks upon human visitors to the forests. He watched over boundaries and property and was regarded as the giver of fruitfulness in gardens and orchards. Their first fruits were offered to him.

Silvanus is generally depicted as an old man of rustic appearance, frequently distinguished by a pruning knife.

Susannah Centlivre of Simon Pure, the real or genuine person or article. The name Simon Pure is taken from a character in Susannah Centlivre's comedy, *A Bold Stroke For A Wife* (1718).

In the play Colonel Fainall, in his attempts to win the consent of the Quaker guardian of his chosen bride, impersonates Simon Pure, "a quaking preacher."

The ruse succeeds, but "the real Simon Pure" immediately appears. The name became a proverbial expression.

Susannah Centlivre (1667–1723) married, as her third husband, Joseph Centlivre, cook to Queen Anne. She was actress as well as dramatist. Garrick made a marked success in her comedy *The Wonder! A Woman Keeps a Secret* (1714). She had a marked sense of theatre, but some of her plays were regarded as immoral.

Simon of Simony. Simony, the buying or selling of ecclesiastical preferment, takes its name from Simon, the sorcerer, who is mentioned in *Acts viii. 9–18*.

He is described as bewitching the people of Samaria, and "giving out that himself was some great one." Simon convinced the people, who attributed to him the great power of God. However, he suffered himself to be baptized by Philip, and continued with him, wondering at the miracles and signs which were done.

When Peter and John were sent to Samaria and laid their hands upon the people, Simon offered them money, saying, "Give me also this power, that on whomsoever I lay hands, he may receive the Holy Ghost. But Peter said unto him, Thy money perish with thee, because thou hast thought that the gift of God may be purchased with money. Thou hast neither part nor lot in this matter: for thy heart is not right in the sight of God. Repent therefore of this thy wickedness, and pray God, if perhaps the thought of thine heart may be forgiven thee. For I perceive that thou art in the gall of bitterness, and in the bond of iniquity.

"Then answered Simon, and said, Pray ye to the Lord for me, that none of these things which ye have spoken come upon me" (*verses 18–24*).

Sisyphus of Sisyphean labour. A Sisyphean task is an endless, heartbreaking toil.

The legendary King of Corinth was a criminal. The crimes attributed to him are varied but in company with others, such as Tantalus, Ixion and the Danaids, his punishment in the infernal regions gave scope for the imagination of the poets.

Sisyphus had to roll a huge stone up a high mountain, but on reaching the top it always rolled down again and Sisyphus's task began anew. The allusion may have been to the sun's daily climbing of the heavens.

(See *Tantalus of Tantalize.*)

Sir Hans Sloane of Sloane Square. The British physician and collector, Hans Sloane, was born in County Down, Ireland, in 1660. He was to be the first medical practitioner to receive an hereditary title when he was created a baronet in 1716.

He was of Scots descent and studied medicine in London and on the Continent. He returned from abroad with a valuable collection of plants and curios. He indulged his interest in natural history when he went to Jamaica as physician to the Duke of Albemarle, who died on arrival. Sloane published elaborate catalogues of his collections.

He became secretary to the Royal Society, and was afterwards President. He was for many years president of the College of Physicians, held the office of Physician-General to the Army and was chief physician to George III.

He amassed considerable wealth and acquired a manor at Chelsea and founded there the Botanical Gardens. His collection of books and manuscripts, etc., was acquired by the nation.

Sloane suffered throughout his life from a consumptive tendency, which had been sufficiently acute to interrupt his education for several years. He kept the disease at bay by a strictly disciplined regimen, but he was noted for a generous hospitality which he could not completely share. His manor was the meeting place of royalty and of distinguished men and women from many countries. He died at the age of ninety-three in 1753.

Hans Place, Chelsea, also perpetuates his name.

Sir John Soane of Soane's Museum. Sir John Soane (1753–1837) was born at Whitchurch, near Reading, of humble parentage. He quickly gained distinction as an architect and won many awards, including a travelling scholarship to Italy.

He married a rich woman and his successful practice enabled him to indulge his taste for the arts.

At his home in Lincoln's Inn Fields, London, he gathered a remarkable collection of pictures, manuscripts and antiquities.

Soane, who was elected R.A. in 1802, was architect to the Bank of England and professor of architecture to the Royal Academy.

Two years before his death he bequeathed his collection to the nation with an endowment for its upkeep. He expressed considerable impatience at the tardy process of the acceptance of the offer.

The Museum, which is still housed in Lincoln's Inn Fields, includes some notable originals by Hogarth.

Bishop Wilberforce of Soapy Sam. The expression "Soapy Sam" to describe an unctuous, persuasive hypocrite derives, apparently unfairly, from Dr. Samuel Wilberforce (1805-73).

He was third son of the great philanthropist and slave emancipator, William Wilberforce.

Samuel was made Bishop of Oxford in 1845 and was translated to Winchester in 1869. He is said to have gained the nickname through an unctuous manner of speaking in his early years. It appears to have been an unfair sobriquet as Carlyle and Froude speak well of the bishop's learning, wit and religious sincerity.

One story ascribes the expression to the fact that the bishop's and the adjoining stall (that of the Principal of Cuddesdon) bore the initials S.O.A.P., representing *S*amuel *O*xon and *A*lfred *P*ort.

The bishop himself is reputed to have said that the allusion arose because he was often in hot water and came out with clean hands.

G. K. Chesterton, incidentally, remarks that the merit of being constantly in hot water is that it keeps one's hands clean.

Socrates of Socratic. Socratic: of, like or pertaining to Socrates; pose of ignorance assumed to lure others into a display of supposed knowledge.

Socrates (469-399 B.C.), the great Greek philosopher, devoted himself to the investigation of virtue and the makings of a good citizen. He conversed with all, especially those of reputed wisdom, many of whom he refuted.

He thus made enemies and on a charge of impiety was sentenced to death by a narrow majority of his judges. He was required to drink hemlock.

Socrates left no philosophic writings, but is known chiefly through the *Dialogues* of Plato. The characteristic of the Socratic method is to ask carefully framed questions in order to reach the conclusion the questioner intended.

Solomon, the personification of wisdom. Solomon, the great King of Israel from 1015 to 977 B.C., was David's successor and his second son by Bathsheba, whom David obtained by setting her husband, Uriah the Hittite, "in the forefront of the hottest battle" (*2 Sam. xi. 15*).

Solomon was noted alike for his magnificence and his fabulous wisdom. His was the golden age of Israel; the splendour of his court and its intellectual achievement were unrivalled, though the people were oppressed by vast schemes.

The Queen of Sheba said to him, "It was a true report that I heard in mine own land of thine acts, and of thy wisdom. Howbeit I believed not the words, until I came, and mine eyes had seen it: and, behold, the half was not told me: thy wisdom and prosperity exceedeth the fame which I heard" (*1 Kings x. 6-7*).

James the First was called "The English Solomon."

Solon, the wise lawgiver or sage. Solon, the great lawgiver of ancient Greece, was one of the Seven Sages. The motto of Solon of Athens was "Know thyself." The other six were

Chilo of Sparta, Thales of Miletus, Bias of Priene, Cleobulus of Lindos, Pittacus of Mitylene and Periander of Corinth.

Solon, who had a wide experience of commerce, was elected archon in 594 B.C. and carried out vast legal, administrative and social reforms and developments.

There are frequent references in literature to Solon's pre-eminence as a lawgiver, notably in Browning's *The Ring and the Book*.

Voltaire was called "The Solon of Parnassus" by Boileau.

The Duke of Somerset of Somerset House.

The original Somerset House was the Palace of Edward Seymour, Duke of Somerset (1506(?)–52), protector of England.

At Somerset's execution the Palace reverted to the Crown. It was extended and improved by Inigo Jones and was used as a palace by several queens.

Somerset House to-day

The present Somerset House, on the same Strand–Thames Embankment site near Charing Cross, was designed towards the end of the 18th century by Sir William Chambers to replace the demolished palace.

It houses many official offices but is chiefly linked in the public's mind with the principal Probate Registry and the Registrar-General of Births, Marriages and Deaths.

Joanna Southcott of Joanna Southcott's Box.

Joanna Southcott (1750–1814) was a religious fanatic born in Devonshire of humble farming stock. She appears to have been in domestic service.

In middle life, after a Methodist background, she announced that she had prophetic gifts and supernatural powers. She identified herself with the woman mentioned in *Rev. xii. 1–5* —"a woman arrayed with the sun, and the moon under her feet, and upon her head a crown of twelve stars . . . and she was delivered of a son, a man child, who is to rule all the nations with a rod of iron."

She wrote prophecies in crude rhyme and obtained a considerable following, the members of which were "sealed" at a remunerative fee.

When in her sixties, Joanna Southcott announced that she would fulfil the visions revealed to St. John and bring forth a son miraculously.

She announced the delivery of Shiloh on October 19, 1814, and some accounts say that she suffered from a disease which gave her the appearance of pregnancy and added to the excitement of the faithful. Fantastic preparations were made for the birth of the messiah and when the child failed to appear it was announced that the prophetess was in a trance.

When she died, in 1814, of a brain disease, she left a box which she directed be opened at a time of national crisis in the presence of all the bishops.

It was opened in 1928 in the presence of a bishop and revealed nothing.

The term "Joanna Southcott's Box" is still in frequent use to describe a promising project which eventually proves worthless.

The followers of the prophetess were said to number several hundreds of thousands and they persisted for years, as did her jumbled religious writings, for the propagation of which a disciple left a large sum of money.

Joanna was buried, after a post-mortem and under a fictitious name, in the burial ground attached to St. John's Wood Chapel, London.

Earl Spencer of Spencer.

The name spencer, applied to a close-fitting bodice and formerly to an outer short coat worn by men and women, was named after the second Earl Spencer (1758–1834), who popularized the garment at a time when most outer coats were tailed.

Frederick Robert Spofforth, the demon bowler.

Prodigious fast bowlers may come and go but new applicants for inclusion are always a new "Spofforth," from F. R. Spofforth (1853–1926). This great Australian cricketer was born in Sydney, New South Wales, and played with each of the first five Australian teams that toured England from 1878.

At Lord's in that year he took ten wickets for twenty runs and several times repeated the feat in first-class matches.

His prodigious speed, his twirling arms and menacing approach, coupled with his remarkable control of delivery, made Spofforth an unforgettable cricket giant, the first and in a sense only "Demon bowler."

He settled in this country and died at Ditton.

The Rev. W. A. Spooner of Spoonerisms.

The transposition of letters or sounds in a word or sentence is technically known as metathesis. The word Spoonerism derives from the Rev. W. A. Spooner, Warden of New College, Oxford, who died in 1930.

While the habit naturally tempted frequent imitators, Spooner himself was responsible for many of the best examples, which are said to include:

Half-warmed fish, for half-formed wish.
The Lord is a shoving Leopard.
Kingkering Kongs their titles take.
The cat popped on its drawers.
You are occupewing my pie.
I was sewn into this sheet.

Zeno of Stoic and Stoical.

Zeno, the Greek philosopher, founded the Stoic school about 308 B.C. It was so called because Zeno gave his lectures in the Stoa Poikile, the "Painted Porch" of Athens. He was born to a merchant career but, losing all in a shipwreck, devoted himself to philosophy.

In contrast with the teaching of Epicurus, the Stoics held that virtue was the supreme good, that passions and appetites should be rigorously subdued and pain endured without complaint, as of no account.

Samuel Butler, in *Hudibras*, refers to

The ancient Stoics in their porch
With fierce dispute maintain their church,
Beat out their brains in fight and study
To prove that virtue is a body.

Zeno lived to a great age and his disciples revealed a high level of integrity and nobility.

Antonio Stradivari of Stradivarius.

The supreme violin-maker was born at Cremona, Italy, in 1644. He was a pupil of Nicolas Amati but soon developed his own designs and produced them with a craftsmanship that has never been surpassed. The secrets of his skill and the recipes of his varnishes have never been revealed. His sons assisted him and the family also produced some notable violas and 'cellos.

Stradivari died in 1737. He is the subject of a poem by George Eliot.

Jack Straw of Jack Straw's Castle.

Straw was the leader of a party of Essex insurgents in the Peasants' Rising in 1381. There have been several inns named after him, the most notable of which is Jack Straw's Castle on Hampstead Heath, but there does not appear to be any historical connection between Straw and the inns.

Emmanuel Swedenborg of Swedenborgian.

Emmanuel

Swedenborg (1688–1772) was born at Stockholm, the eldest son of Jesper Swedberg, Bishop of Skara, Sweden.

Swedenborg was educated at Upsala and Oxford. His primary interest was philosophy, but at twenty-eight, on his return to Sweden, he was appointed assessor of the Royal College of Mines by Charles XII.

After thirty years of scientific research, invention and writing he turned to theology. He wrote also on mathematical, astronomical and marine subjects.

In 1719 the family was ennobled by Queen Ulrica Eleonora, with the name of Swedenborg.

Swedenborg was a mystic and founder of the New Jerusalem Church. He led a simple, abstemious life and received the highest recognition. He never married. He successfully withstood occasional orthodox religious opposition to his doctrines.

His chief works are *An Introduction to the Philosophy of the Infinite, and the Final Cause of Creation* (1734), *The Worship and Love of God* (1745), and *Prodromus Principiorum.*

True Christian Religion embodies the theology of The New Church.

Swedenborg, a man of brilliant and diverse intellectual gifts, was concerned primarily with a knowledge of the soul and the reality of the spirit world, of which the visible world was a faint reflection.

He died in London in his eighty-fifth year.

St. Swithin, the weather forecaster. Popular legend claims that if it rains on St. Swithin's Day, July 15, it rains for forty days thereafter. If the day is fine a fair spell of similar length is assured.

St. Swithin was a 9th-century bishop of Winchester. He desired to be buried in the Minster grounds. At his canonization, a hundred years after his death, the monks sought to honour the bishop by transferring his body to the Choir. The saint's day was chosen for the ceremony, but operations were delayed by consistent rain for forty days. The monks, sensing some supernatural opposition, abandoned the project.

There are similar traditions associated with different saints in several continental countries.

The Sybarites of Sybaritic. The Sybarites were inhabitants of the ancient Greek colony of Sybaris, in Southern Italy, on the Gulf of Tarentum. They flourished in the 7th century B.C., but in 500 B.C. were overrun by the rival colonists of Crotonia.

A legend has it that the Sybarites taught their horses to dance to the pipes and this local knowledge was exploited by the invading Crotonians who advanced playing pipes and benefited by the resulting confusion when the enemy's horses suitably responded.

The fabulous luxury and voluptuousness of the Sybarite colony was known throughout the ancient world. One of them is said to have complained of a sleepless night and discovered a rose petal doubled under him.

The name became synonymous with excessive luxury and sensuousness and to some extent with effeminacy and wantonness.

Tam-O'-Shanter of the hat. The tam-o'-shanter, a round woollen or cloth cap, close fitting at the brow, but large and full above, is taken from Burns's character in the poem of that name: the hat, whose name is often shortened to "tammy," is worn by the poet himself in some representations.

The poem, to which Burns gives the sub-title "A Tale," was written while walking on the banks of the Nith. He regarded it as his "standard performance in the poetical line."

The origin of the character was Douglas Grahame, who farmed Shanter on the Carrick shore.

The story presents Tam o'Shanter, well primed and "holding fast his guid blue bonnet," passing the Kirk of Alloway on his grey mare, Meg.

He sees the Kirk lighted and inhabited by witches and warlocks dancing to the pipes of the devil "in shape o' beast."

Attracted by the antics of one "winsome wench," Tam o'Shanter calls out, "Weel done, Cutty-sark!" And in an instant all was dark "and scarcely had he Maggie rallied, When out the hellish legion, sallied."

Tam escapes from the swarm of witches over the bridge beyond their power but the mare's tail is secured by Cutty-sark while it is still within her domain.

A cutty sark is a short chemise.

Tantalus of Tantalize. Tantalus, in Greek mythology, was a Lydian King who, having tested his friendship with the gods to the point of presumption, was condemned to everlasting torment in the infernal regions.

He was required to expiate his sins by suffering the torments of continual hunger and thirst. Just out of reach above his head, luscious fruits grew.

The waters of the river of Hades, in which he stood up to his neck, receded when he stooped to drink.

In addition to the verb tantalize, the god's name is appropriately given to a spirit stand in which the decanters are visible but not to be handled unless the thirsty one has the key.

(See *Sisyphus of Sisyphean labour.*)

St. Anthony of the Tantony Pig. The smallest pig of a litter is called a Tantony pig from St. Anthony, patron saint of swineherds. The Tantony pig is said to follow its owner anywhere.

St. Anthony, not to be confused with St. Anthony of Padua, was the founder of a 4th-century fraternity of desert ascetics. His day is January 17. He is frequently depicted in art with an accompanying pig, often with a bell at its neck. In consequence the term "Tantony" is often applied to a small church bell or any handbell.

The term "St. Anthony's pig" has also been used in literature to describe a hanger-on or time-server.

Erysipelas was once known as "St. Anthony's fire" from the belief that intercession to this saint was particularly efficacious in the cure of the disease.

Mark Tapley, the invincibly cheery person. Tapley is servant at "The Dragon Inn" in Dickens' *Martin Chuzzlewit* (1843–4).

Tapley leaves the inn to find a post in which his indomitable cheerfulness and good humour will find full scope.

He accompanies Martin to America in search of fortune. Tapley eventually marries the hostess of "The Dragon."

Sir Henry Tate of the Tate Gallery. Henry Tate, born 1819 at

Chorley, Lancashire, was created first baronet in 1898. He was a successful sugar broker in Liverpool, moving to London about 1874. He was an expert art collector and philanthropist, giving large sums to Liverpool University and local hospitals. He also gave four public libraries to Lambeth.

Tate offered £80,000 and a collection of pictures to the nation, and the Trustees of the National Gallery

The Tate Gallery

built the Tate Gallery in Millbank, on the site of the old prison.

It was opened with a collection including sixty-five pictures given by Tate, on July 21, 1897. This collection, offered originally to the National Gallery, was the subject of such wrangling and delay that the contemporary press said that never had a public benefaction been more criticized, scorned and rejected.

Tate died two years later in Streatham.

The Gallery was severely damaged during the Blitz in 1941.

Richard Tattersall of Tattersall's. The famous London horse mart was founded in 1766 by Richard Tattersall (1724–95). He was a native of Hurstwood, Lancashire, but as a young man entered the service of the second Duke of Kingston as stud groom. Later he became an auctioneer.

In 1766 he took a ninety-nine year lease from Lord Grosvenor of premises in Hyde Park Corner, then on the edge of London, and Tattersall's became the centre of interest in the sales of racing and other horses.

Three years later Tattersall bought the famous racehorse "Highflyer" for £2,500, naming his house near Ely, Highflyer Hall. There he was on intimate terms with the Prince of Wales, who visited him from Newmarket and in fact shared, disastrously, in "Old Tatt's" newspaper ownership.

Tattersall's removed to Knightsbridge Green in 1867.

The original Subscription Rooms, reserved for members of the Jockey Club, developed into Tattersall's Committee and the Ring which are, however, unconnected with the horse mart. The Committee is concerned unofficially, but with great power, in the safeguarding of the interests of all occupied with racing in any capacity.

Tattersall's Ring is the name given to the chief betting enclosure on any racecourse under recognized rules. Sales now take place at Doncaster and Newmarket.

The Ring enjoys special immunities by reason of a House of Lords' decision that it is not "a place" within the meaning of the controlling Betting Act of 1853.

St. Audrey of Tawdry. A tawdry object, showy, gaudy, but worthless, derives from St. Audrey's Fair, held annually in the isle of Ely. Cheap, "Brummagem" jewellery was sold and a showy local product known as "St. Audrey's lace."

The name Audrey is a corruption of Etheldrida, 7th century, a Saxon princess, who escaped marriage by taking refuge in a monastery and afterwards founded the monastery which became the Cathedral of Ely.

Shakespeare mentions "tawdry lace and a pair of sweet gloves" in *Winter's Tale, iv. 4.*

Terminus of Terminus. Terminus was one of the field dieties, linked with Pan and Silvanus. His particular protection was concerned with boundaries and landmarks.

King Numa, in order to impress the sanctity of property and boundaries, instituted the festival of Terminalia, held annually on February 23. The owners of land decorated the boundary stones with garlands and offerings were made to the god.

There was a shrine to Terminus in the temple of Minerva.

The great temple of Jupiter is said to contain a statue of Terminus because, when the pressure on space required the removal of several shrines, Terminus himself refused its exclusion. Most of the gods whose removal was planned expressed by means of auguries their willingness to bow to the dictates of the supreme Jupiter.

Themis, one personifying law and justice. In Greek mythology Themis was the second goddess-wife of Zeus. She was one of the Titans and by her Zeus was the father of the Horæ (the Seasons) and the Mœræ (the Fates).

The Horæ were generally represented as three in number, Eunomia, Dice and Irene. The three Mœræ were Clotho (spinner), Lachesis (allocator) and Atropos (inevitable).

Themis, daughter of Uranus and Gaea, symbolizes the goddess of law and order among all things, immortal and mortal. She is also associated with all national and civic assemblies, as typifying law and order. Hospitality also received her special interest.

Themis was often depicted as holding a balance in one hand and a palm branch in the other—the obvious inspiration of many figures that are now called "Justice."

The Doubting Thomas. The allusion is to St. Thomas, the apostle. He expressed doubts recorded in *John xiv. 5*—"How know we the way?" and in *John xx. 25* is his answer after the Resurrection when the other disciples claimed that they had seen the Lord. Thomas said, "Except I shall see in His hands the print of the nails, and put my finger°into the print of the nails, and put my hand into His side, I will not believe."

Eight days later, when Thomas was rebuked by Christ for unbelief and given proof (*John xx. 27*), Thomas replied, "My Lord and my God."

St. Thomas Aquinas of Thomism. St. Thomas Aquinas, "The Angelic Doctor," was a 13th-century Italian of noble birth who became a Dominican monk. He became leader of a famous School among whom he was known as "the dumb ox" on account of his silence at study. His voluminous writings include the notable *Summa Theologiæ*. His controversies with Duns Scotus were an outstanding feature of the scholastic and theological world of his day.

St. Thomas was called by Pope Pius V "the Fifth Doctor of the Church." His theological doctrine, which was given the name Thomism, included the maintenance of the doctrine of predestination and°efficacious grace, but denied the immaculate conception.

Sir Nicholas Throgmorton of Throgmorton Street. Sir Nicholas Throgmorton (or Throckmorton) was born in 1513, head of an ancient Warwickshire family. He was a court favourite in three reigns, but appears to have jeopardized his chances of sustained success by a turbulent spirit and a penchant for intrigue.

He was appointed sewer, or chief butler, to Henry VIII after having been brought up in the household of Catherine Parr. In this office he was required to attend the "marshall'd feast, served up with sewer and seneschal."

Throgmorton distinguished himself at the Battle of Pinkie and was

Queen Elizabeth's Ambassador in France. He was several times, during troublous periods, Ambassador to Scotland.

In 1554 he was sent to the Tower on a charge of complicity in the Wyatt Rebellion. He conducted brilliantly his own defence in what was considered a hopeless case. He secured an acquittal, though members of the jury suffered for their verdict.

In 1569 he was again sent to the Tower, for intrigue in the plot to marry Mary, Queen of Scots, to the Duke of Norfolk.

He died in 1571.

His daughter, Elizabeth, married Sir Walter Raleigh.

Thor of Thursday. Thor, whose day Thursday is, was the god of thunder. Jove, whence the French *jeudi* is derived, was also a god of thunder and on occasion Thursday was called Thunderday.

Sunday is the day of the sun; Monday, the day of the moon. Tuesday comes through *Tiwes*, from Tiw, a god of war. The origin of Wednesday is found in Woden, or Odin, a supreme god in Teutonic mythology, linked with Mercury and associated with wisdom, culture and valour; also with storms.

Friday is associated with Frig, the wife of Odin, or with the Anglo-Saxon *frige daeg*, being a translation of the Roman name of the day, *dies veneris*, the day of the planet Venus. Frig, or Freya, was also the goddess of marriage.

Saturday derives from Saturn, the god of agriculture, later identified with the Greek Cronus. He was said to have ruled over an age of golden innocence and plenty.

The Titans of Titanic, Titanesque, etc. The Titans were a race of mighty, lawless giants. According to Greek mythology they were the children of Uranus, who personified the heavens and was the son and husband of Ge (the earth). Hesiod,

an early Greek poet, says they were twelve in number, six sons: Oceanus, Cœus, Cruis, Hyperion, Iapetus, Cronus; and six daughters: Theia, Rhea, Themis, Mnemosyne, Phœbe and Tethys. They probably represent various forces of nature or ancient vanquished gods. In the *Iliad* Oceanus and Tethys are referred to as the progenitors of the Titans.

The name "Titanic" is nowadays vividly associated with one of the greatest maritime disasters of all time. The White Star liner so named was the largest vessel afloat (about 45,000 tons). In April, 1912, on its maiden voyage to New York, it struck an iceberg during the night of the 14th, and sank in less than three hours. Out of over 2,000 passengers, only 711 were saved and the lost included many distinguished people.

Titian of Titian. The adjective titian, applied particularly to hair of a lustrous bronze, with a characteristic complexion, derives from the types often favoured by the master painter and depicted by him with unrivalled skill.

Titian, the greatest painter of the Venetian school, was born at Pieve about 1477. He became a pupil of Bellini and Giorgione. His works, several of which are in the National Gallery, include portraits, religious, allegorical and mythological subjects. All are remarkable for superb colouring and technical mastery.

Titian died of the plague in Venice in 1576.

Gilbert Talbot of Talbot House (Toc H). Talbot House is known to a world public by the signaller's abbreviation, Toc H.

The first Toc H was a club for soldiers serving in Flanders in the first World War. It was opened at Poperinghe, the nearest habitable town to Ypres, on December 11, 1915. Its "Innkeeper" was an Army Chaplain, the Rev. Philip (Tubby) Clayton, now a Companion of Honour. It was named after Lieutenant Gilbert Talbot. His brother, Senior Chaplain Neville Talbot (afterwards Bishop of Pretoria), chose "Tubby" Clayton for the new club whose "Upper Room" was soon to become a legend and an inspiration.

Lieutenant Gilbert Talbot, son of a bishop, whose name was perpetuated, was a subaltern in the Rifle Brigade. He was killed on July 30, 1915, while leading his men in an effort to regain trenches lost at Hooge when the enemy first used liquid fire.

Talbot and the Hon. G. W. Grenfell, who fell in the same engagement, were among the most brilliant Oxford men of their generation. Talbot was a man of outstanding character and charm for whom a notable career was predicted. Nothing he could have achieved, had he lived, is likely to have transcended the magnificent work of Toc H which bears his name. It is one of the greatest constructive movements born of the First World War.

After the war "Tubby" Clayton revived the spirit of "Toc H" among the survivors of Poperinghe and the vital seed grew, flowered and bore fruit all over the world.

In 1929 Lord Wakefield presented the "Old House" at Poperinghe to "Toc H" and generously endowed it. It survived occupation by the Germans in the second World War and remains the inspiration of the movement.

Tartuffe, the religious hypocrite.
The name is that of the chief character in the comedy *Tartuffe* (1664), by Molière (1622–73). He is a bawdy court sycophant, said to have been drawn from the character of a French abbot. Tartuffe, under pious guise, insinuates himself into the family of one, Orgon, and, failing to seduce the wife, attempts to ruin the family.

The name derives from the Italian word for truffles and Molière is thought to have utilized it to symbolize the sensuous satisfaction displayed by certain religious brethren when contemplating the delicacy.

Torquemada, the Inquisitor.
Thomas Torquemada (1420–98), whose name is a synonym for any cruel persecutor or vicious tyrant, was a Spanish Dominican with influential relations in the Church. He was made Prior of the Convent of Santa Cruz, in Segovia, and it was the Royal visits to Segovia that resulted in Torquemada's being appointed confessor to the young Infanta, Isabella.

When she came to the throne, her spiritual councillor was given great ecclesiastical and civic powers. He believed that the union of the Spains

Torquemada

depended upon the eradication of the toleration towards religious difficulties.

The Inquisition was revived and reorganized with Torquemada as Inquisitor-General. Although his instructions for torture were relatively moderate, as compared with later corruptions and exploitations of them, it is said that over ten thousand people were burnt during his eighteen years in office.

Before he died he had resumed the life of a friar, living and dying in a convent he had built at Avila.

Arnold Toynbee of Toynbee Hall.
Toynbee Hall is a lighthouse in the

path of social reform and education and it derives its first inextinguishable illumination from the man in whose honour it was named.

Arnold Toynbee was born in 1852, the son of a distinguished surgeon. His spirit consumed his frame and he was prevented by ill health from following a planned army career. He was a man of brilliant intellect and remarkable character and leadership.

He was co-worker with Canon Barnett, then rector of St. Jude's, Whitechapel, in pioneer efforts to interest the Universities of Oxford and Cambridge in the social and civic conditions of Whitechapel. He did much to rouse the social conscience of the country. The world-famous Settlement was named after Toynbee, whose early death in 1883 was accelerated by his social zeal and organizing powers.

Barnett was ably assisted in his remarkable educational work by his wife, Dame Henrietta Barnett, who was responsible for the creation of the Hampstead Garden Suburb. At its inception, forty years ago, it was one of the most remarkable and enlightened town planning schemes. It is still the subject of study by town planning experts from many lands.

The link with Whitechapel is sustained in the naming of the Suburb's parish church (designed by Sir Edwin Lutyens) in honour of St. Jude.

George Du Maurier of the Trilby.

The soft felt hat, called almost universally a Trilby for several generations, took its name from George du Maurier's novel *Trilby*, published in 1894. It was later illustrated by the author, who was a famous *Punch* artist.

The novel is the story of Trilby O'Ferral, an artist's model in Paris, with whom several young English students fall in love.

Under the hypnotic influence of Svengali, a Hungarian musician, she becomes a famous singer, but his mesmeric influence ceases at his death, and Trilby languishes and dies.

The background was well known to the author, for he was born and educated in Paris, the son of an English mother. Through this novel he added another word to the English language, for a person of flamboyant hypnotic powers is frequently referred to even to-day as a Svengali.

Du Maurier, who died in 1896, was the father of Sir Gerald du Maurier and grandfather of the two contemporary du Maurier novelists, Daphne and Angela.

The name trilby in the language of hats has now been largely superseded by the term "Anthony Eden," applying to a black felt hat of the type made popular by Anthony Eden, the former Foreign Secretary.

Triton of "A Triton among the minnows."

Triton, in Greek mythology, was the son of Poseidon and Amphitrite. He is generally depicted as a man with a dolphin's tail. His sea shell or conch is a distinguishing symbol. Occasionally Amphitrite is represented as riding on the back of a Triton. Some accounts give the name Triton to a race of minor sea gods, who were to some extent a sea counterpart of the mischievous satyrs of the land. Sometimes Tritons are credited with the forelegs of a horse in addition to the characteristic dolphin tail.

The roar of the sea is said to be caused by the Tritons blowing through their shells.

The phrase "a Triton among the minnows" implies the presence of a dominating personality among small fry.

The Trojans of "To work like a Trojan."

The Trojans are cited as the prototypes of prodigious, courageous workmen and citizens. Troy was a city of Troas, north-west of Mysia, Asia Minor.

The Trojan War, recorded by

Homer in the *Iliad*, was waged by the Greeks for some ten years against Troy. The burning of Troy is described by Virgil in the *Aeneid*.

The wooden horse of Troy, which phrase has come to be used for any deceptive scheme, was made by Ulysses, according to Virgil. The horse, purporting to be an offering to the gods, was hauled within Troy. It was full of Grecian soldiers who, at night, revealed themselves, slew the guards and opened the gates of the city to secure its destruction by fire.

Consistent praise is given in all accounts to the strenuous labours and unremitting courage of the Trojans.

Marie Tussaud of Madame Tussaud's. The name Tussaud is unique in its association with waxworks and as a synonym of a rare accomplishment. The story behind the world-wide association is singularly romantic.

In the 18th century a distinguished Swiss doctor, Christopher Curtius, of Berne, modelled the limbs and organs of his patients in wax to assist diagnosis. As a hobby he produced wax miniatures of his friends. His house came to assume the aspect of a queer museum. Dr. Curtius moved to Paris to devote himself to his novel art, and was patronized by the Prince de Conte, cousin of Louis XV. He experimented successfully with life-size models.

His sister and her daughter, Marie (b. 1760), came to live with him. The child showed marked aptitude for the unusual work. Royal encouragement was forthcoming, and the girl lived for several years at the Palace.

At the Revolution Marie carried on alone. She was forced to make models of heads from the guillotine. She was thrown into prison but was released by influence. Her uncle was dead and most of her friends had disappeared.

She married a French soldier, François Tussaud, and had two sons before her husband left her.

Marie brought all her possessions to England, where travelling waxwork shows were a feature of the contemporary scene.

Madame Tussaud took the old Lyceum Theatre for her exhibition, which was a remarkable success. The waxworks included famous and notorious figures of the Revolution. She toured the country with her show and proved herself not only a fine artist, but an astute business manager. Many models were lost during a storm on the way to Ireland.

She experienced adverse conditions in London until a model of a popular singer, Madame de Malibran, restored attendances. Madame Tussaud's in Marylebone became one of the sights of London. Her sons were already immersed in the business when its creator died at the age of ninety in 1850.

In 1925 the collection was destroyed by fire, but the creator's descendants rebuilt it. It was also damaged during London's blitz and subsequently restored.

Sir Thomas More of Utopian. Sir Thomas More, who derived the title of his most famous literary work, *Utopia,* from the Greek for "no place," succeeded Wolsey as Lord Chancellor in 1529.

Utopia and utopian have since been associated with the ideally perfect place or state of things. The book, virtually a political essay, was written in Latin in 1516 and was subsequently translated into English and several other languages. Its subject is the search for the perfect form of government.

More, who was born in 1478, was a distinguished lawyer, man of letters and an intimate of Erasmus. He was a zealous patron of art.

He was appointed a Privy Councillor by Henry VIII and accompanied the King to the Field of the Cloth of Gold in 1520.

When he succeeded Wolsey, More's conscience and integrity, always keen,

caused him to resign his high office. When he refused to take the Oath of Supremacy he was found guilty of high treason and sentenced to be hanged. The sentence was later commuted to execution and he died at the block, protesting that he died for his religious convictions.

The King, on More's appointment as Lord Chancellor, had praised his admirable wisdom, integrity and innocence, joined with most pleasant facility of wit. These were true attributes of a great churchman and statesman who was much beloved.

When offered a valuable goblet with suspected motives he caused it to be filled with wine, drank the woman's health, and returned the cup. He was given gloves stuffed with a bribe. He returned the gold, protesting that he preferred gloves without lining.

Sir Thomas More was canonized in 1935.

St. Valentine of Valentines. St. Valentine, who has won more popular recognition than perhaps any other saint (and less ecclesiastical attention), was a pagan priest of the 3rd century.

After his conversion he is said to have given aid to persecuted Christians. Some accounts state that he restored the sight of his gaoler's daughter. He was martyred by being clubbed to death and afterwards beheaded.

That was on February 14, 269.

The day has long been associated with the mating of birds and as a result the saint's name was given to a human courting missive, the Valentine.

Such cards, sent by the hopeful of either sex to the desired one, achieved

A typical Victorian Valentine

immense popularity in Victorian times and their use has revived, though on more humorous and less saccharine lines, in recent years. The custom is said to have pagan antecedents connected with the worship of Juno.

The association of St. Valentine with the mating of birds and the budding romance of early spring is referred to by Chaucer in his *Parliament of Foules*, by Shakespeare in *Midsummer Night's Dream*, and by John Donne most happily in the lines:

Hail, Bishop Valentine! whose day this is;
All the air is thy diocese,
And all the chirping choristers
And other birds are thy parishoners.

Sir Anthony Van Dyck of the Beard. The noted Flemish portrait painter was born at Antwerp in 1599, the seventh of twelve children of a silk merchant. He was one of Rubens' most notable pupils. When he was twenty-one he came to England in the employment of James I. After a few years he went to Italy and later Antwerp.

In 1632 he became one of the Court painters to Charles I, receiving the active patronage of the Earl of Arundel. Van Dyck was knighted, appointed principal painter in ordinary and installed at Blackfriars, with a country residence at Eltham Palace. He married a Scotswoman of the house of Ruthven, with royal encouragement.

He painted most of the celebrities in Court circles and was a prominent figure, leading a careless, if not carefree, and lavish life. His beard was considered handsome, distinctive and was much copied.

He found that royal and other art patrons were more eager to commission than to pay, and despite a pension of £200 per annum, bestowed in 1633, he suffered financial embarrassment.

Van Dyck was a businesslike and prolific painter, a brilliant portraitist, though his ambition was to have been an historical painter. He would never give more than an hour at a time to any sitter. He employed assistants for the first painting of the sitter's clothes and favoured for the glazing of the hair a private preparation derived from peach stones.

Van Dyck died at Blackfriars in 1641 and was buried in Old St. Paul's.

Vesta of Vesta. Vesta, the Roman virgin goddess of the hearth, had her Greek counterpart in Hestia. She appears to have been late in coming to veneration as she does not figure in the *Iliad* or the *Odyssey*. The hearth was the altar of domestic life and the place of ritual sacrifices, therefore the goddess assumed guardianship of homes and was associated with the fire of the hearth, hence the appropriateness of the name for certain matches.

Sacred fires were kept burning in her honour, and a temple at Delphi was dedicated to her. Though wooed by many, Vesta retained her virginity and virgins were required to do her service.

The four and later six spotless Vestal Virgins were rigidly disciplined and were buried alive if they lost their virginity. They tended the goddess's perpetual sacred fires and prepared the first fruits of the harvest and the sacrifices for certain great occasions. They were chosen as children, from distinguished families, and served for thirty years, after which period they were released from their vows of virginity.

Shakespeare, in *Midsummer Night's Dream* refers to Queen Elizabeth as "a fair vestal" and Pope in the oft-quoted lines from *Eloisa to Abelard* writes:

How happy is the blameless Vestal's lot!
The world forgetting, by the world forgot.

Queen Victoria of the Victoria Cross.

Queen Victoria (1819–1901) instituted the Victoria Cross on January 29, 1856. It is awarded for conspicuous bravery in the face of the enemy. The ribbon is crimson for all services, but until 1918 it was blue for the Royal Navy. It is worn before all other decorations, on the left breast, and the bronze Maltese cross bears the Royal Crown, surmounted by a lion, in the centre. The inscription beneath is "For Valour."

The medals were struck from the metal of guns captured at Sebastopol.

In 1911 the right to receive the Cross was extended to Indian soldiers and in 1920 a Royal Warrant extended the right to Matrons, Sisters and Nurses and the staff of nursing and allied services and to civilians of either sex regularly or temporarily under the direction of the British Empire Services.

The award carries a special annuity of £10 a year if the recipient is below commissioned rank, with £5 extra for every bar, plus an additional 6d. a day to pension. If the recipient is unable to obtain a livelihood after leaving the service, the annuity may be increased to £75 a year.

The Victoria Cross

St. Vitus of St. Vitus's Dance.

St. Vitus was a Roman saint who suffered martyrdom, together with his tutor, Modestus, and his nurse, Crescentia, during the persecutions of the Emperor Diocletian in the third century. They are commemorated on June 15.

The association of the saint's name with the nervous affliction, generally most evident in childhood and early adolescence, derives from the 15th and 16th centuries. Then it was the custom, which is noted by several contemporary chroniclers, for young people to dance round statues of St. Vitus thereby, it was believed, ensuring good health for the following twelve months. The custom was most prevalent in Germany. The dancing often reached a degree of frenzy and was accordingly associated with the saint's name. His aid was invoked against it and against hydrophobia and kindred afflictions.

St. Vitus's Dance is known medically as chorea.

Sir Richard Wallace of the Wallace Collection.

The Wallace Art Collection is exhibited in Sir Richard Wallace's Hertford House, Manchester Square, London.

Wallace (1818–90) was the natural son of the fourth Marquess of Hertford and was educated in Paris where he became known as a connoisseur of art and a notable collector. During the siege he did great service to the nation and in 1871 he was created a baronet.

His father died leaving him many bequests, including Hertford House and its contents.

Wallace was one of the Trustees of the National Gallery and a British Commissioner àt the great Paris Exhibition.

His widow, the daughter of a French officer, bequeathed his collection to the British nation in 1897.

Josiah Wedgwood of the pottery.

Josiah Wedgwood was born in 1730, at Burslem, Staffordshire, of a long line of potters. In those times English pottery was of little account and most common china was obtained from Delft, in Holland, and fine porcelain from China.

Wedgwood worked in restricted circumstances and with no education. He was debarred from using the potter's wheel by a childhood illness which necessitated the amputation of his right leg. He began modest experiments which eventually revolutionized English pottery standards. He designed and manufactured earthenware for the table, and later a white stone ware which attracted the notice and patronage of Queen Charlotte and many other influential figures.

Wedgwood founded a new industry and developed out of all knowledge the facilities and prospects of the Potteries.

He contributed largely towards the founding of the Trent and Mersey Canal and built the village of Etruria, consisting chiefly of habitations for his workmen.

He discovered the genius of John Flaxman for the decoration of his pottery and collaboration of design.

Wedgwood died in 1795.

Duke of Wellington of the Wellington Boot.

The high boots, over which originally the trousers were fitted tightly, were named after Arthur Wellesley, the famous first Duke of Wellington (1769–1852) and one of Britain's greatest generals.

He entered the army as an ensign and achieved brilliant victories in India, Portugal, Spain and France. After the culminating triumph at Waterloo he began a notable political career and in 1828 George IV called upon him to form an administration.

He died suddenly and was buried in St. Paul's Cathedral.

The Wellington boots were worn extensively in the army and by the fashionable. "No gentleman could wear anything in the daytime but Wellington boots," says a contemporary chronicler. They were often almost completely covered by the close trouser which was strapped under the instep like a spat.

Certain types of hats, coats and trousers were also named after the great soldier.

Werther of Wertherism.

Wertherism, a morbid sentimentality, derives from the characteristics of Werther, hero of Goethe's sentimental romance, *The Sorrows of Werther* (1774). Werther was so overcome by his unrequited love for Lotte that he took his life.

Thackeray parodied the story of the unconcerned girl in *The Sorrows of Werther*, which includes the well-known lines:

Charlotte, having seen his body
Borne before her on a shutter,
Like a well-conducted person,
Went on cutting bread and butter.

John Wesley of **Wesleyan.** John Wesley (1703–91), the founder of Methodism, was born at Epworth Rectory, the fifteenth child of Samuel and Susanna Wesley. He was educated at Charterhouse and Christ Church, Oxford. He was ordained in 1725.

Despite his poor health he set himself a rigorous programme of discipline and financial austerity.

He visited Georgia at the instigation of the Society for the Propagation of the Gospel.

John Wesley

He experienced a revolutionary religious re-orientation when attending a meeting in Aldersgate Street on May 24, 1738, where Luther's *Preface to the Epistle to the Romans* was read.

He began preaching in the open air, considering the world his parish.

At first Wesley's efforts were intended to supplement the services of the Church of England, of which he was an ordained member, but gradually they superseded them. He organized the vast structure of Methodism, travelling extensively and imposing upon himself a life of rigorous abstemiousness and prodigious physical effort. He spent many hours in solitary contemplation.

"I feel and grieve," he wrote, "but by the grace of God I fret at nothing."

He wrote extensively and was his own publisher and bookseller. His organizing and administrative powers were no less remarkable than his preaching ability.

In his forty-eighth year he married Mrs. Vizelle, a rich widow with four children. Wesley stipulated that the marriage should not in any way curtail his religious activities. His marriage was a failure and some biographies have classed Mrs. Wesley in the shrewish category of Xanthippe and the wife of Job.

John Wesley died at City Road in 1791 in his eighty-eighth year.

The Wesley family, one of the most famous in the history of religious organization, came from Somerset and originally spelt their name Westley. Samuel, rector of Epworth, had nineteen children of whom eight did not survive infancy.

Charles (1707–88), the eighteenth child, wrote more than 6,500 hymns, the best of which are among the finest examples of English hymnology.

Samuel Sebastian Wesley (1810–76) was the natural son of Samuel Wesley (1766–1837), a composer and brilliant organist. Samuel Sebastian, grandson of Charles, the hymnologist, was one of the Children of Chapel Royal. He was organist at the Cathedrals of Exeter, Winchester and Gloucester. He conducted the Three Choirs Festival on several occasions. He was one of the most significant forces in the revival of English church music and his anthems, particularly *The Wilderness* and *Blessed be the God and Father*, are still widely sung to-day.

Sir Charles Wyndham of **Wyndham's Theatre.** Sir Charles Wyndham, the noted English actor and manager, was born at Liverpool in 1837, the son of a doctor. He qualified in medicine and served as a brigade surgeon in the U.S. Federal Army. Later he had a remarkable theatrical success in New York, repeating it in England and Ireland.

He played with Sir Henry Irving and Ellen Terry and was noted for his performance as Charles Surface in Sheridan's *School for Scandal*.

Wyndham, who had a long run of successes at the Criterion, opened Wyndham's Theatre in 1899. For many years his leading lady and business partner was Mary Moore.

He was knighted in 1902 and died in London in 1919.

Xanthippe of the shrewish wife. Xanthippe, the wife of Socrates, the great Greek philosopher, has become proverbial as a synonym for the nagging, shrewish wife or woman. There have been some attempts to suggest that she was maligned. Socrates is said to have been unusually ugly. Alcibiades compares him to a figure of Silenus. Xanthippe's temper was the subject of much gossip in Athens.

Fielding, in *Tom Jones*, says, "An errant Vixen of a Wife . . . By this Xantippe he had two Sons," and Shakespeare aptly makes similar allusion to her ill temper in *The Taming of the Shrew, i. 2.*

Be she as foul as was Florentius' love,
As old as Sibyl, and as curst and shrewd
As Socrates' Xanthippe, or a worse,
She moves me not.

Y

Lord Yarborough of the Bridge term. At bridge a Yarborough is a hand in which there are no trumps, trumps having been established, but the term more properly applies to a hand in which there is no card higher than a nine.

The name derives from the second Lord Yarborough, early 19th century, who is said frequently to have laid odds of a thousand to one against the dealing of such a hand.

The mathematical odds are said to be 1827 to 1 against.

Richard James Morrison of Zadkiel. A Zadkiel was for generations the synonym for an astrological almanac, similar to "Old Moore."

The name was taken from the pseudonym, "Zadkiel Tao-Sze," adopted by R. J. Morrison (1795–1874), who became a widely known astrologer after a career in the Royal Navy.

His annual *Almanac* of prediction became an institution under the name of *Zadkiel*.

In a noted libel action in 1863 he maintained his complete belief in the "science." Morrison was also an astronomer and mathematician of some repute.

Zadkiel, in rabbinical tradition, is the angel of the planet Jupiter.

Zephyr, the west wind. Zephyrus was one of the four winds, children of Aurora. The others were Boreas, (north); Eurus, (east); and Notus, (south).

Zephyrus was the welcome harbinger of spring and well favoured so that one of the Horæ was given him as wife. The Romans called Zephyrus Favonius to denote the favourable influence of the west wind upon the course of nature.

The word zephyr is much favoured by poets. Typical instances of its use are:

Fair laughs the Morn and soft the Zephyr blows
Gray, The Bard.

*So near to mute the zephyrs flute
That only leaflets dance.*
Meredith, Outer and Inner.

The Zodiac. The signs of the Zodiac, with the alleged influences conferred on people born under them, are so frequently referred to in fiction that a correct list may be useful.

The zone of the heavens within which lay the paths of the sun, moon and principal planets was divided in

The Signs of the Zodiac

ancient astronomy and astrology into twelve constellations.

They were:
Aries, the Ram.
Taurus, the Bull.
Gemini, the Twins.
Cancer, the Crab.
Leo, the Lion.
Virgo, the Virgin.
Libra, the Balance.
Scorpio, the Scorpion.
Sagittarius, the Archer.
Capricornus, the Goat.
Aquarius, the water-carrier.
Pisces, the fishes.

Zodiac derives from the Greek *zoon*, an animal, and was given because the majority of the signs were named after animals.

Emile Zola of Zolaism. The word Zolaism has a much wider application than association with the works of Emile Edouard Charles Zola (1840–1902). It applies to all excessive detailed realism and absence of reserve, particularly in descriptions of the gross, squalid or immoral.

Zola, the French novelist of Italian and Greek descent, set new standards in realistic, or as he called it naturalistic, writing. His belief was that literature should concern itself with life in the raw and by its realism expose that which should be exposed for the eventual good of the community.

In his early years he worked as a clerk and in a publishing house. He wrote much notable art and literary criticism. His novels fall into two classes, the first concerned with sensational realism and the second in which characterization is overshadowed by the propagation of Socialistic principles and philosophy.

Zola became one of the most noted opponents of anti-semitism by his challenge to the French Government to give Dreyfus a hearing. His challenge, the famous *J'Accuse*, appeared in *Aurore*.

INDEX

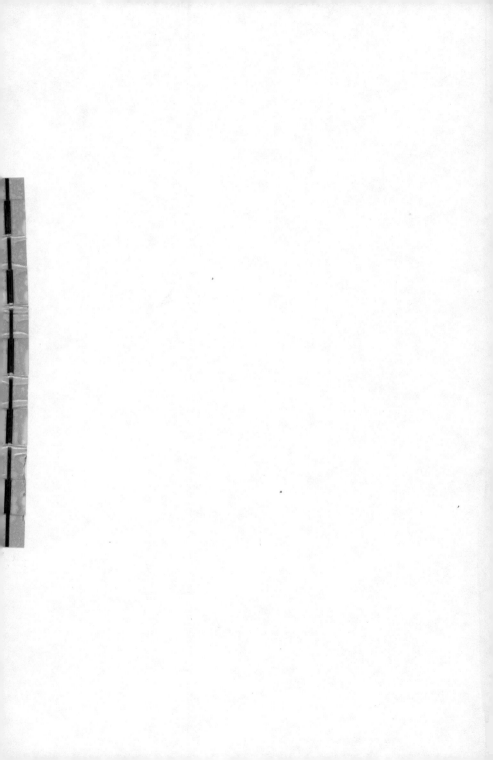

122476